OF BOYS AND MEN

OF BOYS AND MEN

*Why the Modern Male Is Struggling,
Why It Matters, and What to Do about It*

RICHARD V. REEVES

BROOKINGS INSTITUTION PRESS
Washington, D.C.

Published by Brookings Institution Press
1775 Massachusetts Avenue, NW
Washington, DC 20036
www.brookings.edu/bipress

Co-published by Rowman & Littlefield
An imprint of The Rowman & Littlefield Publishing Group, Inc.
4501 Forbes Boulevard, Suite 200, Lanham, Maryland 20706
www.rowman.com

86-90 Paul Street, London EC2A 4NE

Distributed by NATIONAL BOOK NETWORK

Typeset in Janson Text LT Std

Composition by Westchester Publishing Services

The Brookings Institution is a nonprofit organization devoted to research, education, and publication on important issues of domestic and foreign policy. Its principal purpose is to bring the highest quality independent research and analysis to bear on current and emerging policy problems.

British Library Cataloguing in Publication Information Available

Library of Congress Cataloging-in-Publication Data available

Library of Congress Control Number: 2022938978

ISBN: 978-0-8157-3987-6 (hardcover)
ISBN: 978-0-8157-4066-7 (paperback)
ISBN: 978-0-8157-3988-3 (ebook)

The paper used in this publication meets the minimum requirements of American National Standard for Information Sciences— Permanence of Paper for Printed Library Materials, ANSI/NISO Z39.48-1992

For George, Bryce, and Cameron

CONTENTS

Preface   ix

PART I   The Male Malaise

1   Girls Rule   3
     Boys Are Behind in Education

2   Working Man Blues   18
     Men Are Losing Ground in the Labor Market

3   Dislocated Dads   31
     Fathers Have Lost Their Traditional Role in the Family

PART II   Double Disadvantage

4   Dwight's Glasses   45
     Black Boys and Men Face Acute Challenges

5   Class Ceiling   60
     Poor Boys and Men Are Suffering

6   Non-Responders   73
     Policies Aren't Helping Boys and Men

PART III   Biology and Culture

7   Making Men   85
     Nature and Nurture Both Matter

PART IV   Political Stalemate

8   Progressive Blindness   105
The Political Left Is in Denial

9   Seeing Red   117
The Political Right Wants to Turn Back the Clock

PART V   What to Do

10   Redshirt the Boys   133
Boys Need an Extra Year in the Classroom

11   Men Can HEAL   150
Getting Men into the Jobs of the Future

12   New Dads   167
Fatherhood as an Independent Social Institution

Epilogue   183

Acknowledgments   185

Notes   186

Index   234

PREFACE

It is well known that institutions produce books: commercial publishing houses, think tanks, and university presses, for example. But it is also true that sometimes books produce institutions. This is one such case. An earlier edition of this book, in fact, led me to found the American Institute for Boys and Men (AIBM).[1]

That is not what I thought would happen. It is not what many of my closest friends *hoped* would happen. They were worried about me even writing a book on this subject, let alone starting a whole think tank devoted to it. But the conversations I have had since this book was first published have made it clear that when it comes to the challenges facing boys and men, there is not only an intellectual gap but also an institutional one.

There was a turning point in this process in March 2022 during a podcast conversation with Ezra Klein of the *New York Times*.[2] We discussed how the COVID-19 pandemic had a disparate impact on men, not least in terms of a much higher death rate. (The United States, for example, lost almost twice as many male prime-age workers [25 to 54] as female ones.[3]) Ezra agreed that the lack of attention to these male issues reflected an institutional asymmetry. There were many responsible, research-based organizations sounding the alarm about the impact of the pandemic on women but none doing the same for men despite the difference in death rates. Here's what I said to Ezra: "Since I've been out talking about the book, I've become even more aware of the lack of boring institutions looking at the issues of boys and men. That's a problem, because it means that there aren't institutional frameworks through which to have these conversations." In that moment, the American Institute for Boys and Men was effectively born.

My communications colleagues don't always love me saying that our goal is to be boring. (One of my sons, by contrast, said, "You're the man for that job, Dad!") But since then, it has become even clearer to me that in discussions about gender, sex, and masculinity, we need less froth and more facts. Fewer discussions of Tinder, more on technical high schools; less attention to the *Barbie* movie, more attention on the tragic loss of the 40,000 men who take their own lives every year.[4]

The reactions to the messages in this book show there is both an appetite and a need for a more serious conversation. And it turns out that being boring—or, to put it in a way my colleagues might prefer, being *factual*—is valuable not just for policy wonks and researchers but also for boys and men, who can too often feel unseen and unheard.

Shortly after publishing the first edition of this book, I made a video with the *Big Think* team summarizing my arguments. The team there tells me that it is the most successful video in their twelve-year history. A few days later, my wife called me to ask whether I'd read any of the comments about the video. I was in a taxi headed to the Chicago airport. "Of course not!" I replied. "Everyone knows you should never read the comments." She responded, "This time you should." So I pulled up the comments field, and we read some of them together, including this one: "As a 38-year-old man, that oftentimes feels worthless, this video is powerful. Thank you for doing this research. I know this sounds weird, but it makes me feel like I'm not alone when I hear that other men struggle with these issues and doesn't make me feel as hopeless." Here's another: "As a guy that is 17, watching this made me cry for the first time in almost a year. And it seems whenever I say something like this, people tell me, 'Suck it up, you're a man.'" There were many more comments like this. By the end of the conversation, both my wife and I were in tears, too.

Of course, there were a few negative comments. But overall the reaction to the video has been overwhelmingly positive, just as it has been to the book and to the creation of AIBM. People know these problems are real because they are seeing them play out in their own lives. They just need space, and perhaps even permission, to talk about them in a way that does not negate the ongoing problems of girls and women. Once you get past the zero-sum framing that suggests you are allowed to care about only one sex or the other, it's like opening the floodgates.

You may be skeptical that what America needs right now is another think tank with more wonks and webinars. Certainly, that is the position of Senator Josh Hawley. In his own book, *Manhood: The Masculine Virtues America Needs*, published in 2023, Hawley criticizes me as one of those "experts safely ensconced in their think tanks."[5] What provoked his ire was my call for a national effort to increase the share of men in professions like psychology, social work, counseling, and education. Hawley's view is that men are "ill-suited" to such roles, which is just as sexist as claiming that women are "ill-suited" to science or engineering.

Since my book was first published, the share of male teachers has dropped even more and is now down to a 23% share, compared to 33% in 1980.[6] Why were men so much less "ill-suited" to those jobs when Ronald Reagan was president? I'm not a geneticist, but I don't think the Y chromosome evolves quite that quickly.

The emptying out of men from what I call the "HEAL" professions—health, education, administration, and literacy—is a national crisis. It is also a good example of the need for careful, evidence-based research as we examine these occupational trends and draw attention to them. The statistics showing the decline in the share of male teachers do not get any media coverage, even though there are now fewer men teaching in K–12 than women working in STEM fields.[7]

But it's even more important to try to understand what's causing the problem before we identify or generate potential solutions and then propose ways to scale them up. This is exactly the kind of work that needs to be done, even if by us "safely ensconced" think-tank types.

When I argue with conservatives on this issue, part of the challenge is to persuade them that there is still much more to do for women and girls, even as we do more for boys and men. Feminism has not "gone too far" in terms of empowering women. There is no upper limit on how far women should be empowered. When I argue with progressives, on the other hand, the difficulty can be to persuade them that paying more attention to boys and men does not mean backing off the cause of women. In fact, the opposite is true. A world of floundering men will not be one of flourishing women, or vice versa.

As I said in a TED talk on this subject in the spring of 2023, "The future cannot be female. Nor, of course, can the future be male. The future has to be for every single one of us, every boy and girl. We have to rise together."[8]

The gender pay gap has narrowed significantly in recent years, with a marked improvement since the onset of the COVID-19 pandemic, likely because of increased opportunities for flexible work. But it is still a huge problem: for every $100 earned by men, women earn $84.[9] As you will see, I think the solutions here include a more equal allocation of childcare, helped by generous paid leave for both mothers and fathers.

But I am just as worried about the college degree attainment gap in the other direction, which is just one symptom of a large and growing gender gap in education: for every 100 bachelor's degrees awarded to women, 72 are awarded to men.[10] The feminist philosopher Cordelia Fine correctly describes these educational disparities as "a gendered injustice."[11] To tackle them, I propose a range of reforms, including starting boys in school a year later than girls, hiring more male teachers, and expanding vocational education.

In other words, we need to redesign jobs to be fairer to women and reform schools to be fairer to boys. We can hold two thoughts in our heads at once: that is, we can be both passionate about women's rights and compassionate toward vulnerable boys and men.

I was motivated to create a whole new organization for the same reasons as those that led me to write this book. First, there is a growing number of gender gaps in which boys and men are at a disadvantage. The gender gap in college degrees awarded is wider today than it was in the early 1970s, but in the opposite direction. The wages of most men are lower today than they were in 1979, while women's wages have risen across the board.[12] One out of five fathers is not living with his children.[13] Men have a three times higher risk from "deaths of despair," either from suicide or from an overdose.[14]

Second, the boys and men struggling most are those at the sharp end of other inequalities, especially of class and race. The boys and men I am most worried about are the ones lower on the economic and social ladder. Most men are not part of the elite, and even fewer boys are destined to take their place. In 1979, the typical American man who completed his education with a high school diploma earned in today's dollars about $1,000 a week. Today, that wage is about $850.[15]

As *The Economist* puts it, "The fact that the highest rungs have male feet all over them is scant comfort for the men at the bottom."[16] Men at the top are still flourishing, but men in general are not, especially if they are Black. "To be male, poor, and African-American . . . is to confront, on a daily basis, a deeply held racism that exists in every social institution," writes my colleague Camille Busette.[17] "No other demographic group has fared as badly, so persistently and for so long." Black men face not only institutional racism but also gendered racism, including discrimination in the labor market and criminal justice system.[18]

Third, it became clear to me that the problems of boys and men are structural rather than individual, but they are rarely treated as such. The problem with men is typically framed as a problem of men: it is men who must be fixed, one man or boy at a time. But this individualist approach is wrong. Boys are falling behind at school and college because the educational system is structured in ways that put them at a disadvantage. Men are struggling in the labor market because of an economic shift away from traditionally male jobs, and fathers are dislocated because the cultural role of family provider has been hollowed out. The male malaise is not the result of a mass psychological breakdown but of deep structural challenges.

"The more I consider what men have lost—a useful role in public life, a way of earning a decent and reliable living, appreciation in the home, respectful treatment in the culture," writes feminist author Susan Faludi in her 1999 book *Stiffed*, "the more it seems that men of the late twentieth century are falling into a status oddly similar to that of women at mid-century."[19]

Fourth, I was shocked to discover that many social policy interventions, including some of the most touted, don't help boys and men.

The one that first caught my eye was a free college program in Kalamazoo, Michigan. According to the evaluation team, "women experience very large gains" in terms of college completion (increasing by almost 50%), "while men seem to experience zero benefit."[20] This is an astonishing finding—making college completely free had no impact on men. In fact, it turns out that there are dozens of other programs that also benefit girls and women but not boys and men: a student mentoring scheme in Fort Worth, Texas; a school choice program in Charlotte, North Carolina; an income boost to low-wage earners in New York City; and many more. The striking failure of these interventions to help boys or men is often obscured by a positive average result that is driven solely by the positive impact on girls or women. In isolation, this gender gap might be seen as a quirk of a specific initiative, but it is a pattern repeated over and over. Many boys and men are not only struggling but also less likely to be helped by policy interventions.

Fifth, there is a political stalemate on issues of sex and gender. Both sides have dug into an ideological position that inhibits real change. Progressives refuse to accept that important gender inequalities can run in both directions, and they quickly label male problems as symptoms of "toxic masculinity." Conservatives appear more sensitive to the struggles of boys and men but only as a justification for turning back the clock and restoring traditional gender roles. The Left tells men, "Be more like your sister." The Right says, "Be more like your father." Neither invocation is helpful. What is needed is a positive vision of masculinity that is compatible with gender equality. As a conscientious objector in the culture wars, I hope I have provided in this book an assessment of the condition of boys and men that can attract broad support.

Sixth, as a policy wonk, I feel equipped to offer some positive ideas to tackle these problems rather than simply lament them. There has been enough handwringing. In each of the three areas of education, work, and family, I provide some practical, evidence-based solutions to help the boys and men who are struggling most. (It is probably worth saying upfront that my focus is on the challenges faced by cis heterosexual men, who account for around 95% of men.[21])

In part I of this book, I present evidence on the male malaise, showing how many boys and men are struggling in school and college (chapter 1), in the labor market (chapter 2), and in family life (chapter 3). In part II, I highlight the double disadvantages faced by Black boys and men suffering from gendered racism (chapter 4), as well as boys and men at the bottom of the economic ladder (chapter 5). I also present the growing evidence that many policy interventions don't work well for boys and men (chapter 6). In part III, I address the question of sex differences, arguing that both nature and nurture matter (chapter 7).

In part IV, I describe our political stalemate, showing how, instead of rising to this challenge, politicians are making matters worse. The progressive Left dismisses legitimate concerns about boys and men and pathologizes masculinity (chapter 8), whereas the populist Right weaponizes male dislocation and offers false promises (chapter 9). For the partisans, there is either a war on women or a war on men. Finally, in part V, I offer some solutions. Specifically, I offer proposals for a male-friendly education system (chapter 10); for helping men to move into jobs in the growing fields of health, education, administration, and literacy (chapter 11); and for bolstering fatherhood as an independent social institution (chapter 12).

"A man would never get the notion," wrote French feminist Simone de Beauvoir, "of writing a book on the peculiar situation of the human male."[22] But that was in 1949. Now the peculiar situation of the human male requires urgent attention. We rise together.

PART I

THE MALE MALAISE

CHAPTER 1

GIRLS RULE

Boys Are Behind in Education

Carol Frances, the former chief economist at the American Council on Education, describes it as a "spectacular upsurge" and "phenomenal success."[1] Stephan Vincent-Lancrin, senior analyst at the Organization for Economic Cooperation and Development's (OECD's) Centre for Educational Research and Innovation, says it is "astonishing . . . people can't believe it."[2] For Hanna Rosin, author of *The End of Men*, it is "the strangest and most profound change of the century, even more so because it is unfolding in a similar way pretty much all over the world."[3]

Frances, Vincent-Lancrin, and Rosin are all talking about the gender gap in education. In the space of just a few decades, girls and women have not just caught up with boys and men in the classroom—they have blown right past them. In 1972, the U.S. government passed the landmark Title IX law to promote gender equality in higher education. At the time, there was a gap of 13 percentage points in the proportion of bachelor's degrees going to men compared to women.[4] By 1982 the gap had closed. By 2019, the gender gap in bachelor awards was 15 points, wider than in 1972—but the other way around.[5]

The underperformance of boys in the classroom, especially Black boys and those from poorer families, badly damages their prospects for employment and upward economic mobility. Reducing this inequality will not be easy given current trends, many of which worsened during the pandemic. In the U.S., for example, the 2020 decline in college enrollment was seven times greater for male than for female students.[6]

Male students also struggle more with online learning, and as the extent of the learning loss becomes clearer in the months and years ahead, it seems almost certain that it will prove to be greater for boys and men.[7]

The first challenge is to persuade policymakers that in education, it is now boys who are at a disadvantage. Some argue that it is premature to worry about the gender gap in education, when the pay gap still runs the other way. I will have more to say about the pay gap in chapter 2; for now, suffice it to say that the labor market is still structured in favor of workers without major childcare and those workers are mostly men. But at the same time, the education system is structured in favor of girls and women, for the reasons I will set out in this chapter. So we have an education system favoring girls and a labor market favoring men. Two wrongs don't make a right. We need to fix both. Inequalities matter, regardless of their direction. It is also worth noting that while women are catching up with men in the labor market, boys and men are falling further behind in the classroom. One gap is narrowing, the other is widening.

I first describe the gender gaps in K–12 schooling and then point to what I see as their main cause: the very different speeds at which boys and girls mature, especially in adolescence. I then trace some of the resulting inequalities in higher education. My main message here is that there are stark gender gaps at every stage, and all around the world, many of which continue to widen. But policymakers, like deer in headlights, have yet to respond.

GIRLS GETTING THE GRADES

What do you know about Finland? That it is the happiest nation on Earth? Correct.[8] That the school system is superb? Well, half right. Finland does indeed always rank at or near the top of the international league table for educational outcomes—but that's because of the girls. Every 3 years, the OECD conducts a survey of reading, mathematics, and science skills among 15-year-olds. It is called the PISA (Programme for International Student Assessment) test, and it gets a lot of attention from policymakers. Finland is a good place to look at gender gaps in education because it is such a high-performing nation (indeed, one could say that other countries suffer from a bout of Finn envy every time the PISA results are published). But although Finnish students rank very high for overall performance on PISA, there is a massive gender gap: 20% of Finnish girls score at the highest reading levels in the test, compared to just 9% of boys.[9] Among those with the lowest reading scores, the gender gap is reversed: 20% of boys versus 7% of girls. On most measures, Finnish girls also outperform the boys in science and in mathematics. The bottom line is that Finland's internationally acclaimed educational performance is entirely explained by the stunning performance of Finnish girls. (In fact, American boys do just as well as Finnish boys do on the PISA reading test.)

This may have some implications for the education reformers who flock to Finland to find ways to bottle the nation's success, but it is just an especially vivid example of an international trend. In elementary and secondary schools across the world, girls are leaving boys behind. Girls are about a year ahead of boys in terms of reading ability in OECD nations, in contrast to a wafer-thin and shrinking advantage for boys in math.[10] Boys are 50% more likely than girls to fail at all three key school subjects: math, reading, and science.[11] Sweden is starting to wrestle with what has been dubbed a *pojkkrisen* (boy crisis) in its schools. Australia has devised a reading program called Boys, Blokes, Books and Bytes.

In the U.S., girls have been the stronger sex in school for decades. But they are now pulling even further ahead, especially in terms of literacy and verbal skills. The differences open up early. Girls are 14 percentage points more likely than boys to be "school ready" at age 5, for example, controlling for parental characteristics. This is a much bigger gap than the one between rich and poor children, or Black and white children, or between those who attend preschool and those who do not.[12] A 6-percentage-point gender gap in reading proficiency in fourth grade widens to a 11-percentage-point gap by the end of eighth grade.[13] In math, a 6-point gap favoring boys in fourth grade has shrunk to a 1-point gap by eighth grade.[14] In a study drawing on scores from

FIGURE 1-1   **Girls getting the grades**

Gender composition of high school GPA (grade point average) rank (deciles)

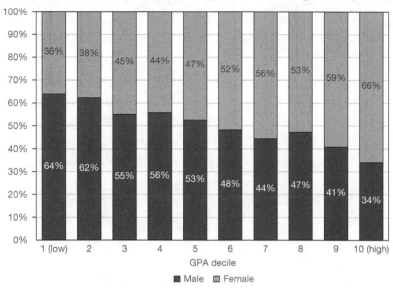

GPA decile

■ Male   ▣ Female

Note: Figure shows total high school GPA for students who were freshmen in 2009. *Source:* U.S. Department of Education, National Center for Education Statistics, High School Longitudinal Study 2009.

the whole country, Stanford scholar Sean Reardon finds no overall gap in math from grades three through eight, but a big one in English. "In virtually every school district in the United States, female students out-performed male students on ELA [English Language Arts] tests," he writes. "In the average district, the gap is . . . roughly two thirds of a grade level and is larger than the effects of most large-scale educational interventions."[15]

By high school, the female lead has solidified. Girls have always had an edge over boys in terms of high school grade point average (GPA), even half a century ago, when they surely had less incentive than boys given the differences in rates of college attendance and career expectations. But the gap has widened in recent decades. The most common high school grade for girls is now an A; for boys, it is a B.[16] As figure 1-1 shows, girls now account for two-thirds of high schoolers in the top

10%, ranked by GPA, while the proportions are reversed on the bottom rung.

Girls are also much more likely to be taking Advanced Placement or International Baccalaureate classes.[17] Of course national trends disguise huge variations by geography, so it is useful to zoom in and look at specific places. Take Chicago, where students from the most affluent neighborhoods are much more likely to have an A or B average in ninth grade (47%), compared to those from the poorest (32%).[18] That is a big class gap, which, given that Chicago is the most segregated big city in the country, means a big race gap too. But strikingly, the difference in the proportion of girls versus boys getting high grades is the same: 47% to 32%. If you're wondering whether grades in the first year of high school matter much, they do, strongly predicting later educational outcomes. As the Chicago researchers who analyzed these data insist, "Grades reflect multiple factors valued by teachers, and it is this multidimensional quality that makes grades good predictors of important outcomes."

It is true that boys still perform a little better than girls do on most standardized tests. But this gap has narrowed sharply, down to a thirteen-point difference in the SAT, and it has disappeared for the ACT.[19] It is also probably worth noting here that SAT and ACT scores matter a lot less in any case, as colleges move away from their use in admissions, which, whatever other merits this has, seems likely to further widen the gender gap in postsecondary education. Here is a more anecdotal example of the gender gap: Every year the *New York Times* runs an editorial contest among middle and high school students, and it publishes the opinions of the winners. The organizers tell me that among the applicants, there is a "2–1, probably closer to 3–1" ratio of girls to boys.[20]

By now it should not be a surprise to learn that boys are less likely than girls to graduate high school. In 2018, 88% of girls graduated from high school on time (i.e., 4 years after enrolling), compared to 82% of boys.[21] The male graduation rate is only a little higher than the 80% among poor students. You might think these were easy numbers to come by, a quick Google search away. I thought they would be when

I started writing this paragraph. But in fact it took a small Brookings research project to figure it out, and for reasons that are instructive. States are required by federal law to report high school graduation rates by race and ethnicity, proficiency in English, economic disadvantage, homelessness, and foster status. These kinds of data are invaluable for assessing trends for the groups at greatest risk of dropping out. But oddly, states do *not* have to report their results by sex. Getting the numbers cited above required scouring the data for each state.

An energetic nonprofit alliance, Grad Nation, is seeking to raise the overall high school graduation rate in the U.S. to 90% (up from 85% in 2017).[22] This is a great goal. The alliance points out that this will require improvements among "students of color, students with disabilities, and low-income students." It definitely will. But they missed a big one—boys. After all, girls are only 2 percentage points from the target, while boys are 8 percentage points below it.

IT'S ALL ABOUT THE TIMING
(OF BRAIN DEVELOPMENT)

What is going on here? There are many potential explanations. Some scholars link the relative underperformance of boys in school to their lower expectations of postsecondary education, surely the very definition of a vicious circle.[23] Others worry that the strong skew toward female teachers—three out of four and rising—could be putting boys at a disadvantage.[24] This matters, for sure. But I think there is a bigger, simpler explanation staring us in the face. Boys' brains develop more slowly, especially during the most critical years of secondary education. When almost one in four boys (23%) is categorized as having a "developmental disability," it is fair to wonder if it is educational institutions, rather than the boys, that are not functioning properly.[25]

In *Age of Opportunity: Lessons from the New Science of Adolescence*, Laurence Steinberg writes that "high-school aged adolescents make better decisions when they're calm, well rested, and aware that they'll be rewarded for making good choices."[26] To which most parents, or anybody recounting their own teen years, might respond: tell me something

I don't know, Larry. But adolescents are wired in a way that makes it hard to "make good choices." When we are young, we sneak out of bed to go to parties; when we get old, we sneak out of parties to go to bed. Steinberg shows how adolescence is essentially a battle between the sensation-seeking part of our brain (*Go to the party! Forget school!*) and the impulse-controlling part (*I really need to study tonight*).

It helps to think of these as the psychological equivalent of the accelerator and brake pedals in a car. In the teenage years, our brains go for the accelerator. We seek novel, exciting experiences. Our impulse control—the braking mechanism—develops later. As Robert Sapolsky, a Stanford biologist and neurologist, writes in his book *Behave: The Biology of Humans at Our Best and Worst*, "The immature frontal cortex hasn't a prayer to counteract a dopamine system like this."[27] There are obvious implications here for parenting, and the importance of helping adolescents develop self-regulation strategies.

Adolescence, then, is a period when we find it harder to restrain ourselves. But the gap is much wider for boys than for girls, because they have both more acceleration and less braking power. The parts of the brain associated with impulse control, planning, future orientation, sometimes labeled the "CEO of the brain," are mostly in the prefrontal cortex, which matures about 2 years later in boys than in girls.[28] The cerebellum, for example, reaches full size at the age of 11 for girls, but not until age 15 for boys. Among other things, the cerebellum "has a modulating effect on emotional, cognitive, and regulatory capacities," according to neuroscientist Gokcen Akyurek.[29] I know; I have three sons. These findings are consistent with survey evidence on attention and self-regulation, where the biggest sex differences occur during middle adolescence, in part because of the effect of puberty on the hippocampus, a part of the brain linked to attention and social cognition.[30] The correct answer to the question so many teenage boys hear, "Why can't you be more like your sister?" is something like, "Because, Mom, there are sexually dimorphic trajectories for cortical and subcortical gray matter!" (Returns to video game.)

While parts of the brain need to grow, some brain fibers have to be pruned back to improve our neural functions. It is odd to think that parts of our brain need to get smaller to be more efficient, but it's true. The brain basically tidies itself up; think of it like trimming a hedge to keep it looking good. This pruning process is especially important in adolescent development, and a study drawing on detailed brain imaging of 121 people aged between 4 and 40 shows that it occurs earlier in girls than in boys. The gap is largest at around the age of 16.[31] Science journalist Krystnell Storr writes that these findings "add to the growing body of research that looks into gender differences when it comes to the brain . . . the science points to a difference in the way our brains develop. Who can argue with that?"[32] (It turns out, quite a few people. But I'll get to that later.)

It is important to note, as always, that we are talking averages here. But I don't think this evidence will shock many parents. "In adolescence, on average girls are more developed by about 2 to 3 years in terms of the peak of their synapses and in their connectivity processes," says Frances Jensen, chair of the department of neurology at the University of Pennsylvania's Perelman School of Medicine. "This fact is no surprise to most people if we think of 15-year-old boys and girls."[33] I don't have any daughters, but I can report that when my sons brought female friends home during the middle and high school years, the difference in maturity was often startling.

The gender gap in the development of skills and traits most important for academic success is widest at precisely the time when students need to be worrying about their GPA, getting ready for tests, and staying out of trouble.[34] A 2019 report on the importance of the new science of adolescence from the National Academies of Sciences, Engineering, and Medicine suggests that "sex differences in associations between brain development and puberty are relevant for understanding . . . prominent gender disparities during adolescence."[35] But this emerging science on sex differences in brain development, especially during adolescence, has so far had no impact on policy. The chapter on education in the National Academies report, for example, contains no specific proposals relating to the sex differences it identified.

The debate over the importance of neurological sex differences, which can be quite fierce, is wrongly framed as far as education is concerned. There are certainly some biologically based differences in male and female psychology that last beyond adolescence. But by far the biggest difference is not in *how* female and male brains develop, but *when*. The key point is that the relationship between chronological age and developmental age is very different for girls and boys. From a neuroscientific perspective, the education system is tilted in favor of girls. It hardly needs saying that this was not the intention. After all, it was mostly men who created the education system; there is no century-old feminist conspiracy to disadvantage the boys. The gender bias in the education system was harder to see when girls were discouraged from pursuing higher education or careers and steered toward domestic roles instead.[36] Now that the women's movement has opened up these opportunities to girls and women, their natural advantages have become more apparent with every passing year.

PINK CAMPUSES

The gender gap widens further in higher education. In the U.S., 57% of bachelor's degrees are now awarded to women, and not just in stereotypically "female" subjects: women now account for almost half (47%) of undergraduate business degrees, for example, compared to fewer than one in ten in 1970.[37] Women also receive the majority of law degrees, up from about one in twenty in 1970.[38]

Figure 1-2 shows the gender gap in the share of degrees awarded at associate's, bachelor's, and graduate degree levels from 1970 to 2019.[39]

Women are earning three out of five master's degrees and associate's degrees, and the rise has been even more dramatic for professional degrees.[40] The share of doctoral degrees in dentistry (DDS or DMD), medicine (MD), or law (JD or LLB) being awarded to women has jumped from 7% in 1972 to 50% in 2019.[41] The dominance of women on campus shows up in nonacademic areas too. In 2020, the law review at every one of the top sixteen law schools had a woman as editor-in-chief.[42]

FIGURE 1-2   The great educational overtaking
Degrees awarded to women for every 100 awarded to men, 1971–2019

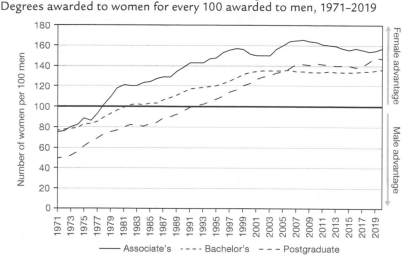

Note: Master's, professional, Ph.D., and law degrees included in postgraduate degrees.
Source: U.S. Department of Education, National Center for Education Statistics,
"Degrees conferred by degree-granting institutions, by level of degree and sex of
student" (2005 and 2020).

As Rosin noted, this is a global trend. In 1970, the year after I was
born, just 31% of undergraduate degrees went to British women. When
I left college two decades later, it was 44%. Now it is 58%.[43] Today, 40%
of young British women head off to college at the age of 18, compared
to 29% of their male peers.[44] "The world is waking up to . . . this problem," says Eyjolfur Gudmundsson, rector of the University of Akureyri
in Iceland, where 77% of the undergraduates are women.[45] Iceland is
an interesting case study, since it is the most gender egalitarian country in the world, according to the World Economic Forum.[46] But Ice-
landic universities are struggling to reverse a massive gender inequality
in education. "It's not being discussed in the media," says Steinunn
Gestsdottir, vice rector at the University of Iceland. "But policymakers are worried about this trend."[47] In Scotland, policymakers are past
the worried stage and into the doing-something-about-it stage, setting
a clear goal to increase male representation in all Scottish universities.[48] Their approach is one that other countries should follow.

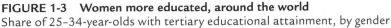

FIGURE 1-3 Women more educated, around the world
Share of 25–34-year-olds with tertiary educational attainment, by gender

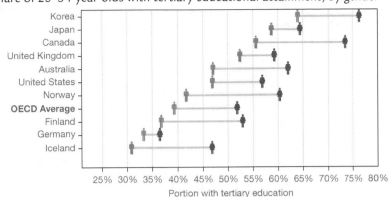

Note: Select OECD countries. Year available varies slightly by country.
Source: OECD, "Educational Attainment and Labour-Force Status: ELS—Population Who Attained Tertiary Education, by Sex and Age Group," data accessed November 15, 2021.

It is true that some subjects, such as engineering, computer sciences and math, still skew male. Considerable efforts and investments are being made by colleges, nonprofit organizations, and policymakers to close these gaps in STEM (science, technology, engineering, and math). But even here the news is generally encouraging. Women now account for 36% of the undergraduate degrees awarded in STEM subjects, including 41% of those in the physical sciences and 42% in mathematics and statistics.[49] But there have been no equivalent gains for men in traditionally female subjects, such as teaching or nursing, and these are occupational fields likely to see significant job growth. (I will be saying more about how to get more men into these HEAL jobs in chapter 11.)

In every country in the OECD, there are now more young women than young men with a bachelor's degree.[50] Figure 1-3 shows the gap in some selected nations. As far as I can tell, nobody predicted that women would overtake men so rapidly, so comprehensively, or so consistently around the world.

AFFIRMATIVE ACTION BY STEALTH

Almost every college in the U.S. now has mostly female students. The last bastions of male dominance to fall were the Ivy League colleges, but every one has now swung majority female.[51] The steady feminization of college campuses may not trouble too many people, but there is at least one group whose members really worry about it: admissions officers. "Once you become decidedly female in enrollment," writes Jennifer Delahunty, Kenyon College's former dean of admissions, "fewer males and, as it turns out, fewer females find your campus attractive." In a provocative *New York Times* opinion piece, plaintively headlined "To All The Girls I've Rejected," she said publicly what everyone knows privately: "Standards for admission to today's most selective colleges are stiffer for women than men."[52]

The evidence for this stealthy affirmative action program in favor of men seems quite clear. At private colleges the acceptance rates for men are considerably higher than for women.[53] At Vassar, for example, where 67% of matriculating students are female, the acceptance rate for male applicants in fall 2020 was 28%, compared to 23% for women.[54] You might be wondering if this is because Vassar was a women's college until 1969. But Kenyon, which was all-male until the same year, has a similar challenge.[55] By contrast, public colleges and universities, which educate the vast majority of students, are barred from discrimination on the basis of sex. This is one reason they skew even more female than private institutions.

You might think that this discrimination on the basis of sex by private colleges is illegal. But read the small print of Title IX, Section 1681 (a) (1), which contains a specific exemption from sex discrimination provisions for admissions to private undergraduate colleges. To be clear, this provision was made to protect the small number of single-sex colleges, rather than to allow discrimination in favor of men in the other institutions. The evidence for the gender bias was so strong that in 2009, an investigation was launched by the U.S. Commission on Civil Rights, despite the Section 1681 loophole. Gail Heriot, the commissioner who instigated the probe, says that there was "evidence of purposeful discrimination."[56] But two years later, the matter was dropped, ostensibly on the grounds of "inadequate data." Nobody knows for sure what happened behind the scenes. But I think Hanna Rosin's assessment is right. "Acknowledging the larger dynamic that would give rise to such discrimination was a whole other kind of threat," she writes. "It meant admitting that in these realms it was in fact men who needed the help."[57]

As Kenyon's Delahunty put it candidly in a September 2021 interview with the *Wall Street Journal*, "Is there a thumb on the scale for boys? Absolutely. The question is, is that right or wrong?"[58] My answer is that it is wrong. Even though I am deeply worried about the way boys and men are falling behind in education, affirmative action cannot be the solution. (Or perhaps I should say, not yet.) To a large extent, the gaps at the college level reflect the ones in high school. Differences in early attainment at college can be explained by differences in high school GPA, for example. Reading and verbal skills strongly predict college-going rates, and these are areas where boys lag furthest behind girls.[59] Equalizing verbal skills at age 16 would close the gender gap in college enrollment in England, according to a study by Esteban Aucejo and Jonathan James.[60] The most urgent task, then, is to improve outcomes for boys in the K–12 school system.

STOP OUTS AND DROPOUTS

But getting more men to college is just the first step. They also need help getting *through* college. With most students now going to some kind of college at some point, the big challenge is completion. Here, too, there is a gender gap. Male students are more likely to "stop out," that is, to take a detour away from their studies, and they are also more likely to "drop out" and fail to graduate at all. The differences are not trivial: 46% of female students enrolling in a public 4-year college have graduated 4 years later; for male students, the proportion is 35%. (The gap shrinks somewhat for 6-year graduation rates.)[61]

In 2019, Matthew Chingos, director of the Center on Education Data and Policy at the Urban Institute, in collaboration with the *New York Times*, created a league table of colleges based on their dropout rates. To judge the performance of institutions fairly, Chingos took into account the kind of students they enrolled, since "on average, colleges have lower graduation rates when they enroll more lower-income students, more Black and Latino students, more men, more older students and more students with low SAT or ACT scores."[62] In other words, colleges should not be penalized for having higher dropout rates because they enroll more disadvantaged students. When I read that article, the addition of "more men" in that category jumped out. It shows that the educational underperformance of half the population is now a routine fact to social scientists, one to be added to the standard battery of statistical controls.

The numbers from Chingos suggest that all else equal, an all-female four-year school would have a graduation rate 14 percentage points higher than an all-male school.[63] This is not a small difference. In fact, taking into account other factors, such as test scores, family income, and high school grades, male students are at a higher risk of dropping out of college than *any other group*, including poor students, Black students, or foreign-born students.

But the underperformance of males in college is shrouded in a good deal of mystery. World-class scholars have pored over the low rates of male college enrollment and completion, piling up data and running regressions. I have read these studies and spoken to many of the scholars. The short summary of their conclusions is: "We don't know." Economic incentives do not provide an answer. The value of a college education is at least as high for men as for women.[64] Even a scholar like MIT's David Autor, who has dug deeply into the data, ends up describing male education trends as "puzzling."[65] Mary Curnock Cook, the former head of the UK's university and college admissions service, says she is "baffled."[66] When I asked one of my sons for his thoughts, he looked up from his phone, shrugged, and said, "I dunno." Which may in fact have been the perfect answer.

One factor that gets too little attention in these debates is the developmental gap, with the male prefrontal cortex struggling to catch up with the female one well into the early twenties. To me, it seems clear that girls and women were *always* better equipped to succeed at college, just as in high school, and that this has become apparent as gendered assumptions about college education have fallen away.[67]

But I think there is an aspiration gap here too. Most young women today have it drummed into them how much education matters, and most want to be financially independent. Compared to their male classmates, they see their future in sharper focus. In 1980, male high school seniors were much more likely than their female classmates to say they definitely expected to get a 4-year degree, but within just two decades, the gap had swung the other way.[68] This may also be why many educational interventions, including free college, benefit women more than men; their appetite for success is just higher. Girls and women have had to fight misogyny without. Boys and men are now struggling for motivation within.

Hanna Rosin's 2012 book had a gloomy title: *The End of Men.* But she remained hopeful, back then, that men would rise to the challenge, especially in education. "There's nothing like being trounced year after year to make you reconsider your options," she wrote.[69] So far, however, there is little sign of any reconsideration. The trends she identified have worsened. There has also been no rethinking of educational policy or practice. Curnock Cook correctly describes this as a "massive policy blind spot."[70] With honorable exceptions—go Scotland!—policymakers have been painfully slow to adjust. Perhaps this is not surprising. The gender reversal in education has been astonishingly swift. It is like the needles on a magnetic compass reversing their polarity. Suddenly, north is south. Suddenly, working for gender equality means focusing on boys rather than girls. Disorienting, to say the least. Small wonder our laws, institutions, even our attitudes, have not yet caught up. But catch up they must.

CHAPTER 2

WORKING MAN BLUES

Men Are Losing Ground
in the Labor Market

In May 2019 I was moderating a panel discussion on inequality at a conference organized by the Federal Reserve. I asked Melissa Kearney, a top-notch economist, whether she was more worried about women or men. She took a moment. I'd sprung the question on her in front of a highly influential audience. "I am really worried about the extent to which men in the U.S. are being pushed to the side of economic, social and family life," she responded. "For 20, 30 or 40 years . . . scholars focused on women and children. Now we really need to think about men."[1]

Kearney was brave to say it, and she is right. If we want a more dynamic economy and a better future for our children, we need to help the men who are struggling. In chapter 1, I described the challenge they face in schools. Here I turn to jobs. Growing numbers of men are detaching from paid work. For most of those who are in a job, wages have stagnated. In fact, one reason that the gender pay gap has narrowed is that median male pay has fallen, surely a suboptimal way to achieve equality. But while women have been catching up with men, workers on the top rungs of the economic ladder—men as well as women—have been pulling away from everyone else. The deepest fissures in the labor market are not those between men and women. They are between white and Black workers and between the upper middle class and the middle class and working class, the subjects of chapters 4 and 5.

"Many in the women's movement and in the mass media complain that men just 'don't want to give up the reins of power,'" writes Susan Faludi. "But that would seem to have little applicability to the situations of most men, who individually feel not the reins of power in their hands but its bit in their mouths."[2]

I describe and explain here the declining economic fortunes of these men. It's very important to see how these result from the fracturing of the labor market, rather than the frailties of the men themselves. It's a structural problem, not a personal one.

MISSING MEN

"Over the last three decades," write economists David Autor and Melanie Wasserman, "the labor market trajectory of males in the U.S. has turned downward along four dimensions: skills acquisition; employment rates; occupational stature; and real wage levels."[3] If that sounds bad, it is. Labor force participation among men in the U.S. has dropped by 7 percentage points over the last half century, from 96 to 89%.[4] Even before COVID cratered the economy in 2020, there were 9 million men of prime working age who were not in employment. (Economists define the "prime" years as beginning at the age of 25 and ending, unnervingly, at 54.) A technical but important point is that most of the men who are not in work don't count in official statistics as "unemployed," because they aren't looking for work. One in three men with only a high school education are now out of the labor force.[5] That is 5 million men, a reserve army of labor twice the size of the People's Liberation Army of China.[6]

If you think of a man hit by economic trends, chances are that you have a middle-aged man in mind. But the problem is not just one for older men. The biggest fall in male employment has in fact been among young men, aged between 25 and 34, as figure 2-1 shows.[7] (Now that *is* prime age.) Scholars are not sure why. Standard economic models struggle to explain it. One popular explanation is the attraction of video games, and it is easy to see how *Assassin's Creed* could seem like a better way to spend your day than in a poorly paid, unappealing job. But there isn't really any good evidence for this. A careful analysis of time-use data

Figure 2-1 Fewer men, more women at work
Change in employment to population ratio, 1979 to 2019

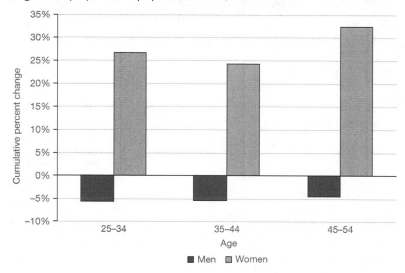

■ Men ■ Women

Note: Seasonally adjusted; ages 25–54; 1979 Q1 to 2019 Q4.
Source: Bureau of Labor Statistics, Employment-Population Ratio series.

by University of North Carolina economist Gray Kimbrough finds that hours spent gaming have increased the most among men in their 20s, but from just three hours a week in 2005, to six hours a week in 2015.[8] Based on my own experience as a father of three sons, I honestly had to double-check that these numbers were really for hours *per week* rather than hours *per day*. The figure does not strike me as justification for a moral panic. Kimbrough also shows that men who leave employment do not increase the hours spent gaming, or at least not immediately.

The economic downturn of 2020 obviously caused employment levels for both men and women to plummet, as lockdowns put the economy into a state of suspended animation. In the space of just a few weeks, female employment fell by 16%, and male employment dropped by 13%.[9] The difference was partly the result of more women taking time away from employment to care for children, especially as schools and childcare providers closed, and the downturn was quickly dubbed a "she-cession."[10] Certainly the 2020 recession was a departure from recent economic downturns in which "women's employment declines were barely perceptible," as Michigan economist Betsey Stevenson observes.[11] Most previous recessions have in fact been he-cessions, hitting male employment hardest.

But since the 2020 downturn was generated artificially by a pandemic, rather than by the usual economic cycle, the recovery was extremely rapid too. The COVID-19 recession was very sharp but very short, lasting just two months, less than any previous downturn in U.S. history. The gender gap closed very quickly too. By October 2021, the 1.2 percentage point decline in labor force participation rates since the start of the pandemic was evenly divided between men and women.[12] There was some good news too: the proportion of female senior executives rose to 24% in 2020, up from 21% in 2019.[13]

ROBOTS AND TRADE

Male employment has not fallen because men have suddenly become feckless or work-shy, but because of shifts in the structure of the economy. Simply put, male jobs have been hit by a one-two punch, of automation and free trade. Machines pose a greater threat to working men than to women for two reasons. First, the occupations most susceptible to automation are just more likely to employ men, as my colleague Mark Muro shows. "Men . . . make up over 70 percent of production occupations, over 80 percent of transportation occupations, and over 90 percent of construction and installation occupations," he writes.[14] And these are "all occupational groups with current task loads that have above-average projected automation exposure." By contrast, women make up most of the workforce in relatively automation-safe occupations, such as health care, personal services, and education.

Second, men often lack the skills required in an automating world. According to Andy Haldane, chief economist at the Bank of England, "the high-skill, high-pay jobs of the future may involve skills better measured by EQ (a measure of emotional intelligence) than IQ."[15] There is already evidence that the female advantage in "soft skills" is giving them an additional boost in the U.S. labor market, and that they are switching more quickly than men to "robot-proof" occupations.[16] It is important to note, however, that there is a lot of uncertainty about the likely impact of automation. Empirical estimates vary widely.[17] Fears about automation have been around for a long time, and they are often a proxy for broader pessimism about economic trends.

One thing is certain. The long-run shift away from jobs requiring physical strength is going to continue. Fewer than one in ten jobs now require what the Bureau of Labor Statistics describes as "heavy work," which requires "occasionally lifting or carrying 51–100 pounds or frequently lifting or carrying 26–50 pounds."[18] As the muscular demands of work decline, men are becoming physically weaker; one study of grip strength, a good marker of overall strength, shows a sharp decline among men.[19] Meanwhile, and perhaps more surprisingly, women are getting physically stronger. In 1985, the average man in his early 30s could squeeze your hand with about 30 pounds more force than a similarly aged woman. Today, their grip strength is about the same.

The goal here is not to bring back brawny jobs for men, it is to help men adapt. Most of the occupations set to grow the most in coming years are female dominated.[20] There has been a commendable and largely successful push to get more girls and women into jobs that require STEM (science, technology, engineering, and math) skills. But it is now even more important to encourage men into what I call HEAL (health, education, administration, and literacy) jobs, which are dominated by women.

Male workers are challenged on one side by robots, and on the other by workers in other countries. Free trade has become a hot political topic in recent years, especially in the U.S. and the UK. It is hard to untangle the empirical knots here. There is no doubt that Chinese imports caused declines in U.S. manufacturing employment, of around 2 to 3 million jobs.[21] Arguments continue, however, over whether there were offsetting increases in other kinds of jobs; how much the impact was restricted to certain places, especially the Midwest; whether the shock was short term, for just a few years after 2001 when China joined the World Trade Organization, or has had longer-lasting effects; and whether the reduced geographical mobility of workers has made matters worse. In other words, it is complicated. It is also very difficult to get a good economic measure of the benefits of cheaper Chinese goods for tens of millions of consumers (as well as for workers in China, of course—but that is a different argument).

I will say that the political elite spent decades complacently arguing that on net, and in the long run, free trade is good. And so it is. By definition, however, this means that *some people*, in *some places*, are being hurt *right now*. Not much was done to help these people, even by center-left politicians who claimed to be on the side of the working class. The assumption in policy circles that some of the winnings from free trade would be redistributed to the losers proved mostly false. The victims were basically left behind, told to buck up their ideas, engage in some "lifelong learning," and get with the program. Up until 2017, for every dollar the U.S. government was spending on Trade Adjustment Assistance for workers, $25 were being spent on tax subsidies toward the endowments of elite colleges.[22] (The Tax Cuts and Jobs Act of 2017 imposed a tax on the biggest of these funds.) In the populist backlash, the technocratic elite largely reaped what they sowed.

For men who are in work, pay levels are typically lower than in the past. The median real hourly wage for men peaked sometime in the 1970s and has been falling since. While women's wages have risen across the board over the last four decades, wages for men on most rungs of the earnings ladder have stagnated. Only men at the top have seen strong earnings growth. Men who entered the workforce in 1983 will earn about 10% less, in real terms, across their working life than those who started out in 1967. For women, by contrast, life-time earnings have risen by 33% over the same period (these numbers are at the median).[23] In the dry words of the U.S. Bureau of Labor Statistics, "The long-term trend in men's earnings has been quite different than that for women."[24]

BUT WHAT ABOUT THAT GENDER PAY GAP?

When I hire a new research assistant, I ask them to read two books. The first is *How to Write Short: Word Craft for Fast Times* by Roy Peter Clark, an excellent guide to sharp communication in a world of blogs and tweets (and yes, I am aware that the book you're holding is rather long). The other is *Factfulness: Ten Reasons We're Wrong about the World—and Why Things Are Better Than You Think* by Hans Rosling, who is something of a hero to me. Rosling, who died in 2017, was a Swedish physician who became obsessed with statistical illiteracy. In *Factfulness*, he describes various biases, including the "straight line instinct," an assumption that a historical trend line will continue unaltered into the future; the "negativity instinct," which is a tendency to think things are likely getting worse; and the "gap instinct," which is a "basic urge to divide things into two distinct groups, with nothing but an empty gap in between."[25] As Rosling puts it, "We love to dichotomize."

The gap instinct leads to two errors of perception. First, we fail to see how much overlap there is between two groups. Second, we fail to see the bigger gaps that typically exist within groups, rather than between them.

The gender pay gap is a case in point. A woman at the middle of the female wage distribution (for full-time, year-round workers) earns 82% as much as a man at the middle of the male one: in 2020, $891 and $1,082 a week, respectively.[26] When we hear about this gap, the thought that naturally gets generated is "women earn less than men." But in fact, the distribution of women's wages looks strikingly similar to the distribution of men's wages, and a lot more similar today than just a few decades ago; figure 2-2 shows the wage distribution for men and women in 1979 and in 2019.

As you can see, the distributions now overlap rather tightly. In fact, 40% of women now earn more than the typical man, up from just 13% in 1979. That two in five women are earning more than what 50% of men earn seems counterintuitive to many people. In June 2021, I polled my Twitter followers, asking them what proportion of female workers they thought earned more than the median man: 10%, 20%, 30%, or 40%. The poll got just 264 votes, so I'm not going to make any scientific claims here. But my followers, being an academic kind of crowd, are likely better informed on this kind of thing than most. But still the votes were, in order, for 20%, 10%, 30% and, finally, the correct answer of 40%. The gap instinct is strong.

The wage charts in figure 2-2 illustrate the other danger of gap-instinct thinking, which is to miss the extent of differences *within*

FIGURE 2-2 The shrinking pay gap

Male and female wage distributions 1979 and 2019

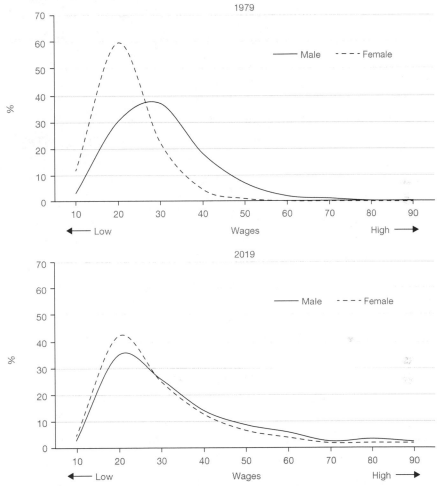

Note: 2019 dollars, adjusted for inflation with CPI-U-RS. The figure shows a smoothed line with the share of workers in each hourly $10 wage bin as displayed on the x-axis.
Source: Current Population Survey, author's calculations.

groups. The wage distributions of men and women overlap more than in 1979, but they are also much more spread out. The gap between high-wage women and low-wage women, and to a lesser extent between high-wage and low-wage men, has widened dramatically. The closeness of the male and female wage distributions is of course stupendously good news on the gender equality front. The last half century has seen what Claudia Goldin calls a "grand gender convergence," with a dramatic narrowing in the gap between men and women, not only in earnings but in employment levels, hours worked, and occupation type.[27] It is also true that in recent years, however, progress on closing the pay gap has slowed, despite women's successes in the classroom.

So, what is causing the remaining gap? The answer to this question matters a lot, especially when it comes to potential solutions.

The basic facts are not in dispute. As I have already said, the typical (i.e., median) full-time female worker earns about 82% as much as the typical man. The question is why. Here things quickly get heated. For the feminist Left, the pay gap proves patriarchy. "The wage gap is a blatantly unfair vestige of a patriarchal labor system that haunts women's economic potential throughout their lives," says Toni Van Pelt, president of the National Organization for Women.[28] Conservatives, meanwhile, dismiss the idea of a pay gap as a feminist myth, used to create the impression of inequalities that simply do not exist. The wage gap is a "massively discredited factoid," says Christina Hoff Sommers of the American Enterprise Institute.[29] Sommers is not alone. In a 2019 survey, 46% of men and 30% of women said the problem of unequal pay was "made up to serve a political purpose."[30]

The pay gap accurately describes the difference in the economic resources available to individual men and women in the middle of their respective wage distributions. It is not a myth. It is math. The real disagreement is not over whether the typical woman earns less than the typical man but *why*. Conservatives point to studies showing that once a range of factors influencing pay are taken into account—hours, industry, experience, seniority, location, and so on—the pay gap almost evaporates.[31] Various studies of this kind put the adjusted gender pay gap at around 5%. In a foreword to a 2009 study commissioned by the federal government, Deputy Assistant Labor Secretary Charles James concluded that "the raw wage gap should not be used as the basis to justify corrective action. Indeed, there may be nothing to correct."[32]

There is certainly very little evidence that women are paid less than men for doing the same work in the same way. Women are paid less because they do different work, or work differently, or both. But, of course, that is not the end of the story. Women may earn less because they occupy fewer senior positions, but that fact itself may be the result of institutional sexism. Similarly, it is true that women tend to be more clustered than men in lower-paying occupations and industries, which explains perhaps a third of the pay gap. But that may reflect socialized gender roles, not least in terms of family responsibilities, or a devaluation of work that is done by women, or both. In any case, while there is a pay gap between occupations, there is as big a gender pay gap *within* occupations.

THE PAY GAP IS A PARENTING GAP

The one-word explanation for the pay gap is: children. Among young adults, especially if they are childless, the pay gap has essentially disappeared.[33] "There's remarkable evidence that earnings for men and women move in sync up until the birth of a couple's first child," says economist Marianne Bertrand. "This is when women lose and they never recover."[34] To make matters worse, the crucial years for wage gains are from the mid-30s onward, which, as Michelle Budig, another top economist in the field, points out, is "the same period when intensive family responsibilities, particularly for mothers, are in full force."[35] The earnings trajectory for women who do not have children looks similar to that for men. The one for mothers does not. The more children women have, the further behind they fall in terms of both employment and earnings.[36]

Some of the best proof that the gender pay gap is mostly a parenting pay gap comes from innovative studies in Sweden and Norway comparing new mothers in same-sex relationships with those in heterosexual relationships. Ylva Moberg, from the Swedish Institute for Evaluation of Labour Market and Education Policy, shows that the impact on earnings for the birth mother is almost identical in both family types.[37] Meanwhile, the nonbirth mothers in the lesbian couples show a similar earnings pattern to fathers in the heterosexual ones. Over time, the inequality seems to balance out in the lesbian couple if they have more than one child, as each takes their turn at being the birth mother. For heterosexual couples, by contrast, the gap gets wider with each child.

A study of bus and train drivers working for the Massachusetts Bay Transportation Authority (MBTA), by Valentin Bolotnyy and Natalia Emanuel, a duo of Harvard economists, provides some strong evidence here too.[38] Women account for 30% of the drivers, and on average earn $0.89 for every dollar earned by their male peers. By focusing on men and women doing the same job for the same employer, Bolotnyy and Emanuel can tease out the various factors contributing to wage differences. They conclude that the pay gap "can be explained entirely by the fact that, while having the same choice sets in the workplace, women and men make different choices."[39] The men were twice as likely to work overtime (which pays extra), even at short notice. They also took fewer hours of unpaid leave, and so on. Among train drivers with children, the gaps were even wider. Fathers wanted even more overtime pay; mothers wanted more time off.

In some ways, it makes most sense to look at women at the top of the ladder, since they have the widest choices and the greatest economic power. Take women who leave Harvard with a professional or postgraduate degree, arguably members of the most elite educational group in the world. Fifteen years after graduating, only half of these women are working full time. What happened? "After facing down so many obstacles, after gaining countless freedoms, the obstruction that had always been there became crystal clear," writes Claudia Goldin, who has studied this group in detail.[40] "The barrier is the time bind. Children require time; careers require time." Or take University of Chicago MBAs. Straight out of the business school, women earned about 12% less than their male classmates, a gap largely explained by the kind of jobs chosen. Thirteen years later, the difference had widened dramatically, to about 38%.[41] But one subgroup of the female MBAs had not fallen further behind. By now you don't need me to tell you which: the ones without children.

For most women, having a child is the economic equivalent of being hit by a meteorite. For most men, it barely makes a dent. The question arises as to whether these different roles are freely chosen or not. I will dig into this question more later. For now, I will say that the mothers of young children seem to want more time at home. In the Chicago MBA study just cited, the women most likely to reduce their working hours were those with the highest-earning husbands. But even if there is a real preference being expressed here, two points need to be added. First, the labor market price paid for this choice doesn't need to be as high as it is. Second, once children are older, there is a good case for fathers doing more on the home front.

THE $2 TRILLION WOMAN

We have women to thank, and especially mothers to thank, for fueling economic growth for at least a generation. In 2019, women accounted for 47% of all workers.[42] The U.S. economy is $2 trillion larger than it would have been had women's economic participation remained at 1970s levels, according to a 2015 report from the Council of Economic Advisers. For families on modest or low incomes, the rise of women's work and wages has also blunted some of the pain of men's economic decline. As the Council concluded, "Essentially all of the income gains that middle-class American families have experienced since 1970 are due to the rise in women's earnings."[43]

The biggest change in employment has been among married women with children. In 1970, most mothers were not in paid work—today, almost three out of four are.[44] Even among the mothers of preschoolers, paid work is now the norm rather than the exception. Women account for around half the managerial positions in the U.S. economy.[45] Many previously male-dominated professions, including medicine and financial management, are rapidly tilting female, especially among younger professionals. The proportion of women lawyers has increased tenfold, from 4% in 1980 to 43% in 2020.[46] The shift has taken place not just in economic activities but in economic aspirations and expectations. In 1968, only 33% of young women in their teens and early 20s said they expected to be in paid work at the age of 35. By 1980, the share was 80%.[47] (The question has now been dropped from the survey.) The idea that women will pursue professional and economic goals has gone from novelty to commonplace. When was the last time you heard the term *career woman*?

"The 200,000 year period in which men have been top dog is truly coming to an end," wrote Hanna Rosin in *The End of Men*. "The global economy is becoming a place where women are more successful than men."[48] Wait, what? Women becoming *more* successful than men? No wonder Rosin got so much heat when her book was published. "Feminists don't like the argument," Rosin observed later, "because they say it makes it seem as though women have totally won and there isn't anything more to worry about."[49] This is not Rosin's view, however—and it is not mine either. There is plenty to worry about in terms of women's opportunities, including in the higher reaches of the economy. Just one in five C-suite company directors is a woman, and just forty-one of the Fortune 500 firms have a female CEO.[50] That is certainly better than the number in 1995, which was zero. But it is still shockingly low. The share of venture capital money going to female founders is 3%.[51] So yes, there is more work to do for women, especially at the apex of the economy. But lower down the economic ladder, it is often the men who are struggling.

Over the last few decades, girls and women have shot past men in school and on college campuses. On the economic front, many men—though not the elite ones—have also lost ground, as women have surged ahead. This has had important consequences for broader culture, especially in terms of family life. The economic rise of women has dramatically altered the terms of trade between the sexes. Many men are struggling to adjust.

CHAPTER 3

DISLOCATED DADS

Fathers Have Lost Their Traditional
Role in the Family

In June 1955, Adlai Stevenson, former Illinois governor and two-time presidential candidate, addressed the all-female graduating class at Smith College. On a warm Massachusetts afternoon, he told them that as future wives, they had an important role to play in ensuring that their husband was "truly purposeful, to keep him whole."[1] At the time, this seemed an innocuous enough statement, even from the leading progressive of the day. (Stevenson was a favorite of Eleanor Roosevelt, among others.) Sixteen years later, the commencement speech was given by a woman who had been a Smith junior when Stevenson spoke. It was markedly different, labeling God as a "she," highlighting the political significance of the female orgasm, and most importantly, describing marriage as an institution designed for "the subjugation of women."[2] Her name was Gloria Steinem.

For Steinem, as for most feminists of her generation, marriage was a relationship of crippling dependency. Her message to the young women on the lawn at Smith was to make their own way in the world and to be able to pay their own bills. "Dependence represents a lack of alternatives," wrote Margaret Mead, a few years after Steinem's speech. "A woman equipped to earn her own living need never feel trapped. . . . Independence begins with economic independence."[3]

The women's movement is about liberation. (That is why it was called women's lib.) Above all, this meant *economic* independence from men. This goal has been largely accomplished in advanced economies, turning marriage into a social choice rather than an economic necessity. Until the 1970s, the typical female college graduate had become a wife within a year of graduation.[4] Among today's Smith graduates, only about half are married by their mid-30s.[5] A husband may be nice, but he is no longer necessary. Steinem was right about the importance of breaking the economic chains. But—and this is obviously much harder to say—Stevenson was right too. A man who knows he must provide for a wife and children has a clear sense of how to be "purposeful" and "whole."

In this chapter, I argue that the role of mothers has been expanded to include breadwinning as well as caring, but the role of fathers has not been expanded to include caring as well as breadwinning. Specifically I argue the following: (1) the male role has long been culturally defined as that of a provider, and based on the economic dependence of mothers on men; (2) this traditional role has been dismantled by the securing of economic independence by women; (3) culture and policy are stuck on an obsolete model of fatherhood, lagging way behind economic reality; and (4) this is resulting in a "dad deficit," with men increasingly unable to fulfill the traditional breadwinner role but yet to step into a new one.

The economic reliance of women on men held women down, but it also propped men up. Now the props have gone, and many men are falling.

DADS AS PROVIDERS

Concluding a sweeping survey of a number of cultures from the Mediterranean basin to Tahiti to South Asia, published in *Manhood in the Making: Cultural Concepts of Masculinity*, David Gilmore writes, "To be a man in most of the societies we have looked at, one must impregnate women, protect dependents from danger, and provision kith and kin. . . . We might call this quasi-global personage something like 'Man-the-Impregnator-Protector-Provider.'"[6] Gilmore argues that this Ubiquitous Male should be seen as nurturing, just in a different way than the typical female. Men are expected to put others before themselves in a variety of ways, including by giving up resources to the group, as well as risking injury or even death in its defense. One of the central ideas here is that of a surplus. Mature men generate more resources than they need for their own survival, and these are shared with the clan, tribe, or family. "The idea of the provider is a major element in the construction of a masculine identity," writes sociologist David Morgan. "It is a moral as well as an economic category."[7]

For at least the last few thousand years, men could essentially describe their role in four words: "providing for my family." For much of this period, the family was an extended one. But in recent centuries, especially in the West, it has evolved into a more narrowly defined social institution, often labeled the nuclear family: father, mother, and children. As a result, the roles of father and husband became so tightly bound together as to be virtually indistinguishable. A good husband and father was one who provided for his family, which consisted of himself, his wife or partner, and their children. This provider role successfully connected men to familial and social life, as the British sociologist Geoff Dench describes in *Transforming Men: Changing Patterns of Dependency and Dominance in Gender Relations*: "What it does is formally to incorporate men into the interpersonal support structures, the chains of dependency, which lie at the core of any human society."[8]

Dench is right as a matter of history. But the question going forward is how to maintain "chains of dependency" between fathers and children, in a world where the ones between men and women have been successfully broken. The traditional family model provided a "'package deal' in which a father's relationship with his child is contingent on his relationship with the mother," write Laura Tach and coauthors.[9] The traditional family was an effective social institution because it made both men and women necessary. But it also rested on a sharp division of labor. While mothers had a direct, primary caring relationship with their children, fathers had an indirect, secondary, providing one. I am not suggesting that this was all there was to it, of course. My own father fulfilled the traditional provider role, but he was much more besides— swimming coach, driving instructor, moving man, chauffeur, academic adviser, you name it. But his bedrock duty was that of all the fathers of his generation: breadwinner.

The traditional contract between caring mothers and providing fathers was expressed through marriage. A breadwinner–carer marriage is part of what Gilmore described as a "special moral system . . . required to ensure a voluntary acceptance of appropriate behavior in men."[10] This is one reason conservatives tend to worry most about declining marriage rates. For them, the dependency relationship between husbands and wives is precisely what makes marriage work, including as a mechanism for harnessing male energy to positive social ends. Feminists by contrast see marriage as an oppressive institution, "the citadel of the enemy," according to John Stuart Mill and a mechanism for "locking women up" in Gloria Steinem's assessment.[11] This critique is sustained by many contemporary feminist writers.[12]

The point on which both sides agree is that marriage bound women to men, but also men to women, and thereby to children. Where they differ is on whether this was a good thing. Conservatives are right that as a social institution, marriage "worked" in the past. Feminists are right that it did so by curtailing women's autonomy. The question is what we do now and, especially, what we do with the men. Certainly, the answer is not to try to roll back the gains of the women's movement, as Dench and other conservatives suggest. A reinvention of fatherhood based on a more direct relationship to children is the answer, and I set out some ideas on this in chapter 12.

It is important to note, however, that life has not always been rosy for men in traditional families. There is a certain desolation to a life that is designed for you. The postwar angst of the "Organization Man" in his gray flannel suit, shuttling between a suburb and an office five days a week, hints at this potential hollowness. Witness the quiet desperation of Willy Loman in Arthur Miller's *Death of a Salesman*, who has to "suffer fifty weeks of the year for the sake of a two-week vacation" and who can only fulfill his role as breadwinner, in the end, by taking his own life.[13] Men's freedom has often been stifled by patriarchy too, with tightly prescribed roles and oppressive expectations.

BICYCLES IN A WORLD OF FISH

Irina Dunn's statement that "a woman needs a man like a fish needs a bicycle," later popularized by Gloria Steinem, was a memorable rallying cry of the women's movement, an evocative description of a world where women do not need men.[14] "Being able to support oneself allows one to choose a marriage out of love and not just economic dependence," Steinem said in 2004.[15]

Women are now the main breadwinner in 41% of U.S. households.[16] Some of those are single mothers, but by no means all; three in ten wives now out-earn their husbands, twice as many as in 1981.[17] Most mothers now work full time, and in almost half of families where both parents work full time, mothers earn as much or more than fathers.[18] Mothers have also received growing support from the welfare system, allowing even those with low or no earnings to be freer of the need for a breadwinning husband. As the British politician and scholar David Willetts writes in his book *The Pinch*, "A welfare system that was originally designed to compensate men for loss of earnings is slowly and messily redesigned to compensate women for the loss of men."[19]

A more positive way to make the same point is that governments increasingly see their role as supporting women raising children, in part so that they are *not* trapped in a dependent relationship with a man. At the same time, there has been a liberalization of divorce law, with the rise of "no fault" or "unilateral" divorces that allow either party to end a marriage on any grounds. These laws remain the subject of heated debate, but they are clearly here to stay.[20]

Marriage and motherhood are no longer virtually synonymous. About 40% of births in the U.S. now take place outside marriage, up from just 11% in 1970.[21] A particularly striking trend is the decline in "shotgun" marriages. Half a century ago, pregnancies outside marriage were common, but the couple went to the registry office or church before the maternity ward. No longer. In fact, the decline in shotgun marriages is the biggest single cause of the rise in nonmarital births to first-time mothers since 1960, according to research from the Joint

Economic Committee. The greatest change has occurred at the bottom of the socioeconomic ladder. In 1977, 26% of pregnancies among women with low levels of education resulted in a marriage before the birth. By 2007 the figure was just 2%.[22]

Social norms about maternal employment have shifted so fast that the term *working mother* already sounds antiquated. According to the General Social Survey, three quarters (74%) of U.S. adults now agree that working mothers can establish as "warm and secure" a relationship with their children as a stay-at-home mother, compared to 48% in 1977.[23]

From a feminist perspective, these are marvelous developments. But what do they mean for men? The old script, mostly centered on breadwinning, has been torn up. In an influential 1980 essay, "Why Men Resist," William Goode observed that "the underlying shift is toward the decreasing marginal utility of males."[24] True. But, ouch.

Many men are left feeling dislocated. Their fathers and grandfathers had a pretty clear path to follow: work, wife, kids. But what now? What is a bicycle for, in a world of fish? Half a century may seem like a long time to an individual, especially if they are young. But in terms of cultural history, it is the blink of an eye. The transformation of the economic relationship between men and women has been so rapid that our culture has not yet caught up.

CULTURE LAGS ECONOMICS

While the role of mothers has been modernized almost beyond recognition, fatherhood remains stuck in the past. "We have a cultural lag," says Johns Hopkins sociologist Andrew Cherlin, "where our views of masculinity have not caught up to the changes in the job market."[25] The economic numbers have changed. The social norms have not. Four out of five American adults (81%) with a high school education or less still believe that "for a man to be a good husband or partner, being able to support a family financially is very important" (compared to 62% of those with a bachelor's degree).[26]

So the very men who are least able to be traditional breadwinners are the most likely to be judged by their breadwinning potential. What this means is that men who fare poorly in the labor market are also likely to suffer in the marriage market, especially in the working class.[27]

Husbands without jobs are at much higher risk of seeing their marriages end today than in the past, according to work from Alexandra Killewald. "Expectations of wives' homemaking may have eroded," she concludes, "but the husband breadwinner norm persists."[28] Marianne Bertrand and her coauthors show that marriage markets have been hit hard by the social expectation that a man will not just earn, but will earn more than his wife. "Our estimates imply that aversion to having the wife earn more than the husband explains 29 percent of the decline in marriage rates over the last thirty years," they write.[29] (It is worth noting that the aversion was found among both men and women.) In other words, as women have earned more, relative to men, they have become less likely to marry. Sociologist Steve Ruggles estimates that 40% of the drop in marriage among Americans aged 25 to 29 from 1960 to 2013 can be explained by the fall in male earnings relative to men of the previous generation.[30] Notably, this dampening effect on marriage was strongest among those with less education.

The old models of marriage and family, based on the economic dependency of women on men, have been largely deconstructed. This is good news, for all the reasons Steinem gave. But even great blessings can be mixed. The traditional way worked well for children by encouraging the creation of fairly stable families. And it was mostly functional for men. As the sole or at least main provider, a man would be joined to a female carer, usually through marriage, in order to raise children. "The family may be a myth," writes Dench, "but it is a myth that works to make many men tolerably useful."

Dench worried that without the traditional provider role, men would "struggle to get full acceptance and risk anomie and short-termism."[31] Given the difficulties of many men today, this fear cannot be dismissed as scaremongering. The success of the women's movement has not caused the precariousness of male social identity, but it has exposed it. The question is where we go from here.

Conservatives urge a restoration of traditional marriage. David Blankenhorn, author of the influential 1996 book *Fatherless America*, argues that fatherhood has rested securely on two foundations, "co-residency with children and a parental alliance with their mother."[32] That is true as a matter of history. But the "co-residency" was something women used to have little choice about. Now they do. Blankenhorn argued that in order to tie fathers back to children, they needed to be bound back into marriage. But given the seismic cultural changes of recent decades, this is an unrealistic prescription. Rather than looking in the rear-view mirror, we need to establish a new basis for fatherhood, one that embraces the huge progress we have made toward gender equality.

For many couples, marriage now serves primarily as a "capstone" to a series of educational, social, and economic achievements, as Andrew Cherlin puts it.[33] Fewer than one in five American adults think that marriage is essential to living a fulfilling life, and of those who are married, just one in seven say that financial reasons were a major factor in the decision to tie the knot.[34]

But having lost their status as breadwinners and resident fathers, many men find themselves a little lost. The economists Ariel Binder and John Bound, after a painstaking study of falling labor market attachment among less-educated men, conclude that "the prospect of forming and providing for a new family constitutes an important male labor supply incentive."[35] Men who are not providers, or at least do not see themselves as such, work less. After an in-depth study of working class men in New Jersey, published as *The Dignity of Working Men* in 2000, Michèle Lamont concluded that "being hardworking is a mode of expressing manliness." Work signaled the fulfillment of the central male role of "providing for and protecting the family" and was part of the "disciplined self" that constitutes mature masculinity.[36]

In 1858 and 1859, a light-hearted poem appeared in newspapers across the U.S., from Virginia and North Carolina to California.[37] It was titled "What Is A Bachelor Like?"

> *Why a pump without a handle,*
> *A mouldy tallow candle,*
> *A goose that's lost its fellows,*
> *A noseless pair of bellows,*

A horse without a saddle,
A boat without a paddle;
A mule—a fool,
A two-legged stool!
A pest—a jest!
Dreary—weary—
Contrary—unchary—
A fish without a tail,
A ship without a sail . . .

Economically independent women can now flourish whether they are wives or not. Wifeless men, by contrast, are often a mess. Compared to married men, their health is worse, their employment rates are lower, and their social networks are weaker.[38] Drug-related deaths among never-married men more than doubled in a decade from 2010.[39] Divorce, now twice as likely to be initiated by wives as husbands, is psychologically harder on men than women.[40] One of the great revelations of feminism may turn out to be that men need women more than women need men. Wives were economically dependent on their husbands, but men were emotionally dependent on their wives. For all their jokes about the ball and chain, many men seem to know this. In a 2016 poll, more men than women ranked being married, either now or in the future, as "very important to me" (58 v. 47%).[41] Men do not want to be ships without sails.

In 2017, the Pew Research Center asked Americans a difficult question: What is the meaning of life? Specifically, they asked respondents an open-ended question, "What about your life do you currently find meaningful, fulfilling, or satisfying? What keeps you going, and why?" One of their most striking discoveries was that women find more meaning in their lives, and from more sources, than men. Women and men are equally likely to say that their job or career provides "a great deal of meaning and fulfillment" (33% and 34%).[42] But in almost every other domain, there was a marked gender gap: 43% of women across all age groups mentioned children or grandchildren as a source of current meaning, for example, compared to just 24% of men.

Someone with multiple sources of meaning and identity would be seen by a psychologist as having high "self-complexity." Being a complex self has costs. You may have to spend time and energy transitioning between different aspects of your identity, for instance. The term *code-switching* is often used for this in the context of race. Women may have to shift between being a mother and a worker, for example, with each identity being "activated" or "deactivated" as circumstances require. They may feel torn between the two. But the benefits are generally bigger. If there is a setback in one domain, according to psychologist Janet Hyde, "women activate the other identity, thereby restoring a positive sense of self, which supports the benefits of self-complexity."[43] If you have a bad day as a mom, you can make up for it by nailing it at work, or vice versa. Or at least, that is the theory.

Right now, men have a narrower range of sources of meaning and identity, which makes them particularly vulnerable if any one of the sources is damaged. Men seem to take a bigger dent in their happiness, for example, if they lose their job.[44] As well as being good for children, a stronger role for fathers would provide many men with a powerful extra source of meaning and purpose in their lives.

A DAD DEFICIT

"Too many fathers . . . are . . . missing—missing from too many lives and too many homes," said Barack Obama, on Father's Day in 2008. "And the foundations of our families are weaker because of it."[45] This was a blunt, brave message coming from a presidential candidate, especially to a Black audience. Obama was criticized for not paying enough attention to the structural barriers facing men, especially Black men. But it is important not to lose sight of his central message, which was a much more positive one. Fathers matter. They are not dispensable. They are, he said, "teachers and coaches. They are mentors and role models."

Obama was also right to point out that many children grow up without a strong relationship with their father. Within 6 years of their parents separating, one in three children never see their father, and a similar proportion see him once a month or less.[46] As these statistics show, the main reason for the dad deficit is the growing likelihood that fathers are not living with the mothers of their children. Missing from their children's home, they end up missing from their lives. This is particularly true for the most disadvantaged. Among fathers who did not complete high school, 40% live apart from their children, compared to just 7% of fathers who graduated from college.[47] In 2020, one in five children (21%) were living with a mother only, almost twice as many as in 1968 (11%).[48]

Attitudes toward unmarried parenthood have become much more relaxed. Eighty-two percent of women aged 25–34 say that "it is okay for an unmarried female to have and raise a child," and 74% of their male peers agree.[49] Most children in the U.S. will not spend their whole childhood with both biological parents.[50] The liberalization of social norms and practices with regard to marriage and childbearing are in many ways a positive development. But it is vitally important that fathers are not benched as a result. Women have expanded their role, and the range of choices that they can make. Too many men are stuck with the narrow provider role, which is now badly obsolete, not only in theory but also in practice.

The result is that the separation of men from women too often means the separation of fathers from children. This is bad for men, bad for women, and bad for children. Just as women have largely broken free of the old, narrow model of motherhood, so men need to escape the confines of the breadwinner model of fatherhood. Fathers matter to children even if—perhaps especially if—they are not married to their mother. The social institution of fatherhood urgently needs an update, to become more focused on direct relationships with children. Along with the obvious challenges there is a big opportunity here too, for an expansion in men's roles.

The stakes here are high. Fatherhood is a fundamental social institution, one that shapes mature masculinity more than any other. "A man who is integrated into a community through a role in a family, spanning generations into the past and future, will be more consistently and durably tied to the social order than a man responding chiefly to a charismatic leader, a demagogue, or a grandiose ideology of patriotism." That's George Gilder writing in 1973.[51] Gilder was an arch conservative, for sure. But given recent political history, it is hard to say that he was wrong.

PART II

DOUBLE DISADVANTAGE

CHAPTER 4

DWIGHT'S GLASSES

Black Boys and Men Face Acute Challenges

A few years back, I was delighted to see my godson wearing glasses. It makes me feel better to know others are aging too. Judge me if you like. "Don't feel too bad, Dwight," I said with faux sympathy. "It happens to all of us in the end." Dwight laughed. "Oh no," he said, "these are clear lenses. I just do more business when I'm wearing them." Dwight sells cars for a living. I was confused. How does wearing unnecessary glasses help him sell more cars? "White people especially are just more relaxed around me when I wear them," he explained.

Dwight is six foot five. He is also Black. It turns out that this is a common tactic for defusing white fear of Black masculinity. When I mentioned Dwight's story in a focus group of Black men, two of them took off their glasses, explaining, "Yeah, me too." In fact, I have yet to find a Black American who is unaware of it, but very few white people who are. Defense attorneys certainly know about it, often asking their Black clients to put on glasses. They call it the "nerd defense."[1] One study found that glasses generated a more favorable perception of Black male defendants but made no difference for white defendants.[2]

Dwight's statement was one of those moments when your whole view of the world shifts on its axis. It was like that evening over dinner when I asked him if he often gets stopped by the police. "No, not really," he said. Then, "maybe every few months?" And after a pause: "I *was* handcuffed by them a little while back though. Mistaken identity, they said." At times like this, I realize that *I do not have the faintest idea* what it is like to be Black in America, and specifically to be a Black man. And so, an advisory warning: as a British-born white guy, my perspective on American racism will need to be discounted appropriately. For what it is worth, however, I am convinced that one of the principal impediments to equity in the U.S. today is the combination of racism and sexism faced by Black men.

In Part 1, I discussed some of the broad challenges facing boys and men in education, work, and family life. In Part 2, I will focus on those facing the starkest challenges, especially Black boys and men in this chapter, and working-class boys and men in chapter 5. In chapter 6, I describe the troubling evidence of social programs not working for males.

Like many Black men in America, Dwight has had a tough journey. He grew up in one of the toughest neighborhoods of West Baltimore. He cannot remember his father, who died when Dwight was young. Given the profound, specific challenges faced by Black men in almost every aspect of American life, from criminal justice to education and employment, putting on a pair of clear tortoiseshell frames may seem trivial. Certainly, Dwight is nonchalant about it. "It is what it is," he says. But I think it says almost everything. Knowing they are perceived as a threat, Black men resort to unneeded eyewear, not to see us, but so that we might see them.

REVERSE SEXISM

In the late 1980s and 1990s, a breakthrough occurred in the study of inequality and discrimination with the development of "intersectionality." Pioneered by Kimberlé Crenshaw, this framework was initially grounded in Black feminism, but it provides a way to examine how different forms of oppression operate in combination. Rather than seeing inequality in binary terms, such as male/female, Black/white, rich/poor, or gay/straight, Crenshaw insists on the "complexities of compoundedness."[3]

The power of intersectional thinking derives from its inescapable pluralism. Each of us are "multiply" identified. You may be a Black heterosexual Jewish socialist lawyer; I may be a white gay atheist libertarian coal miner. This insistence on plural identities echoes centuries of progressive liberal thought, from John Stuart Mill and Harriet Taylor Mill in the nineteenth century to Amartya Sen and Martha Nussbaum in the twenty-first.

Crenshaw centers her work on Black women, but the framework can be used more broadly, and the position of any particular group is not fixed in relation to that of another group. As my colleague Tiffany N. Ford, a public health scholar, writes of intersectional approaches, "Social categories are contextual. Fundamental traits are not fixed, but rather constantly changing over time."[4] What it means to be queer, or Black, or male is not fixed in relation to what it means to be straight, or white, or female. Patterns of advantage and disadvantage are not set in stone. So anti-Black gendered racism hurts Black men and Black women, but not in the same way. Gender is racialized, and race is gendered, in different ways, in different places, and at different times.[5] Consider the conservative archetype of the "welfare queen," a gendered lens through which to pathologize Black women receiving public assistance.[6]

Black men face different intersections of disadvantage, many of which may be more acute than those faced by Black women. As Tommy Curry, chair of Africana Philosophy and Black Male Studies at the University of Edinburgh, writes, "In liberal arts fields it is assumed that because Black and brown men's gender is masculine, there is an innate advantage they have over all women and are patriarchal."[7] But Curry argues that the opposite is true. In *The Man-Not: Race, Class, Genre and the Dilemmas of Black Manhood*, he argues that Black males in the U.S. are "oppressed racialized men."[8] Curry urges the creation of a new scholarly field of Black male studies, on the grounds that the accounts offered by existing feminist and intersectional scholars are missing the mark when it comes to the specific forms of gendered racism faced by Black men.

But the challenge is not just in academia. Efforts to focus on the specific challenges of Black boys and men are often viewed with suspicion, as distractions from the challenges of Black women or people of other races and ethnicities. I want to be clear about my own position.

I believe that the deepest American prejudices are rooted in anti-Black racism, specifically toward the people that legal scholar Sheryll Cashin calls "descendants," African Americans who "descend from the long legacy of slavery."[9] For this reason, among others, I don't much like the term *people of color*, or the idea that the main dividing line is between white Americans and everybody else. I understand the need to build coalitions. I also understand the desire not to appear to be downplaying racism for other groups. But the idea that all people who are not white are in a similar position to that of Black Americans is both morally offensive and empirically wrong. Anti-Black racism is the main challenge, and it is at least as great for Black men as for Black women.

HARD FACTS ON BLACK MEN

Dwight spent the first 11 years of his life living in Rosemont, West Baltimore. Or as the U.S. Census Bureau would put it, Tract 24510160700. It was a Black neighborhood then. It is a Black neighborhood now. By Baltimore standards, the outcomes for children from Rosemont are not too bad. But this is not the same as saying that they are good; in terms of adult outcomes, Baltimore is one of the worst places in America to grow up as a boy.[10] Among the boys born around 1980 into low-income families (Dwight's cohort) in Rosemont, one in seven (16%) were in prison on April 1, 2010. To be clear, not that they had *been to* prison by April 1, but that they were *in prison* on that date.[11] In fact, more of these boys became prisoners than became husbands: the marriage rate for this cohort by their mid-30s was just 11%. One in three were still living in the neighborhood, which means their children will likely go to the local Belmont Elementary School. All of Belmont's students are Black. To say that outcomes from the school are poor would be an understatement. At the elementary school my children attended in Bethesda, 82% of the students cleared Maryland's proficiency standards in math in 2019. Statewide, the proportion was 58%. At Belmont, it was 1%.[12] The scale of our failure here is almost incomprehensible.

When Dwight was 11, stray gunshots were fired through his bedroom window. Working two full-time jobs, his mother managed to move the family out of the neighborhood, and he won an athletic scholarship to a private Catholic school and then to two colleges. As an upwardly mobile, well-educated, economically successful Black man, Dwight is an exception that proves the rule. Raj Chetty and his team at Opportunity Insights have crunched the numbers on 20 million Americans born around 1980, to look closely at intergenerational patterns of poverty and mobility. They find that Black men are much less likely than white men to rise up the income ladder, while Black and white women raised by poor parents have similar rates of upward intergenerational mobility. Chetty and his team conclude that the overall Black–white intergenerational mobility gap "is entirely driven by differences in men's, not women's, outcomes."[13]

But of course Black women also suffer from the poor economic outcomes of Black men, not least in terms of household income. "Black women continue to have substantially lower levels of household income than white women, both because they are less likely to be married and because Black men earn less than white men," write Chetty and his team.[14] In similar research, Scott Winship, a scholar at the American Enterprise Institute, and I find that marriage rates are a small part of the story.[15] The main problem is the low incomes of Black men, especially of those raised in poverty. This means that despite some impressive progress made by Black women, their children are still much more likely to grow up poor, reinforcing intergenerational inequality. Breaking the cycle of poverty for Black Americans will require a transformation in the economic outcomes for Black men.

Chetty has provided some sharp new statistics, but the insight is hardly new. "Many of those who escape do so for one generation only," wrote Daniel Patrick Moynihan in his 1965 report on the Black family. "As things now are, their children may have to run the gauntlet all over again."[16] One way to avoid running the gauntlet again is by getting a good education. But as the figures for Belmont Elementary dramatize, quality schools and colleges remain less accessible to Black Americans.[17]

And the boys and men are at a particular disadvantage here. As Jerlando F. L. Jackson and James L. Moore write in a special issue of the *Teachers College Record*, "Throughout the educational pipeline— elementary, secondary, and postsecondary— . . . African American males lag behind both their African American female and White male counterparts."[18]

Black women are seizing educational opportunities long denied to them, and on some fronts they have overtaken white men. Black girls are more likely than white boys to have graduated from high school; young Black women aged 18 to 24 are more likely than young white men to be enrolled in college; and a higher proportion of Black women aged 25 to 29 hold postgraduate degrees than white men of the same age.[19] The gaps here are modest, but they illustrate the important educational gains made by Black women in recent years. The gender gap in education between Black women and Black men is much wider than the one between white women and white men, as figure 4-1 shows. For every Black man getting a college degree, at all levels, there are two Black women.[20]

Black men face particularly acute challenges in the U.S. But there are similar patterns in other countries. In the UK, for example, the gender gap in education is most pronounced among Black students, with Black boys lagging Black girls in all subjects at all ages.[21] (It is worth noting here, however, that the group doing worst at British schools are white boys from lower-income backgrounds.)

Black men therefore enter the world of work with fewer educational credentials than almost any other demographic group. Then they face a greater risk of discrimination in many parts of the labor market, as well as higher rates of incarceration.[22] As a result, there are more Black women than Black men in the labor force, in contrast to every other racial or ethnic group.[23] This is not just an issue of poverty. As Chetty reports, Black men raised in relatively affluent families have lower employment rates than white men raised in poverty.[24]

Those Black men who are in work receive some of the lowest wages; the weekly wage of the typical Black male worker in 1979 was $757 (in today's dollars). Today it is $830. That is a gain of just 10%.

FIGURE 4-1   Black men lag Black women in education
Gender composition of degrees awarded to Black students

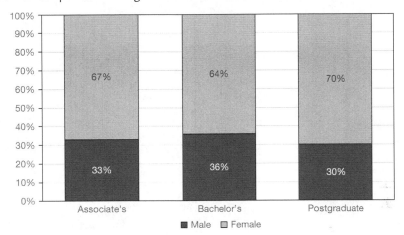

Note: Data are for the 2018–2019 academic year.
Source: National Center for Education Statistics, IPEDS. *Digest of Education Statistics*
Tables 321.20, 322.20, and 323.20, and 324.20.

Again, it is important to look at race and gender together here. White women have seen the most dramatic economic gains in recent decades, as figure 4-2 shows. In 1979, white and Black women earned the same. Now Black women earn 21% less. White women caught up with Black men by the 1990s and have had faster-rising earnings ever since. Black men now earn 14% less than white women (and 33% less than white men).

Gender gaps in the labor market are narrowing while race gaps widen. The overall gender pay disparity is closing because the wages of women, especially white women, are rising rapidly. Meanwhile the Black–white pay gap is widening, as Black workers, especially Black men, see painfully slow growth in wages. Given these trends, it should not be a surprise to learn that Black women are more likely than Black men to be the main family breadwinner, again in contrast to every other racial group.[25]

In terms of upward mobility, employment, wages, and breadwinning status, the status of Black men is starkly different from that of white men, and on most measures also lagging behind Black women.

FIGURE 4-2   White women now earn more than Black men
Median weekly earnings in 1979 and 2020, by race and gender

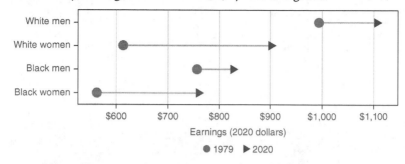

Note: Median weekly earnings for workers aged 16+, in 2020 dollars adjusted for inflation.
Source: Bureau of Labor Statistics, Current Population Survey, Table 3.

None of this is to suggest that Black women have somehow sprung free of racism or sexism, or achieved anything close to equality. Black women face a different combination of disadvantages than Black men; there is some evidence, for example, that Black women experience greater discrimination when they become mothers.[26] They face gendered racism too, albeit of a different kind.

But there is a particular pain point for Black boys and men, not in spite of their gender, but because of it. A summary of Chetty's research in the *New York Times* concludes that "there is something unique about the obstacles black males face."[27]

This is one reason why President Obama launched his 2014 initiative, My Brother's Keeper, which lives on as the MBK Alliance in the Obama Foundation.[28] This focus on boys and men has been criticized, for example, by the Institute for Women's Policy Research, for drawing attention away from the challenges faced by Black women.[29] But it seems right to me, given both the stark disparities as well as the general lack of institutional investment in issues facing boys and men. There are, after all, many organizations, both public and private, focused on women, many of which also address some of the challenges faced by Black women. In recent years, some foundations and think tanks have also paid more attention to Black men. But the response still looks tepid given what

Camille Busette describes as an "appalling crisis." We need, she says, nothing less than a "New Deal for Black Men."[30]

THE THREAT STEREOTYPE

Many Black men, including Dwight's former neighbors in Baltimore, end up in what Ta-Nehisi Coates calls the "Gray Wastes" of the American prison system. One in four Black men born since the late 1970s have been in prison by their mid-30s.[31] Among those who dropped out of high school, it is seven out of ten. These men hit young adulthood just as the imprisonment boom began in the 1980s and 1990s as part of the bipartisan war on drugs.

The problem starts with the perception that Black men are dangerous. Black men are "uniquely stigmatized," according to studies of implicit bias conducted by political scientists Ismail White and Corrine McConnaughy. One in three white Americans rank "many or almost all" Black men as "violent," compared to just one in ten who say the same of white men.[32] According to McConnaughy and White, "The gender modifier does unique work in accessing negative notions of black men."[33] In other words, Black men are discriminated against *because* they are men. It hardly needs saying that this is an old problem. "Keeping the Negro 'in his place' can be translated as keeping the Negro male in his place," Moynihan noted in 1965. "The female was not a threat to anyone."[34]

These perceptions constrain the lives of Black men in very specific ways. My colleague Rashawn Ray, a sociologist, shows for example that middle-class Black men are less likely to be physically active in neighborhoods that are mostly white. Why? Because Black men are trying to avoid being seen as a threat. "Black men have a different social reality from their black female counterparts," he writes. "The perceptions of others influence black men's social interactions with co-workers and neighbors [and] structure a unique form of relative deprivation. . . . In this regard, the intersectionality framework becomes useful for illuminating black men's multiplicities and vulnerabilities."[35]

This is intersectionality as a matter of life and death. On February 23, 2020, Ahmaud Arbery was shot dead while out for a run in his neighborhood. His killers were Gregory McMichael, a former police officer, and McMichael's son, Travis. Despite irrefutable evidence, they were not arrested for 2 months. Ibram X. Kendi, a scholar from American University, wrote of his own experience of running. "They don't need to figure out who I am. All they see is what I am. A black male. And what I am pronounces who I am. A criminal. The embodiment of danger. The producer of fear."[36]

Seen as more threatening, Black men are more likely to be stopped by the police, more likely to be frisked, more likely to be arrested, and more likely to be convicted. The wars on drugs and crime became in effect a war on Black men, who are more than three times as likely to be arrested for a drug crime than white men (though no more likely to use drugs) and nine times more likely to end up in a state prison as a result of a drug offense.[37] For Black men, even more than for men in general, masculinity is a double-edged sword. Black masculinity was seen as "toxic" long before the term was applied more broadly, as shown by the use of terms like *superpredator* and *wolf pack* to describe Black male offenders.[38]

One of the most striking aspects of anti-Black gendered racism, as directed against boys and men, is its physicality. As Ta-Nehisi Coates has written, this is a history of bodily theft and destruction, of "carriage whips, tongs, iron pokers, handsaws, stones, paperweights or whatever might be handy to break the black body, the black family, the black community, the black nation."[39] And now, of guns too. In July 2016, three Black men were shot by police officers on three successive days in three different cities: Delrawn Small in Brooklyn, New York; Alton Sterling in Baton Rouge, Louisiana; and Philando Castile in Saint Paul, Minnesota.

On the third day, a close colleague came to my office, ostensibly to talk about a work project. She is a Black mother and was in tears within a few minutes, worried sick about her boys, and perplexed by the way all the people around her were managing to go about their daily tasks as if there was nothing wrong. Until she walked through my door, I had been one of those people too.

One of the reasons Black men are less likely to be in the workplace is simply that they are so much more likely to be in jail. And even when they are released, their chances of finding work are massively reduced. This is not just because they have a criminal record—it is because employers are more likely to view Black men as criminals anyway.[40] One striking study showed that a Black man *without* a criminal record is less likely to be hired than a similarly qualified white man *with* a criminal record. This is why reforms to "Ban the Box" (i.e., remove the requirement to declare a criminal record when applying for a job) do not seem to improve the chances of Black men being hired.[41] As Devah Pager writes, "Effectively, the job market in America regards Black men who have never been criminals as though they were."[42]

The criminalization of Black men in America has resulted in millions of workless men and millions of fatherless families. But men struggling in the labor market often struggle in the marriage market too, leading to higher rates of single parenthood. President Barack Obama describes the "hole" in his heart left by the absence of his father.[43] Many Black men suffer from "post-traumatic missing daddy disorder," according to Jawanza Kunjufu, author of *Raising Black Boys*.[44] Before their 14th birthday, one in four Black children see a parent go to jail or prison, usually their father.[45] Daniel Beaty, a writer, actor, and poet, recalls a childhood game he played until he was 3. When Beaty's father knocked at his bedroom door in the morning, Beaty would pretend to be asleep, before jumping gleefully up into his father's arms. Until the morning his father did not knock, because he was in prison. Three decades later, Beaty performed his poem "Knock, Knock," which includes the following lines:

> *Twenty-five years later I write these words for the little boy*
> *in me who still awaits his papa's knock. . . .*
> *Papa, come home cause I miss you*
> *I miss you waking me up in the morning and telling me you love me.*
> *Papa, come home, because there are things that I*
> *don't know and I thought maybe you could teach me:*
> *how to shave, how to dribble a ball, how to talk to a lady, how*
> *   to walk like a man. . . .*[46]

I will have more to say about the importance of fathers in chapter 12. But for now, I will note that Black boys seem to benefit even more than others from engaged fatherhood, and that on many measures, Black fathers are more engaged than fathers of other races, especially when they are not married to or living with the mother.[47]

THE BLACK FAMILY UNDER STRESS

Black women have always played a more important economic role in the family, especially compared to white women. Even today, inequality shapes racial differences in family life. Half of Black women raising children are doing so without a husband or cohabiting partner, in stark contrast to women of other racial groups, especially whites. Black mothers are three times as likely as white mothers to be single parents (52% v. 16%), and half as likely to be living with a spouse (41% v. 78%).[48] Most births to Black women take place outside marriage (around 70%), compared to about half the births to Hispanic women, and 28% of those to white women.[49]

A comprehensive study of marital trends by Kelly Raley, Megan Sweeney, and Danielle Wondra concludes that "compared to both white and Hispanic women, Black women marry later in life, are less likely to marry at all, and have higher rates of marital instability."[50] Black women in their early 40s are five times as likely as white women of the same age to have never married (34% v. 7%). Black marriage has been undermined by anti-Black racism, including by the specific challenges faced by Black men. In his sociological classic *The Truly Disadvantaged*, published in 1990, William Julius Wilson argued that dire economic conditions create a smaller pool of "marriageable men," so fewer couples tie the knot.[51]

I have always been uncomfortable with this argument, because male "marriageability" is based on stereotypical assumptions. To be marriageable, a man has to be a breadwinner. How outdated and sexist! The trouble is that most people, including most Black people, agree with Wilson. Breadwinning potential is highly prized in a potential mate: 84% of Black Americans say that in order to be a good husband or partner, it is "very important" for a man to be "able to provide for their family financially," compared to 67% of white respondents.[52] But the gap is even wider when it comes to female providers: 52% of Black Americans say it is very important for *women* to be able to financially support their family, compared to just 27% of white Americans. Given the economic challenges facing Black women and men, this is not surprising. But while Black women are seeing some improvement in their educational and economic positions, and therefore their ability to fill the breadwinning role, Black men are falling way behind.

I hope it is clear that I am not arguing for somehow elevating Black men *above* Black women, even if that were possible, but just to help them to keep up. More needs to be done to clear the obstacles in the path of Black women. But even more now needs to be done for Black men. This is not a zero-sum game, and it is vitally important that it is not framed as such, as Moynihan did in a letter to President Johnson in 1965. "Men must have jobs. We must not rest until every able-bodied Negro male is working," he wrote, before adding, fatally, "even if we have to displace some females."[53] Of course, Moynihan was writing more than half a century ago. He was also a white man and an establishment figure. But we should not just dismiss the comment. Even today, there is a fear that helping men means hindering women, whether by design or by happenstance. But it is not true. It is important to strive for equity in terms of gender, class, *and* race—as Heather McGhee argues in her book *The Sum of Us*.[54] Raising men up does not mean holding women down, or "displacing" them. It means rising together.

FREE MEN

On August 9, 2014, Michael Brown, an unarmed Black teenager, was shot and killed by a white police officer in Ferguson, Missouri, part of the St. Louis metro area. The next day, August 10, Dr. Sean Joe arrived in the city. He had come to fill the post of professor of social development at Washington University. Joe was already planning to work on the issues confronting Black boys and men. Now, as the city reeled from Brown's death and its aftermath, his work took on a new urgency. He created a new Race and Opportunity Lab and an initiative, Homegrown

STL, focused on improving the prospects of the 60,000 Black boys and men aged between 12 and 29 who lived in the area. Following Brown's death, a commission of local leaders was charged by the governor of Missouri with the task of conducting "a wide-ranging, in-depth study of the underlying issues brought to light by the events in Ferguson." In October 2015, the commission issued a hard-hitting report on the history and impact of racism in the city, and provided almost 200 recommendations for reform.[55]

But Sean Joe was disappointed. "The report talks about racial equity in general—but says nothing about Black boys and men specifically," he told me. "We need to be able to talk confidently about the issues facing Black boys and men. This is what Michael Brown represented. It was not just the fact that he was Black that mattered—it was the fact that he was a Black *male*. People just don't want to *talk* about that." The report is indeed silent on gender. This is not an uncommon problem. Race equity is now on the agenda of many institutions and communities. But there is a real reluctance to focus on the particular challenges faced by Black boys and men. The fact that Black males are disadvantaged *because* of their gender doesn't fit into the binary models of racism and sexism that many are comfortable with. Given the weight of evidence now available on the specific plight of Black men, this just won't do.

There are some signs of hope. In 2020, a rare piece of bipartisan legislation established the Commission on the Social Status of Black Men and Boys. This is a nineteen-member permanent commission within the United States Commission on Civil Rights, charged with investigating "potential civil rights violations affecting black males" and "studying the disparities they experience in education, criminal justice, health, employment, fatherhood, mentorship and violence."[56] Modeled on a similar initiative in Florida, the Commission is required by law to report annually to Congress with policy recommendations and advice.[57] There was some resistance to the Commission's creation from congressional Democrats, again fearing, wrongly I think, that it would distract from women's issues. As then-Senator Kamala Harris said, "It is time that we come to terms with the fact that America has never fully addressed the systemic racism that has existed in our country—particularly toward black men and boys."[58] The gendered racism faced by Black boys and men is unique in its level of harm, and it is time to face it squarely. Many of the proposals I make later in this book have this goal in mind.

After a long conversation about his own challenges, I asked Dwight what he most wanted for his three sons. "I just want them to be free, you know?" he said. "Free of the fear, free of just the crushing awareness of it all. Just free."

CHAPTER 5

CLASS CEILING

Poor Boys and Men
Are Suffering

In 2017, a new phrase entered the lexicon of social science: "deaths of despair." Popularized by the scholars Anne Case and Angus Deaton, the term refers to mortality from drug overdoses, suicides, and alcohol-related illnesses. In an academic paper and subsequent 2020 book, Case and Deaton highlight the rise in deaths of despair among middle-aged, less-educated whites.[1] They argue that declining economic fortunes in the working class have combined with various forms of social breakdown—especially in family life—to create patterns of "cumulative disadvantage," or more bluntly, "the collapse of the white working class."[2] But this is a story about gender too. Overall, deaths of despair are almost three times higher among men than women.[3]

I have argued that Black boys and men face particular disadvantages because of gendered racism. This is why it is vitally important to examine gender through the lens of race, and vice versa. But the same is true of social class. At the top of the economic ladder, especially in the top 20% of the income distribution, both women and men are flourishing on almost all measures, from their growing wealth to the lengthening spans of their lives. (This was the focus of my previous book, *Dream Hoarders*.) Below this top bracket, men are working less than in the past, and at lower wages.

The wage gap between men and women has narrowed, but the gap between highly paid workers and everyone else has widened. In 1979, the earnings of the typical woman were 63% those of the typical man.

By 2019, this had risen to 82%. By contrast the wages of the typical worker (i.e., at the median) fell from 54% of the wages of a high earner (i.e., at the 90th percentile) to 42% by 2019.[4] By these measures, then, the gender pay gap narrowed by 19 percentage points, while the class pay gap widened by 12 percentage points.

Class warriors downplay gender concerns, focused only on the oligarchy. Gender warriors downplay class concerns, focused only on the patriarchy. But inequalities of class and gender have to be considered together, especially when they pull in different directions. "Policymaking is not a zero-sum game in which you have to choose between caring about female disadvantage or the socio-economic gap or male underachievement," write Nick Hillman and Nicholas Robinson. "All three matter."[5] Focusing too narrowly on the remaining barriers facing women can distract attention from the much deeper class divides that have opened up in our society. We might lean in, but fail to look down.

In this chapter I set out the evidence on male deaths of despair; show how the economic difficulties of working class men ends up hurting families and putting more pressure on women; and describe how many of these men have lost connection to social institutions that once anchored male identity, including marriage. I also describe how childhood disadvantage hurts boys more than girls, resulting in a corrosive, intergenerational cycle. As working-class men struggle, their families become poorer; and in these families, boys suffer most, which damages their prospects in adult life. The male malaise becomes an inherited condition.

It might seem odd to put so much stress on economic inequality in a book about boys and men. But I have come to see the two problems as inseparable. There is simply no way to reduce economic inequality without improving the fortunes of less advantaged boys and men.

DEATHS OF DESPAIR

When Donald Trump talked about "American carnage" in his inaugural address, I admit to having rolled my eyes.[6] I thought it was ridiculous hyperbole. Now I think it was only hyperbole. Trump knew who he was talking to. The counties with the most deaths of despair were the ones who swung most decisively to him in 2016, compared to Mitt Romney's performance in 2012.[7] These are also the communities where employment has declined most sharply, especially for men.

"Men in particular felt the loss not only of income but also of dignity that accompanied a good job," write Nicholas Kristof and Sheryl WuDunn, authors of *Tightrope: Americans Reaching for Hope*, a study of communities hit hardest by recent economic trends. "Lonely and troubled, they self-medicated with alcohol or drugs, and they accumulated criminal records that left them less employable and less marriageable. Family structure collapsed."[8]

The work from Case and Deaton and others on deaths of despair shows that drug-related deaths have risen sharply. Opioids are obviously a big part of the story here, and men account for almost 70% of the opioid overdose deaths in the U.S.[9] Almost half the prime-age men out of the labor force in 2016 said they had taken pain medication the previous day, mostly at prescription strength, according to a survey analyzed by Princeton economist Alan Krueger. He suggested that the increase in opioid prescriptions from 1999 to 2015 could account for almost half (43%) of the drop in male employment over the same time period.[10] Of course, poor job prospects might be fueling opioid use, as much as the other way around. A review of employment trends by the Maryland economists Katharine Abraham and Melissa Kearney concludes that "although it seems clear that the problems of depressed labor force participation and opioid use are interrelated, the arrows of causality run in both directions."[11]

I think opioids are just as much a barometer of social problems as they are a cause. Opioids are not like other drugs, which might be taken to artificially boost confidence, energy, or illumination. There is a reason people take MDMA in a dance club or psychedelics on a spiritual quest. Opioids are taken simply to numb pain—perhaps physical pain at first, then existential pain. They are not drugs of inspiration or rebellion, but of isolation and retreat. One reason that so many people die from opioid overdoses is that users are typically indoors, and very often alone.[12]

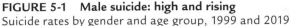

FIGURE 5-1   Male suicide: high and rising
Suicide rates by gender and age group, 1999 and 2019

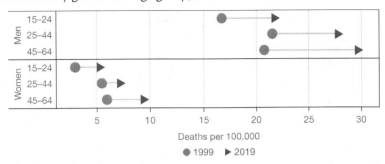

Note: Suicides identified using International Classification of Diseases, 10th Revision.
Source: National Center for Health Statistics, National Vital Statistics System, Mortality.

Men are also much more likely to commit suicide than women. This is a worldwide, long-standing pattern. But the gender gap is widest in more advanced economies, where men are about three times more likely than women to take their own life.[13] Suicide is now the biggest killer of British men under the age of 45.[14] In the U.S., suicide rates have risen fastest among middle-aged men, but there has also been a big increase in recent decades among adolescent and younger men, as figure 5-1 shows. Suicide rates for women have increased too, from a much lower starting point, but remain well below those for men.[15]

In a 2019 essay on masculinity published in *Harper's Magazine*, Barrett Swanson noted how many of his male friends and neighbors seemed dislocated in one way or another. "Several of these men struggled with addiction and depression, or other conditions that could be named," he writes, "but the more common complaint was something vaguer—a quiet desperation that, if I were forced to generalize, seemed to stem from a gnawing sense of purposelessness."[16]

In a study of suicides, Australian researcher Fiona Shand and her colleagues looked at the words or phrases that men who have attempted suicide most often used to describe themselves.[17] At the top of the list were *useless* and *worthless*. The true cause of the male malaise, I believe, is not lack of labor force participation but cultural redundancy.

FAMILY MISFORTUNES

When men struggle, families become poorer. One of the most striking facts about recent economic history is that it is only women who have kept American families financially afloat in the last few decades. And even then, just barely. Except for the richest families (i.e., the top fifth), all the growth in household income since 1979 resulted from the increased working hours and earnings of women. As Heather Boushey, appointed in 2021 to the Council of Economic Advisers, and Kavya Vaghul write, "Women's contributions saved low-income and middle-class families from steep drops in their income."[18]

We should not make the mistake of assuming that women were somehow forced into work against their will, just to keep food on the table. No doubt this was true in some cases. But most women, including mothers, *want* to earn a living, and certainly want to have that option, rather than being dependent on a man. The point here is simply that if men were doing better, most families would benefit.

Since women continue to take most responsibility for childcare, they often also end up working what the sociologist Arlie Hochschild labeled a "second shift," of domestic labor on top of their job.[19] The double shift is most acute, of course, for those who are raising children alone. In the U.S., one in four children under 18 are being raised by a single adult, 82% of whom are mothers.[20] These women, by definition, shoulder a heavier burden. But they are also often reluctant to commit to a relationship. Sociologists Kathryn Edin and Maria Kefalas show in their book, *Promises I Can Keep: Why Poor Women Put Motherhood before Marriage*, that many women in poor neighborhoods have come to see men, including the fathers of their children, as just another mouth to feed, an inversion of the men's expected role.[21] With the rise in female earning power, men need to clear a higher bar to be seen as husband material. Women are more likely to go it alone than partner with a man who is in a weak economic position. As Edin's and Kefalas's ethnographic work illustrates, many women decide that "I can do bad by myself."[22] In the bottom fifth of the income distribution, seven out of ten mothers are now the main breadwinner—usually because they are the *only* one.[23] This growing class gap in family life shows how economic factors, especially the position of men, both in absolute terms and relative to women, influences family formation.[24] The falling earnings power of noncollege males is one reason for their falling marriage rates, according to David Autor and Melanie Wasserman.[25]

Even as marriage has weakened as an economic institution, it has retained much of its symbolic power.[26] In 2015, after a long fight, lesbian and gay couples won the right to wed in the U.S. Within 2 years, three out of five cohabiting same-sex couples were married.[27] But as one gap closed, another opened up, by social class. Marriage rates among well-educated, affluent Americans have held steady, at quite high levels, in recent decades—but have fallen for everyone else.[28] In 1979, there was almost no difference in marriage rates by social class. Today there is a wide gap.[29] The marriage rate of men aged 40–44 with a high school education or less has dropped by more than 20 percentage points over the past 40 years, compared to 6 percentage points for those with college education.[30] As my colleague Isabel Sawhill has written, "Family formation is a new fault line in the American class structure."[31]

Most births to women with only a high school diploma now occur outside marriage (59%), but the same is true for just one in ten births to women with a 4-year college degree.[32] Andrew Cherlin's work shows that even if college-educated women are not married when they have their first child, they are quite likely to be married by the time they have their second, usually to the man who is the father of both children. "Marriage remains more central to the family lives of college educated Americans than to those without college educations," Cherlin concludes.[33]

There is something of a paradox here. The women who have achieved the greatest degree of economic independence, with high levels of education and earning potential, are the ones who are now *most* likely to get married and stay married. I don't think Gloria Steinem or anyone else thought that this was how things would unfold. Even she eventually got married, at the age of 66, explaining, "We are at an age when marriage can be chosen and not expected."[34]

I think educated Americans have transformed marriage from an institution of economic dependency into a joint venture for the purpose of parenting. Marriage here serves primarily as a commitment device for shared investments of time and money in children. I call these high-investment parenting, or HIP, marriages.[35] Affluent, highly educated parents have more flexibility at work, more money to outsource domestic labor, and more wealth or credit to buy time at home if they choose. If one of them takes time out of the labor market, the family finances will survive. That study of MBA graduates I cited in chapter 2, showing how time taken to care for children caused the gender pay gap, also found that women with the highest-earning husbands were the most likely to take time out of the labor market.[36] This underscores the differences in the position of men of different classes. College-educated men have been largely insulated from the labor market shocks that have derailed so many others. With high and rising earnings, they have remained attractive marital prospects, even for women who are themselves flourishing in the labor market. These men have not, by and large, become stay-at-home dads, however.

Even at the top of the ladder, there is a lot to be said for sharing the breadwinning between two winners. Educated Americans have also heard and absorbed the messages about the importance of family stability for children's prospects. Professional men have modernized enough to be good partners, without having to give up the traditional trappings of male status, especially as providers. Life is very different for men with waning wages and truncated job prospects. Equality is easier for the affluent.

The class gap in family life reflects and reinforces social and economic inequality. High earners are pooling resources in households shared with other high earners; low earners, not so much. "When considering all households," write economist Shoshana Grossbard and coauthors, "the factor accounting most for the increased inequality during this period [1973–2013] is an increased tendency for individual men and women to remain single."[37] Affluent couples are also able to invest much more heavily in their children. The result is diverging destinies among children, greater economic responsibility and independence for women, and a growing number of men who are "unburdened and unmoored," according to Shelly Lundberg and her coauthors.[38]

THE HAPHAZARD SELF

Without a script, there is no choice for many men except to improvise. But improvising a successful life is a very difficult task. "A model of stable masculinity," writes David Morgan, "would include a relatively high degree of congruence between public discourses about masculinity and the public and private practices of masculinity. For individual men, there would be a sense of ontological security."[39] This is not a great slogan. "What do we want? Ontological security! When do we want it? Now!" But this is in fact *exactly* what many men are seeking; a more solid social anchor, more certainty about how to *be* in the world.

Over the course of 13 years, a team of qualitative researchers led by Kathryn Edin conducted in-depth interviews with men in four American cities. In the resulting 2019 paper, "The Tenuous Attachments of Working-Class Men," they chart the erosion of key institutional frameworks for mature masculinity, especially work, family, and religion. These core institutions, Edin and her coauthors write, "created the attachments, investments, involvements, and beliefs that guided and gave meaning to human activity in specific social domains." They also "organized social activity into common patterns of behavior, [and] supplied norms, beliefs, and rituals that legitimated such patterns."[40]

As the title of their paper implies, many working class men are now only tenuously attached to these institutions of work, faith, and family. In these circumstances, "a few may craft lives that are more rewarding than those of prior generations, but the majority will struggle."[41] The result is an increased number of men with what the team labels "a haphazard self," oscillating between different plans and priorities, struggling to stay on any particular track, and often slipping backward.

In Coal Brook, anthropologist Jennifer Silva's label for a town in the anthracite region of Pennsylvania, "massive transformations in gender, work and family . . . have ripped open men's lives and left them scrambling to put them back together." Here, in the run up to the 2016 election, Silva reports that Donald Trump was viewed positively as a "man's man." Silva shows how some of the men in Coal Brook are attempting, against the odds, to "sustain the masculine legacy of provision, protection, and

courage that they inherited."[42] Others seek alternative routes to masculine identity, including commitments to religion or individually focused self-improvement. Some have succumbed to white nationalism,
others to the temporary escapism of opioids. In one way or another, all
are trying, in Silva's words, "to piece the self back together."

ALL THE LONELY MEN

Very often, they are doing so alone. Men have fewer friends than women
and are at greater risk of isolation. The gap has widened in recent years.
A 2021 report from the Survey Center on American Life identified a
male "friendship recession," with 15% of men saying they have no close
friends, up from 3% in 1990.[43] Unsurprisingly, these are also the men
who are most likely to report feeling lonely.

Daniel Cox a scholar at the American Enterprise Institute who conducted the survey, writes, "In 1990, nearly half (45%) of young men reported that when facing a personal problem, they would reach out first to
their friends. Today, only 22% of young men lean on their friends in
tough times. Thirty-six percent say their first call is to their parents."[44]
This may in part be because the men are more likely to be living under
the same roof as Mom and Dad. In 2014, one in three young adult men
(35%) were living with their parents, more than were living with a wife or
partner.[45] For women, it is the other way around.

I once heard a stand-up comedian in New York open his routine by
describing himself as a "stay-at-home son," and then riffing off that
theme. Like most jokes, it was funny because it had the sharp edge of
truth. Many of these men are the inhabitants of the place sociologist
Michael Kimmel labels "guyland."[46] The failure to launch is not just a
trope. It's a fact. A tragicomic sketch from *Saturday Night Live* aired in
November 2021, showing women taking their male partners to a "man
park" in order to socialize with other men. "Which one's yours?" asks
one woman of another.

Why the friendship deficit among men? For one thing, men tend to
invest less in their friendships than women, and they often rely on girl-
friends or wives not only to organize social lives but as their principal

confidant.[47] When a marriage breaks up, women seem to do better in maintaining and building networks of friends.[48] There is a reason why Ernest Hemingway, and then Haruki Murakami, almost a century later, chose the title *Men without Women* for their collections of short stories.[49] Men on their own tend to be men alone. "A guy needs somebody—to be near him," says Crooks in John Steinbeck's *Of Mice and Men.* "A guy goes nuts if he ain't got nobody. . . . I tell ya a guy gets too lonely an' he gets sick."[50]

At the extreme are the young men who retreat from society altogether. The trend is most pronounced in Japan, where the rising number of *hikikomori* (shut-ins) has prompted widespread national concern, and even some government action in the form of online support.[51] Some hikikomori have been living in one room for years. This is not a formal medical condition, and many are not obviously mentally ill, but the term "severe social withdrawal" is often used. There are now more than half a million of these modern-day hermits, according to a survey from the Japanese Cabinet Office.[52]

Some desperate parents are paying "rental sisters," to write notes to and talk on the phone with their hikikomori sons, in the hope that this will lead them back into mainstream society. Nor are these just young men—or at least, not anymore: a third are over 40. On one level, the hikikomori are conducting a silent rebellion. Many cite the workaholic culture of the nation as one of the reasons for their withdrawal. But the dangers are obvious. "The longer the hikikomori remain apart from society, the more aware they become of their social failure," says Maika Elan, who photographed many of them for a *National Geographic* story. "They lose whatever self-esteem and confidence they had, and the prospect of leaving home becomes ever more terrifying. Locking themselves in their room makes them feel 'safe.'"[53]

The concern among some scholars is that where Japan leads, other nations may follow. An organization to work with Italian hikikomori has been established.[54] A U.S. researcher, Alan Teo, associate professor at Oregon Health and Science University, believes that hikikomori may be more widespread than many believe. He has worked to define and measure the syndrome with a new twenty-five-item questionnaire

(HQ-25).[55] Even if relatively few men will totally withdraw, there are many more who are some way along the hikikomori spectrum, Teo believes. "We have a large number of people [in the United States] in their early 20s living in the basement bedroom," he says. "Oftentimes it is younger men. Struggling with work. Struggling with launching. There is some element of still being stuck in an earlier developmental stage."[56]

MALE ORCHIDS

Is your child a dandelion or an orchid? An odd question, I know, but psychologists use these terms to distinguish between children who are pretty resilient, mostly able to cope with adversity and stress (dandelions), and those who are more sensitive to their conditions (orchids).[57] If things are just right, orchids will really bloom. If not, they will suffer. Psychologists are still arguing over how far the orchid/dandelion dichotomy can be applied at the individual level. But in the meantime, social scientists are piling up the evidence that boys suffer worse consequences from childhood adversity.

Boys raised in families in the bottom fifth of the income distribution, for example, are less likely to escape poverty as an adult than girls from similarly poor homes.[58] If Horatio Alger were writing his rags-to-riches stories today, his principal characters would need to be girls. This is not just a U.S. phenomenon. In Canada, for example, boys born into the poorest households are about twice as likely as girls to remain poor as adults, according to Miles Corak an economist at The Graduate Center, CUNY.[59] Perhaps even more striking, in the U.S., boys raised poor are less likely than girls to be in paid work at the age of 30.

"Gender gaps in adulthood have roots in childhood," write Raj Chetty and his coauthors, who conducted the U.S. study, "perhaps because poverty and exposure to disadvantaged neighborhoods during childhood are particularly harmful for boys."[60]

Boys do especially badly if they are raised not only in poor families but in poor places. There is growing evidence that neighborhoods matter for long-term outcomes. But they seem to matter more for boys than girls. Boys do badly, for example, if they are raised in neighborhoods with high levels of crime, and a large share of single-parent households seem to be particularly detrimental to boys. This is why boys seem to fare particularly poorly in certain cities, including Baltimore, as well as places like Detroit and Fresno, while outcomes for girls are less influenced by their zip code. On the plus side, Black boys raised in neighborhoods with a high proportion of fathers have better prospects as adults. The bottom line, according to Chetty, is that "neighborhoods matter more for boys than girls."[61]

There is a similar dandelion/orchid story in education. The developmental gap between boys and girls starting kindergarten is much wider for children from homes with less educated mothers and less involved fathers. In high school, boys' academic performance is much more affected by family background—measured in terms of income, parental education, and marriage—than girls'.[62] The bigger impact of class position on boys and men is also clear in postsecondary education: girls raised in the poorest families (i.e., the bottom fifth of the distribution) are 57% more likely to get a 4-year college degree than boys from similar backgrounds, compared to a difference of just 8% among those from affluent (top fifth) families.[63] In the UK, the gender gap in college attendance is widest for those who are eligible for free school meals.[64]

Last but not least, boys suffer more from family instability, especially from the exit of biological fathers.[65] Boys raised by single parents, especially single mothers, have worse outcomes than girls (including their own sisters) at school and lower rates of college enrollment, in part because of bigger differences in behavioral problems in the classroom.[66] "Boys do especially poorly in broken families," write Marianne Bertrand and Jessica Pan.[67] Boys also benefit much more than girls from successful placement into a foster family, rather than remaining in a group home, according to an analysis by Stanford's Cameron Taylor.[68]

Looked at from every angle, then, the pattern is clear. Economic and social disadvantage hurts boys more than girls. This is an extremely important fact, and one that has yet to receive nearly enough attention. The problems of men are not only *fueling* social and economic inequality but also being *caused* by it. "A vicious cycle may ensue," write David Autor and Melanie Wasserman, "with the poor economic prospects of less-educated males creating differentially large disadvantages for their sons, thus potentially reinforcing the development of the gender gap in the next generation."[69]

NEW GENDER ECONOMICS

The dominant narrative of gender equality is framed almost exclusively in terms of the disadvantages of girls and women. But if we consider gender equality in the context of both race and class, a different picture emerges. Especially at the bottom of the economic ladder, it is boys and men who are falling behind girls and women. "Public policy needs to be informed by a new gender economics, at least when it comes to social mobility," writes Miles Corak. "There are important differences between the life prospects of boys and girls from less advantaged families."[70]

Any serious effort to improve rates of upward mobility or reduce economic inequality must take into account the specific challenges being faced by boys and men. Otherwise, patterns of male disadvantage will repeat across generations. That will be bad for everyone, including women, and children, especially boys. This will require more than a policy tweak here or a quick initiative there. These problems run deep and require a commensurate response.

The good news is that the clear connection between economic inequality and the male malaise provides the possibility of bipartisan action. Conservatives worried about boys and men need to be concerned about economic inequality. But liberals worried about inequality must pay more attention to boys and men.

CHAPTER 6

NON-RESPONDERS

*Policies Aren't Helping
Boys and Men*

"Women are just naturally smarter than men, and now they are on the rise." That's Jonathan, a college junior. We are discussing why women are doing so much better in college than men. "You know, the motivation for men is just not there anymore," he adds. "It's a mental thing."

Jonathan and I are talking over coffee in his hometown of Kalamazoo, Michigan. Kalamazoo is a special place, especially to policymakers. Not because of the Glenn Miller song "(I've Got a Gal In) Kalamazoo," but because of its unique free college program. Thanks to an anonymous benefactor, students educated in the city's K–12 school system get all their tuition paid at almost any college in the state.[1] There are similar initiatives in other cities, but the Kalamazoo Promise is unusually generous. It is also one of the very few to have been robustly evaluated, by a trio of scholars at the Upjohn Institute, Timothy Bartik, Brad Hershbein, and Marta Lachowska.[2] They find that the Promise made a big difference—bigger than other Promise-type programs.

But the average effect disguises a stark gender divide. The program put rocket boosters on female college completion rates, increasing the number of women getting a bachelor's degree by 45%. But men's rates didn't budge. A cost–benefit analysis shows an overall gain of $69,000 per female participant—a return on investment of at least 12%—compared to an overall *loss* of $21,000 for each man (in other words, it was expensive and didn't work). The philosopher Bertrand Russell said the mark of a civilized man was the ability to weep over a column of numbers. For a policy wonk, the numbers in these regression tables might just do it.

But it is not just the Kalamazoo Promise. I have discovered a startling number of social programs that seem to work well for girls and women, but not for boys and men. I describe some of them here, first in education and training, and then in job programs. This seems to me to be a big deal. But it is getting barely any attention, not least because almost nobody knows about it.

I asked Brad Hershbein what was behind the massive gender gap in Kalamazoo. Because he is a true scholar, Brad's answer was, "We don't know." What he means is that the gap cannot be explained statistically, at least with easily observable factors like test scores or family background. As I noted in chapter 1, there is still a good deal of mystery surrounding the worse educational outcomes for men. But I think Jonathan is on the right track with his observation about the "mental thing." If we want answers, we won't find them in the metrics, but in the minds of the young men themselves.

That is one reason why I went to Kalamazoo to meet some of the men the Promise is designed to help. Maybe they would know why it did not.

IMMUNE TO INITIATIVES: EDUCATION

"I just felt like I was wasting my time in college," says Quamari, another of my interviewees. "I was depressed a lot. I just didn't have much of a drive." After dropping out of Kalamazoo Valley Community College, he got a job working in a bank, and then he was fired. So he returned to his studies, this time at Michigan State University in Lansing, 70 miles to the northeast. Quamari hopes that a smaller, quieter city will make it easier for him to crack the books. After all, as he says, "There is not a lot else to do here." Quamari has had a staccato journey through higher education, stopping, switching, restarting. He has changed his major many times, from accounting to orthodontics (he says, "I know it sounds weird, but I like teeth and I had braces"), to interior design and then to sociology. Now he is hoping to go into psychology, having discovered music and art therapy as a potential career path. His story fits with the research suggesting that men are more likely to zig-zag through the college years, while women follow a straighter path.[3] "Females are just working harder, doing better, asking more questions," he says. Jalen, one of Kalamazoo's male success stories, agrees. He graduated with a BA from Western Michigan University and says he always sought out female-dominated study groups because "you just knew they would get it done."

One of the other studies that jumped off my desk was an evaluation of a mentoring and support program called Stay the Course, at Tarrant County College, a 2-year community college, in Fort Worth, Texas.[4] Community colleges are a cornerstone of the U.S. education system, serving around 7.7 million students, largely from middle-class and lower-income families.[5] But there is a completion crisis in the sector. Only about half the students who enroll end up with a qualification (or transfer to a 4-year college) within 3 years of enrolling.[6] Many produce many more dropouts than diplomas. The good news is that there are programs, like Stay the Course, that can boost the chances of a student succeeding. The bad news is that, as the Fort Worth pilot shows, they might not work for men—who are most at risk of dropping out in the first place. Among women, the Fort Worth initiative "tripled associate degree completion."[7] This is a huge finding. But as with free college in Kalamazoo, it had no impact on college completion for male students.

Why? Again, the evaluators can only speculate. James Sullivan, one of the scholars who is examining the program, says, "We don't know."[8] That phrase again. His research team does note that the case managers assigned to work with students, called "navigators" (great name by the way), were all women. When a program relies heavily on a close one-to-one relationship, matching the gender of the provider and recipient may be important. This is consistent with research showing that when the racial or gender identities of teachers and learners or mentors and mentees match, results are often better.[9]

The Stay the Course program and the Kalamazoo Promise are just two among dozens of initiatives in education that seem not to benefit boys or men, including the following:

- An evaluation of three preschool programs—Abecedarian, Perry, and the Early Training Project—showed "substantial" long-term benefits for girls, but "no significant long-term benefits for boys."[10]
- Project READS, a North Carolina summer reading program, boosted literacy scores "significantly" for 3rd grade girls— giving them the equivalent of a 6-week acceleration in learning. But there was a "negative and insignificant reading score effect" for boys.[11]
- Students who attended their first-choice high school in Charlotte, North Carolina, after taking part in a choice lottery, had higher GPAs, took more AP classes, and were more likely to go on to enroll in college. But "these overall gains are driven entirely by girls."[12]
- A new mentoring program for high school seniors in New Hampshire almost doubled the number of girls enrolling in 4-year college, but it had "no average effect" for boys.[13]
- Urban boarding schools in Baltimore and Washington, DC. boosted academic performance among low-income Black students, but only the girls. "Taken literally, the point estimates imply that our findings are driven entirely by the female . . . applicants," note the evaluators.[14]
- College scholarship programs in Arkansas and Georgia increased the number of women getting a degree, but had "muted" effects on white men, and "mixed and noisy" results for Black and Hispanic men.[15]
- Project STAR, which provides extra learning support and financial assistance for college freshmen, gave a big boost to women's academic performance—higher GPA, more credits and lower rates of academic probation—but had "no effect on men."[16]

MIT's Josh Angrist, a Nobel Prize winner in economics, studied this last program and has spent a lot of time in this field. He tells me he "has no theory" about the gender gap. (This is a more formal way of saying "I don't know.") I think the main issue is the lower levels of engagement and motivation that the young men in Kalamazoo talked about a lot. These are not things that can easily be fixed externally.

Back in 2009, Angrist and his coauthors wrote, "These gender differences in the response to incentives and services constitute an important area for further study."[17] They do indeed. But as far as I can see, nobody has heeded this call. At the very least, these results suggest that policymakers and scholars need to be much more sensitive to differential effects by gender, and the potential implications for program design.

Of course, there are programs that do show positive results for both genders, such as another well-evaluated community college mentoring scheme, Accelerated Study in Associate Programs (ASAP), some other early education programs, and so on.[18] But where there is a difference by gender, it is almost always in favor of girls and women. The only real exception to this rule is vocationally oriented programs or institutions, which do seem to benefit men more than women, which is one reason why we need more of them.

IF YOU CAN MAKE IT HERE: WORK

New York City is the urban expression of America's "can-do" spirit. "Make your mark in New York," wrote Mark Twain, "and you are a made man."[19] The perfect place, then, to test a new program to help more men to make their mark. The Paycheck Plus pilot provided around 3,000 childless participants with a wage bonus of up to $2,000, with the main policy goal being to lift employment rates. A rigorous evaluation of the pilot by the MDRC research group found "a relatively large positive effect on employment rates among women," but "no detectable effect among men."[20] Female participants got healthier too; the men did not.[21]

The MDRC team describe the result for men as "somewhat disappointing."[22] This is something of an understatement, given the hopes for the project and the falling wages and employment levels of less-skilled men.[23] There are broader policy implications here too. Paycheck Plus is seen as a trial run for a possible shift in national policy, to make the Earned Income Tax Credit available to childless adults. This would not be cheap. A similar EITC expansion in the 2021 Build Back Better bill had a price tag of $13.5 billion a year.[24] An explicit goal of EITC expansion is to help less-skilled men. Gene Sperling, former national economic adviser to Presidents Bill Clinton and Barack Obama, argues that the policy change is "important to incentivizing younger men . . . to participate in the formal economy."[25] But the Paycheck Plus pilot suggests that higher wage subsidies may attract more single women than single men into work. To be clear, I am not saying this is a bad thing, just that it is not a stated principal goal of the reform.

If wage subsidies don't work so well for men, what about worker training? Sadly, the evaluation studies here make for grim reading. It is hard to find examples of government-funded training programs that work well for anyone, male or female.[26] But the few programs that have managed to move the needle often skew toward women, including the following:

- A training program in Milwaukee, funded as a public–private venture, had a positive, statistically significant, impact on the employment rates and earnings for participating women at the two-year mark—but not for the men.[27]
- Programs for dislocated workers funded by the Workforce Investment Act had "greater benefits for participation for women . . . with the quarterly earnings increment exceeding that of males." The value of training also had greater long-run positive impacts on earnings and employment for women.[28]
- Workplace-based training programs and job search assistance programs funded under the Job Training Partnership Act of 1982 produced "significant positive impacts" for the earnings and educational attainment of female participants—but not for the male ones.[29]

As I've said, the overall pickings are pretty slim when it comes to effective training programs. But even among the few that do show some positive impact, there is often a gender gap. If a training program works, it generally works for women, but not always for men.

There is a clear, recurring pattern in evaluation studies of policy interventions, with stronger effects for girls and women than for boys and men. This has profound implications for research and policy. Most obviously, evaluators must include results disaggregated by gender. And when differences are found, they should be highlighted. Right now, they are often given scant attention. In the research brief based on the evaluation of the trio of public–private training programs undertaken by Public Private Ventures and published through the Aspen Institute, the gender gap in outcomes was not mentioned.[30] Even in the main report, the difference was only visible to readers who made it to appendix D, table 5, on page 72.[31]

Given the evidence that many programs simply do not work for half the population, it is irresponsible for policymakers not to question whether this money is being well spent. There is certainly enough evidence here to challenge any presumption in favor of gender-blind programs and services. It is no good to note these "disappointing" findings, shrug our shoulders, and keep on spending.

ASPIRATION GAPS

The hard question, of course, is *why* these initiatives have not worked for boys or men, and what might work instead. The empirical evidence on this is weak. But Tyreese, a young Black man making his way through community college in Kalamazoo, has thought hard about this question. Tyreese is exactly the kind of person the Kalamazoo Promise is intended to help. His father died when he was 5. Two of his brothers are in prison. He observes four big differences between the women and men around him. First, motivation: "The women are so driven. They know they have to provide for their family." Second, independence: "They [the women] don't really need a relationship, they can do it on their own." Third, persistence: "When stuff gets hard, the guys tend to run away, the girls don't." Fourth, planning: "Women tend to live in the future, men tend to live in the present." Put these together—motivation, independence, persistence, and planning—and it is no wonder, to Tyreese at least, that women are doing better in school.

It seems clear to me that motivation and aspiration, almost impossible to capture quantitatively, are a big part of the story here. Young women are seizing opportunities with much greater zeal than young men. Take studying abroad as another example. In recent decades, this has become much more popular (at least until the pandemic) with increasing numbers of undergraduates now grabbing their passports and phrase books and heading overseas, most often to Europe.[32] And why not? Going to another country for a few months is a great opportunity. In a joint report, the American Institute for Foreign Study and the Institute of International Education extol the value of studying abroad.[33] They would, of course. But it looks like they are right. Employers do seem to like hiring graduates with broader horizons, and many of the skills honed in a foreign country seem to be useful later in life. But strikingly, female students are more than twice as likely to study abroad as their male peers.[34] There is a similar gap in European countries.[35] Perhaps you are thinking, "Ah, but maybe that is just because women are more likely to be in subjects offering more study-abroad options, like languages and arts." But no—the gender gap can be found in all subjects.

Once again, this gap has left researchers stumped. What we do know is that women seem to be motivated to study abroad by all kinds of factors, including having educated parents, or classes focused on human diversity and difference. None of the factors have any impact on men. One thing that did seem to influence men's decision whether to study abroad was "peer interactions," but in a negative direction.[36] Men appear to motivate each other to stay put, rather than hit the road. The report stresses the need for a diverse and representative pool of students heading to other countries, and serious efforts have gone into lowering barriers for nonwhite students, who now make up three in ten study-abroad students. There is no mention, however, of the 2:1 ratio of female to male students.

It is not just studying overseas. There generally seems to be a greater spirit of adventure among young women. The same 2:1 gender imbalance can be seen in the numbers signing up for the Peace Corps, as well as the domestic equivalent, Americorps.[37] The gap is even greater in the UK's Voluntary Service Overseas program.[38] Young women today have wider horizons than the men. Forget all the old stereotypes about men with wanderlust, out on the road. Women are the explorers now. And as so often, nobody has a good explanation why. It is not that men have fewer opportunities. It is that they are not taking them. The problem seems to be a decline in agency, aspiration, and motivation. But this hasn't happened in a vacuum. I think it is the result of a whole range of structural challenges. I have already shown that the education system is less suited to boys, and that the labor market has become a tougher place for men. But there are deeper, cultural causes too. In particular, the dramatic rebalancing of power relations between men and women over the last few decades has rendered old modes of masculinity, especially as family breadwinner, obsolete. But nothing has yet replaced them.

"Women are becoming more independent," reflects Quamari, back in Kalamazoo. "More headstrong, willing to work for it. They know they need other options." By his own admission, Quamari struggles with this new world. He supports equality but is part of a Christian denomination teaching that men should be the head of the household. He is torn between being the kind of man he has been told to be, and the kind of man the world needs now. He is not the only one. A common thread running through many of the challenges facing men is the culture shock represented by women's economic independence. To truly understand what's going on with boys and men, we need anthropologists at least as much as economists. And we need policymakers willing to face the facts, including the facts about which programs work best. Otherwise the danger is that some of our boys and men won't just fall behind but will end up beyond our reach.

PART III

BIOLOGY AND CULTURE

CHAPTER 7

MAKING MEN

Nature and Nurture Both Matter

Every religion has a story to tell about how or why we are created male and female. In Judaism and Christianity, it all starts with Adam and Eve. Islamic theology teaches that men and women are "made in pairs," from a single soul. In the Hindu tradition, Brahma asks Rudra to divide into male and female, so that creation can continue. These creation stories reflect the most fundamental dichotomy in human biology, the one between male and female.

Sex differences in biology shape not only our bodies, including our brains, but also our psychology. We are not blank slates. Some of these differences are more about the timing of development than about the end results. I have already described how girls' brains mature much earlier, for example, one reason for the gender gap in education. But many differences are enduring. Men are typically more aggressive, take more risks, and have a higher sex drive than girls and women.[1] Of course this is not a comprehensive list. There are other traits that tend to be found more often in men than in women. Males are a bit more interested in things, for example, while women are a bit more interested in people; the guy tinkers in the garage, his wife chats with a friend.[2] But these three—aggression, risk, sex—are where the differences are most pronounced, and the ones I will say more about here.

In this chapter I describe the evidence for natural sex differences, especially in terms of aggression, risk, and sex drive. I'll then argue that both our immediate environment and broader culture matter greatly as well, shaping the ways in which biological differences develop and are expressed. Occupational choice, especially the so-called STEM paradox, provides an example of the need to take both our immediate environment and the broader culture into account. Nature and nurture *both* matter, and they also interact in important ways. I think we can safely leave this tired debate to one side. Finally, I point to the dangers of ignoring biology altogether, especially in applied fields like psychology.

The idea that there is a natural basis for sex differences is, however, politically charged. So I'd better get the caveats in right away. First, while certain traits are more associated with one sex than the other, the distributions overlap, especially among adults. After using MRI scans to examine sex differences in a sample of over 5,000 people in the UK— the largest study of its kind to date—psychologist Stuart Ritchie and his coauthors conclude that "for every brain measure that showed even large sex differences, there was always overlap between males and females: even in the case of the large difference in total brain volume there was 48.1% sample overlap."[3] In other words, the differences are dimorphic—different but overlapping—rather than binary. (Watch for that gap instinct I mentioned in chapter 2.) The typical male has a greater willingness to take risks, for example, than the typical female (especially in adolescence). But some women are more risk-taking than some men. Most studies find the biggest differences are at the tails of these distributions, rather than for the majority of people. A large majority of the *most* aggressive people are male, but the differences in aggressiveness in the general population are much smaller.

Second, these sex differences can be magnified or muted by culture. Some cultures valorize violence, while others do not. I'm pretty sure that I would be more physically aggressive if I had been born in Sparta a couple of thousand years ago. There's just not that much use for it at the Brookings Institution. These cultural variations matter a lot for how, and how far, natural tendencies are expressed in behavior. Culture and biology do not develop separately from each other. They coevolve. Neither biology nor culture can provide the whole story. But understanding the role of biology is necessary for keeping it in its place. "Biology does represent the foundation of our personalities and behavioral tendencies," writes Louann Brizendine in her book, *The Female Brain.* "If in the name of free will—and political correctness—we try to deny the influence of biology on the brain, we begin fighting our own nature. If we acknowledge that our biology is influenced by other factors . . . we can prevent it from creating a fixed reality by which we are ruled."[4]

Third, these sex differences typically have a rather modest impact on day-to-day lives in the twenty-first century. There are now much bigger drivers of behavior, including not only culture but personal agency. In modern societies, there is much more room, thankfully, for individuality. Breaking free of narrow definitions of what it takes to be a man or woman is a mark of progress, both as societies and as individuals. But this does not require us to deny any natural differences, simply to address them responsibly. The neuroscientist Gina Rippon warns that "a belief in biology brings with it a particular mindset regarding the fixed and unchangeable nature of human activity."[5] But it is perfectly possible to have a "belief in biology" without mindlessly assuming that human nature is "fixed and unchangeable," or that culture and environment are irrelevant. It is hard to find a responsible scientist who is either an outright determinist or an outright denier on the question of biology. The real debate is not about whether biology matters, but *how much* it does, and *when* it does.

Fourth, average sex differences do not justify the institutionalization of gender inequality. There is a fear that biology can be used to provide an intellectual foundation for sexism. This is well founded, given our history. In the wrong hands, evidence for natural differences can indeed be used to justify oppression. But denying science altogether is not useful; the truth always comes back to bite you eventually. The rather boring truth is that masculine traits are more useful in some contexts and feminine ones in others, and neither set is intrinsically better than the other.

Fifth, average differences between groups should not influence how we view individuals. That is what most people call stereotyping and economists call statistical discrimination. Even if, on average, women are wired to be a little more nurturing (which they are), it does not mean that my son cannot be an excellent, caring, and empathetic teacher of young children (which he is). You can probably think of some women who are not very nurturing. If you are hiring into a job where nurturing is important, focus on the individual, not their sex.

It is important, then, to keep the role of biology in perspective, and to be careful to avoid potential misuse. There is always a danger of succumbing to the "naturalistic fallacy," presuming that everything that is natural must necessarily be good. But nor is it helpful to deny or dismiss the reality of natural sex differences. "I want [my daughters and son] to understand that there are differences between the sexes that are not shaped by culture but are more fundamental, rooted in evolution and biology," writes the anthropologist Melvin Konner, in *Women After All*. "I don't want any of the four of them—or my hundreds of students a year, or any young people, or anyone at all—to live with the great disadvantage of missing that fact."[6]

TESTOSTERONE: AGGRESSION

It is ironic that in most of the religious creation myths, the male comes before the female. In biology, the opposite is the case: in the beginning was the female. The initial genetic plan for all humans, as for all mammals, is for a female. In an XY combination, the job of the short but industrious Y chromosome is to disrupt that carefully laid female plan. Men are "basically genetically modified women," in the words of Oxford geneticist Brian Sykes.[7]

Task number one for the Y, about 7 weeks from fertilization, is to get the testes growing. Next, the embryo is subjected to a bath of the androgen testosterone, which sets it down the path toward manhood. Androgens masculinize the brain. Next, under orders from SOX9 in the Sertoli cells, a two-man team of genetic workers—AMH on chromosome 19p13.3 and AMHR2 on chromosome 12—represses the development of female reproductive body parts. The male hormones then take a break for a few years, until puberty, when testosterone is needed again, among other things to grow the penis and the prostate.

The whole process of sex determination is so extraordinarily complex that it is amazing it goes according to plan almost all the time. But it does. Almost all of us are born definitively male or female. Occasionally, an XX embryo gets exposed to more male hormones than usual, either as a result of a genetic anomaly or certain medications taken during pregnancy, which can lead to being defined as *intersex* rather than male or female. This part of the spectrum of sexual development is, as Konner puts it, "like some exotic glass sculpture—small but beautiful and strange."[8] Historically, however, intersex people themselves have been treated more as strange than beautiful, and subjected to victimization, unwanted surgery, and shame. Even today, their human rights are often violated.[9] There is no single definition of intersex, and there are varying estimates of prevalence, but applying the broadest definition, a reasonable upper-end estimate is of around one in a hundred people.[10] Intersex people with more typically female anatomy are often assigned female at birth, but many are in fact more at home with a male identity, and they often transition later.[11] This provides important evidence that sex is strongly determined by what happens in the womb, rather than after birth.

One result of the testosterone bath of male brains is a greater tendency toward physical aggression, not just in humans but in almost all primates and mammals. Human males are more physically aggressive in all cultures at all ages.[12] Boys are five times more likely than girls to be frequently aggressive by the age of seventeen—seventeen *months*, that is.[13] The gap widens until early adulthood before narrowing again.[14] Worldwide, men commit over 95% of homicides and the overwhelming majority of violent acts of other kinds, including sexual assault.[15] But the relationship between testosterone, masculinity, and aggression is complex. For one thing, it looks as if testosterone does not directly trigger aggression but amplifies it.[16] How far this amplification takes place depends a lot on the circumstances. As Carole Hooven shows in her book *Testosterone: The Story of the Hormone That Dominates and Divides Us*, the innate tendency toward aggression in boys and men is real but not necessarily expressed. We are not slaves to our cells.

It is also important to note that most societies have become much less violent over time, and that there are big differences in crime rates among countries today. "That all these factors matter is not evidence that the relationship between T and aggression is weak," Hooven writes, "rather, it shows us that it's complicated, as is the research that looks into how the relationship works."[17] Nobody denies that culture and socialization matter. It would otherwise be difficult to explain the dramatic differences in levels of male violence between different places and in different eras. But it is equally silly to deny that biology matters here too, not least in the differences between men and women.

DAREDEVILS: RISK

These sex differences are not the result of some cosmic accident. Humans are, as Desmond Morris put it, "risen apes, not fallen angels."[18] The traits that get passed on are the ones that have been reproductively effective. That is what sexual selection is all about. The optimal reproductive strategies have been different for men and for women, with long-run consequences for our psychology. Men, for example, have a greater appetite for risk. This is not a social construct. It can be identified in every known society throughout history, as Joyce Benenson shows in her book *Warriors and Worriers: The Survival of the Sexes*.[19] "Sex differences exist in virtually every area in which risk has been studied, with males engaging in more risk-taking than females" write a team of scholars studying leadership styles. "Similar findings have been reported from hunter gatherers to bank CEOs."[20]

Like aggression, risk-taking is one of the differences between male and female psychology that has clear roots in our evolutionary history. Taking risks must then make more sense for men. But why? Bluntly, because men are much less likely than women to reproduce at all. In fact, we have twice as many female ancestors as male ones.[21] This can take a minute to get your head around. After all, genetically speaking, everyone must have a mother and a father. But of course one man can father many children with many women, while others father none at all. This is exactly what has happened historically. Genghis Khan, a direct ancestor of 1 in 200 people today, is perhaps the most famous example. The polite way to put this is that "males have higher variance in reproductive success than females."[22] Psychologist Roy Baumeister makes the point more bluntly: "To maximize reproduction, a culture needs all the wombs it can get, but a few penises can do the job. There is usually a penile surplus."[23]

Add the fact that most human societies have been polygynous, allowing men to have multiple wives, and you end up with what Harvard evolutionary psychologist Joseph Henrich calls the "math problem of surplus men."[24] This is where risk comes in. Men who are in danger of becoming evolutionary duds will be willing to take serious risks in order to gain access to a mate, perhaps by committing a crime to get more resources, or fighting in a potentially lucrative war. Even a 50/50 chance of success looks pretty good to a man who is otherwise unlikely to have any children at all. As a result, Henrich writes, "Men's psychology shifts in ways that spark fiercer male–male competition."

Recent evidence for this claim comes from a study of China's one-child policy, which was introduced at different times in different provinces, providing a chance for researchers to examine the impact. Because families preferred to have a boy, once the rule was in place the sex ratio tilted sharply toward males. The economist Lena Edlund shows that 18 years after the introduction of the policy in each area, as the surplus boys became men, crime rates started to rise. Not modestly, either: arrest rates almost doubled.[25] Edlund's work underlines a crucial point. Even though male psychology is more wired for risk, this usually tips into antisocial forms of risk-taking (such as crime) only in circumstances of intense competition.

It hardly needs to be said that the male attitude toward risk comes with many downsides. When I look back through the eyes of a middle-aged father at some of the "games" my male friends and I would play as teens, I shudder. The one where we tried to be the last one to dash across a highway in front of an oncoming truck particularly stands out. (I was *never* last.) But the willingness of men to put their lives on the line also has some upsides. Men seem to demonstrate a greater willingness to take risks in order to save others, which again makes perfect evolutionary sense given the relatively greater importance of female bodies for reproduction.

Each year, the Carnegie Hero Fund, founded in 1904, issues medals to civilians for courageous acts, specifically risking their life to save a stranger. In 2021, 66 of the 71 medals awarded went to men.[26] Medalists for that year included Lucas Y. Silverio Mendoza, aged 19, killed while attempting to guide a 3-year-old from a burning building, and 17-year-old Christian Alexander Burgos, who drowned after saving the life of a 9-year-old boy and his mother. We can seek to reduce the downsides of the greater male willingness to take risks, but also encourage and celebrate the benefits it can bring. As Margaret Mead wrote, "It is essential that the tasks of the future should be so organized that as dying for one's country becomes unfeasible, taking risks for that which is loved may still be possible."[27] (As I write, however, the prospect of dying for one's country is only too real in war-torn Ukraine.)

SEX ON THE MALE BRAIN

Given that the differences between male and female psychology have emerged in large part through sexual selection, perhaps it should not be a surprise that the biggest difference between men and women is with regard to sex itself. As a matter of biological fact, men are just lustier—or have what Konner labels more "driven sexuality"—than women.[28] A comprehensive review of 150 studies found overwhelming evidence that men have a higher sex drive, "reflected in spontaneous thoughts about sex frequency and variety of sexual fantasies, desired frequency of intercourse, desired number of partners, masturbation, liking for various sexual practices, willingness to forego sex, initiating versus refusing sex, making sacrifices for sex, and other measures."[29] As Billy Crystal's character says in the movie *City Slickers*, "Women need a reason to have sex. Men just need a place."

Again, there is a good evolutionary reason for this difference. With a much higher chance of failing to father any children, men have had to be ready to take almost any opportunity for procreation. "Physically, men in their prime are hardwired to be in a state of near-perpetual readiness to couple with any female in their environment who is likely to be able to conceive and bear children," writes Marianne Legato, director of the Foundation for Gender-Specific Medicine.[30] That is why Legato and others see erectile health as a proxy for overall health in men.

The commercialization of the male sex drive is as old as recorded history; there are twenty-five words for "prostitute" in Latin.[31] It is almost entirely men who pay for sex, and there are about 1 million prostitutes working in the U.S. today, far outnumbering priests and pastors.[32] A study in New York found that opening a strip club or escort agency reduced sex crime in the surrounding neighborhood by 13%.[33] More money flows through the sex trade than drugs and guns combined, according to a study of eight cities by the Urban Institute.[34] The reality of the male sex drive means, whether we like it or not, that sex workers will always be with us. Policymakers should recognize this fact, rather than engaging in magical thinking about the prospects of a change in male sexuality. (Decriminalizing prostitution would be good, not least to improve conditions for sex workers themselves.[35])

Pornography is also not new. An erotic ivory figurine, discovered in 2008, dates back about 35,000 years.[36] Every technological revolution, from the printing press to the camera and movies, means more porn. But the internet has been a force multiplier. In 2021, PornHub and Xvideos, the two largest online porn sites, had an average of 694 million and 640 million visitors each month, respectively, in the U.S. alone. For context, that is more than Netflix (541 million) or Zoom (630 million). The title of a comprehensive review undertaken for the UK's Office of the Children's Commissioner summarized the situation well: "Basically . . . porn is everywhere."[37] Some women watch porn too of course, but much less than men.[38]

When the *New Yorker* writer and CNN commentator Jeffrey Toobin became famous for being seen masturbating in a break during a long Zoom meeting, the reaction of most of my female friends was along the lines of, "What was he thinking, in the middle of a meeting, in the middle of the day?" For most of the men it was, "What was he thinking, not checking that his camera was turned off?" I think one of the reasons that porn use can cause such a strong negative reaction is that it highlights vividly the nature of male sexuality. Typically, young men report watching porn 2 or 3 days a week, almost always to accompany masturbation, and usually not for very long (6 minutes seems to be the average visit length). Men who are in committed sexual relationships masturbate to porn much less frequently.[39] As with gaming, the problem is among the small numbers of heavy users who may become addicted.

Again, it hardly needs adding that, for good or ill, culture hugely influences the expression of the driven sexuality of men. One of the most important things young men learn from their surrounding culture is how to express their sexual desire in an appropriate way. But greater male lust is a fact of life.

CULTURAL ANIMALS

I hope to have convinced you now that while sex differences in biology are not determinative of behavior, they do matter, and that little good will come from denying it. But our environment and culture weigh heavily too. It is not nature *or* nurture. It is nature *and* nurture. "We don't have a 'get out of evolution free' card," writes Kevin Mitchell, a neurogeneticist at Trinity College, Dublin, "but we are also not meat robots whose behavior is determined by the positions of a few knobs and switches, independent of any societal forces."[40] Some of the most fascinating recent research in this area shows how our immediate environment, especially during childhood, shapes the way in which genetic predispositions are expressed. Growing up in a stressful or unstable family environment, for example, appears to influence the capacity of the brain to metabolize serotonin, which helps to reduce aggressive behavior.[41] Differing life trajectories of identical twins influence how far genes associated with risk-taking are dampened or amplified.[42] Children with fathers in prison see a shortening of the length of their telomeres (the ends of chromosomes), which increases the risk of health problems in adulthood. Boys with genes that make them more sensitive to their environment do worse when their biological father leaves the household, but also benefit most if their biological father *joins* the household, an example of how being an orchid can bring benefits as well as costs.[43] There are countless other examples of the complex, two-way relationship between physical biology and the social environment.

The fact that biology matters does not make culture less important. In fact, it makes it more important. Culture determines how we manage, channel, and express many of the natural traits I have described here. Biology influences culture, but culture also influences our biology. As Joseph Henrich argues, it makes most sense to think of the *coevolution* of nature and nurture. "Culture rewires our brains and alters our biology" he says, "without altering the underlying genetic code."[44] When humans learned how to use fire, we started to eat more meat, for example, and our digestive systems adapted. Literacy changed the psychology of many people who became what Henrich calls WEIRD (Western, educated, industrialized, rich, and democratic).

One striking example is the role of marriage, which Henrich describes, rather brutally, as "a testosterone suppression system."[45] (I've been almost continuously married for thirty years.) Testosterone levels are highest among young single men, and those with higher T are actually more likely to become fathers. But testosterone levels then fall among men who settle down with a wife and children, and the drops are sharpest among men who do more childcare. One group of scholars studying this evidence concludes that "human males have an evolved neuroendocrine architecture shaped to facilitate their role as fathers and caregivers as a key component of reproductive success."[46] There are broader social implications here too. As the institution of monogamous marriage spread, the number of men directly involved in raising families rose. The collective impact, via reduced testosterone levels, was to dramatically reduce overall levels of male violence. This is a good example of the complex interactions between biology, immediate environment, and broader culture.[47]

FRAGILE MANHOOD

Anthropologists all agree: Manhood is fragile. Womanhood is more robust because it is more determined by women's specific role in reproduction. As the feminist anthropologist Sherry Ortner writes, "It is simply a fact that proportionately more of woman's body space, for a greater percentage of her lifetime . . . is taken up with the natural processes surrounding the reproduction of the species."[48] Womanhood is defined more by biology, manhood more by social construction. This is why masculinity tends to be more fragile than femininity. When was the last "crisis of femininity"? That's right: never.

Masculinity is defined at least as much by behavior as biology. "I learned very early on that what a man does . . . is even more important than who he is," wrote the British psychiatrist Anthony Clare in his book *On Men: Masculinity in Crisis.*[49] Clare was referring specifically to paid work in a modern capitalist society, but the general observation holds for almost every known human society. Manhood is a continuous achievement, rather than just a single milestone. In many cultures, rites of initiation—often involving physical duress or risk—have marked the transition from boy to man. As the American poet Leonard Kriegel wrote, "In every age, not just our own, manhood was something that had to be won."[50]

But what can be won can also be lost. Hence the fragility. The making of masculinity is an important cultural task in any society, especially during periods of rapid social change like our own. "Manliness is a symbolic script, a cultural construct," writes the anthropologist David Gilmore.[51] "Real men do not simply emerge naturally over time like butterflies from boyish cocoons; they must be assiduously coaxed from their juvenescent shells, shaped and nurtured, counseled and prodded into manhood."[52] This is not to suggest that there is a single blueprint for making men. To say that men have to be made does not mean there is only one set of instructions. What makes for a "real man" varies greatly across cultures.

Human behavior is driven by a combination of *nature* (our instincts based in biology), *nurture* (the instructions we get from our surrounding culture), and *agency* (our personal initiative). Much of the drama of human life stems from the tension between these three forces. As Shakespeare's Coriolanus declares: "I'll never / Be such a gosling to obey instinct; but stand, / As if a man were author of himself, / And knew no other kin."[53]

He is trying to ignore both nature, the gosling-like instinct, as well as his social duties to his kin, and just go his own way. He fails, of course. Nobody can simply break free of biology or culture to be a fully autonomous agent. Even enlightened moderns are animals underneath. All we can do is try to strike an appropriate balance. The good news is that as societies progress, first culture, and then individual agency become increasingly important. The kaleidoscope of our life choices becomes more colorful. But we should not make Coriolanus's error and think we can escape our culture. We are, as Roy Baumeister argues in *The Cultural Animal*, evolved for culture. "Human beings are shaped—first by their genes and then by their social environment," he writes, "to live in culture."[54]

Culture has played a particularly important role in channeling the energy of men toward positive social ends, especially by teaching them to care for others. But "this behavior, being learned, is fragile," warned Margaret Mead, "and can disappear rather easily under social conditions that no longer teach it effectively."[55] This is a warning we should heed.

THE STEM PARADOX

I have already stressed that an average difference between groups on any given characteristic typically offers limited information about any particular individual. But aggregated across whole populations, these differences will lead to certain patterns, for example, in occupational choice. There has been a strong movement to get more girls and women into STEM careers, in science, technology, engineering, and mathematics. It has been pretty successful too; women now account for 27% of workers in these occupations, a big jump from the 8% share in 1970, though still of course a long way from parity.[56] But should we expect to get to 50/50 gender parity in all these jobs? Probably not. On average, remember, men are more attracted to things, women to people.[57] Even under conditions of perfect gender equality, more men than women will likely choose these career paths. Not because of sexism or socialization but because of real differences in preferences.

In 2018, two researchers, Gijsbert Stoet and David Geary, showed that in more gender-equal countries, such as Finland and Norway, women were less likely to take university courses in STEM subjects. Stoet and Geary called this the "gender-equality paradox."[58] They speculated that in countries with high incomes and strong welfare states, the economic incentives to pursue STEM careers may be lower, allowing women to choose courses and jobs that more closely matched their personal preferences. Some related research offers support for Stoet and Geary's conclusions. Armin Falk and Johannes Hermle studied sex differences in certain preferences, such as a willingness to take risks, patience, altruism, positive and negative reciprocity, and trust, across a range of countries. Sex differences were largest in richer and more gender-equal countries, with each having an independent effect. They conclude that "a more egalitarian distribution of material and social resources enables women and men to independently express gender-specific preferences."[59] A similar study using different data sources came to the same conclusion. "A possible explanation is that people in more progressive and equal countries have a greater opportunity to express inherent biological differences" says one of the authors, Petri Kajonius. "Another theory is that people in progressive countries have a greater desire to express differences in their identity through their gender."[60]

It is important to note that none of these studies has a design allowing for a clear causal interpretation. But at the very least, this work should make us cautious about holding out for perfect gender parity in every single domain of life. Some of the differences we observe may be the result of informed personal agency—and if so, we should respect those choices. While conservatives sometimes suggest that women who don't conform to traditional roles are denying their nature, many on the Left insist that women who do must be surrendering to sexism. But I think the *Atlantic* writer Olga Khazan gets it right: "The upshot of this research is neither especially feminist nor especially sad. It's not that gender equality discourages girls from pursuing science. It's that it allows them not to if they're not interested."[61]

Two points bear repeating here. First, average differences between groups should never influence the treatment of individuals. Even if

FIGURE 7-1 Sex differences in job interest and job choice
Predicted and actual share of women, select STEM fields.

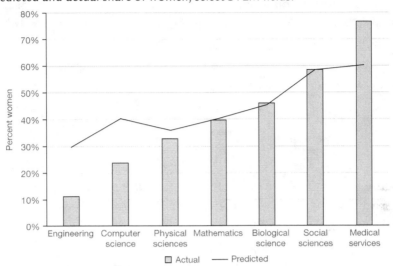

Note: Based on an updated table from personal communication with Dr. Su on February 1, 2022.
Source: Rong Su, James Rounds, Patrick Ian Armstrong, "Men and things, women and people," Table 4 and Figure 1, see note 2 in this chapter.

somewhat fewer women than men are interested in a job in engineering, this is no justification for discrimination against any particular woman. Second, the distributions of these attributes still substantially overlap. In one major study of sex differences on the people-versus-things dimension, for example, almost half (47%) of the male and female distributions overlapped with the other.[62] This means that a nugatory representation of either sex in a particular profession cannot plausibly be attributed to natural preferences. One fascinating study by psychologists Rong Su and James Rounds compared the proportion of women who would be expected to be in various occupations, based on gender differences in interests, with the actual numbers. Some of their results are reproduced in figure 7-1.[63]

Su and Rounds found a good match in many fields, such as mathematics (with 40% representation) and the biological sciences (45%). But there was a significant underrepresentation of women in engineering: around 30% of engineers would be female if interests alone were driving occupational choice, according to their estimates, but the actual number of women engineers was half that. At the other end of the scale, there is a heavy overrepresentation of women in the medical services field, which includes nursing. In chapter 11, I will argue strongly that many more men could—and should—be working in the health and educational sectors.

PSYCHED

The mission of the American Psychological Association is to "benefit society and improve lives."[64] But the association failed against this benchmark with its 2018 guidelines on working with boys and men. The summary of the guidelines states that "traditional masculinity—marked by stoicism, competitiveness, dominance and aggression—is, on the whole, harmful."[65] The APA report also describes the related problem of a "masculinity ideology," defined as "a particular constellation of standards that have held sway over large segments of the population, including: anti-femininity, achievement, eschewal of the appearance of weakness, and adventure, risk, and violence."[66]

The association quickly came under attack from conservative critics, who said the guidelines amounted to "conversion therapy" similar to that once offered to lesbian women and gay men.[67] A clarification was tweeted: "The guidelines support encouraging positive aspects of 'traditional masculinity,' such as courage and leadership, and discarding traits such as violence and sexism, while noting that the vast majority of men are not violent."[68] This was false. The guidelines contain not a single reference to these positive aspects of masculinity.

Some people on the political Right overreacted, perhaps. But there is no question that the APA put out a bad document. The guidelines fail to recognize any biological basis at all for male psychology. Testosterone, for example, is not mentioned. As far as the APA is concerned, it seems, masculinity is entirely socially constructed. "By the time he reaches adulthood," the report states, "a man will tend to demonstrate behaviors as prescribed by his ethnicity, culture, and different constructions of masculinity."

The complete absence of biology here contrasts with the association's equivalent report on girls and women, which usefully discusses the potential psychological implications of puberty, childbirth, and menopause.[69] So while girls and women are treated as flesh and blood, boys and men are treated as blank slates. This is obviously absurd. But it is also damaging, not least because of the poor guidance it provides to psychologists, 80% of whom are women, as they seek to help boys and men.

The APA is not the only institution that seems to have developed something of a science aversion when it comes to sex and biology. In 2015, the MacArthur Foundation issued a forty-seven-page report on the implications of the latest science on adolescent development for juvenile justice.[70] The report correctly drew attention to racial disparities. But despite the huge differences between adolescent girls and boys in terms of brain development, especially with regard to risk-taking and aggression, the report made not a single reference to sex or gender. The fear of "sex determinism" seems in these cases to have led to an unwillingness to engage with, or even acknowledge, the evidence for natural influences on behavior. When this blinkered approach is taken by professional bodies or research institutions, things have gone badly awry.

DANCES AND SHIPWRECKS

J. F. Roxburgh, the first headmaster of Stowe School, a private boys' school in England, described his goal as cultivating men who would be "acceptable at a dance and invaluable in a shipwreck."[71] He wanted men who could make the kind of sacrifices made by the awardees of the Carnegie Hero medals. Perhaps he had in mind the heroism of many men on the *Titanic*, which famously sank in 1912, with a survival rate of just 19% for the male passengers, compared to 75% for women.[72] But the first half of Roxburgh's formulation is even more important. Men who are "acceptable at a dance" are those who have learned how to conduct themselves in company, how to treat women respectfully and as equals. They are, in short, mature.

One of the primary functions of human culture is to help young people to become responsible, self-aware adults. Maturity means, among many other things, an ability to calibrate your behavior in a way that renders it appropriate to the circumstances. To be a grown-up means learning how to temper our own natures. We learn to go to the bathroom. We learn not to hit each other when we are upset. We learn not to act on impulse. We learn empathy, restraint, reflection. It takes time, at least a couple of decades. It takes boys a little longer than girls. But most of us manage it in the end. Boys become men, even gentlemen. The boy is still with us, he is just not in charge anymore.

PART IV

POLITICAL STALEMATE

CHAPTER 8

PROGRESSIVE BLINDNESS

The Political Left Is in Denial

My sons attended a school with a "culture of toxic masculinity." It was perhaps not the first place you would look for it. Bethesda-Chevy Chase High School serves an affluent, liberal, highly educated suburban community just outside Washington, D.C. A third of the adults in the county have a graduate degree.[1] Four out of five voted for Joe Biden.[2] In 2019, the school district added a third option for student gender.[3] If there is a liberal bubble, this is the bubble inside that bubble.

But in 2018 an incident occurred at the school that generated widespread media coverage, including CBS's *This Morning*, ABC's *Good Morning America*, and NBC's *Today* show ("a reckoning on sexual harassment"), as well as in the *Washingtonian* magazine and *Washington Post*.[4] The *Daily Mail*, a British newspaper, picked up the story.[5] Here's what happened. A boy at the school created a list of his female classmates, ranked in terms of their attractiveness, and shared it with a number of his friends, some of whom added their own opinions. Months later, one of the girls saw the list on another boy's laptop. A number of girls complained to the school administration. The boy who created the list was reprimanded and given detention. A protest ensued. "It was the last straw, for us girls, of this 'boys will be boys' culture," one of the young women involved told the *Washington Post*.[6]

Part of a statement read out at a protest outside the principal's office was the following demand: "We should be able to learn in an environment without the constant presence of objectification and misogyny." Large meetings were held in the school to discuss culture. The boy who created the list apologized personally to the girls in question, and to the *Washington Post*. The school principal and two of the female students later participated in a panel discussion of the issue aired on C-SPAN.[7]

This was one incident, at one school, at a particular moment in time. It blipped more loudly on my radar because it happened to take place at our local school. But what was instructive about the incident was the way it was immediately framed, especially in media coverage, as an example of "toxic masculinity." If that is really the case, the term has acquired such a broad definition that it can be applied to almost any anti-social behavior on the part of boys or men.

It is one thing to point out that there are aspects of masculinity that in an immature or extreme expression can be deeply harmful, quite another to suggest that a naturally occurring trait in boys and men is intrinsically bad. Indiscriminately slapping the label of "toxic masculinity" onto this kind of behavior is a mistake. Rather than drawing boys into a dialogue about what lessons can be learned, it is much more likely to send them to the online manosphere where they will be reassured that they did nothing wrong, and that liberals are out to get them. Adolescent girls are after all capable of similar kinds of bullying and disrespect, often toward other girls, but it is not instantly cast as "toxic femininity."

This incident at our high school highlights the first of four major failings of the political Left on issues related to boys and men, which is a tendency to pathologize naturally occurring aspects of masculine identity, usually under the banner of toxic masculinity. The second progressive flaw is individualism; male problems are seen as the result of individual failings of one kind or another, rather than of structural challenges. Third is an unwillingness to acknowledge any biological basis for sex differences. Fourth is a fixed conviction that gender inequality can only run one way, that is, to the disadvantage of women. I will address each of these four progressive failings in turn here, before turning in chapter 9 to the equally harmful response of the political Right.

INVENTING TOXIC MASCULINITY

Until around 2015, the phrase *toxic masculinity* warranted just a handful of mentions in a couple corners of academia.[8] According to sociologist Carol Harrington, the number of articles using the term prior to 2015 never exceeded twenty, and almost all mentions were in scholarly journals. But with the rise of Donald Trump and the #MeToo movement, progressives brought it into everyday use. By 2017, there were thousands of mentions, mostly in the mainstream media. Harrington points out that the term is almost never defined, even by academics, and is instead used to simply "signal disapproval."[9] Lacking any coherent or consistent definition, the phrase now refers to any male behavior that the user disapproves of, from the tragic to the trivial. It has been blamed, among other things, for mass shootings,[10] gang violence,[11] rape,[12] online trolling,[13] climate change,[14] the financial crisis,[15] Brexit,[16] the election of Donald Trump,[17] and an unwillingness to wear a mask during the COVID-19 pandemic.[18] Lumping together terrorists and delinquents, it ultimately poisons the very idea of masculinity itself. Interviewing dozens of adolescent boys and young men for her book *Boys and Sex*, Peggy Orenstein always asked them what they liked about being a boy. She says most drew a blank. "That's interesting," one college sophomore told her. "I never really thought about that. You hear a lot more about what is *wrong* with guys."[19]

Toxic masculinity is a counterproductive term. Very few boys and men are likely to react well to the idea that there is something toxic inside them that needs to be exorcised. This is especially true given that most of them identify quite strongly with their masculinity. Nine in ten men and women describe themselves as either "completely" or "mostly" masculine or feminine.[20] These gender identities are held quite strongly too. Almost half of men (43%) said their sex was "extremely important" to their identity. In another survey by Pew Research Center, a similar proportion of men (46%) said that it was either very or somewhat important for others to see them as "manly or masculine."[21] (In both surveys, the numbers were even higher for women.)

In other words, most people identify pretty strongly as either masculine or feminine. It is a bad idea to send a cultural signal to half the population that there may be something intrinsically wrong with them.

"The toxic masculinity . . . framing alienates the majority of nonviolent, non-extreme men," argues the feminist writer Helen Lewis, "and does little to address the grievances, or counteract the methods, that lure susceptible individuals toward the far right."[22] Given the survey results just described, it may not be great politics either. Half of American men and almost a third of women (30%) now think that society "punishes men just for acting like men," according to a survey by the Public Religion Research Institute.[23] There is a partisan split, as you might expect. Three in five Republicans agree, compared to only about one in four Democrats.[24] Religion plays a role too. Half of both white Protestants and Black Protestants, for example, agree that men are punished for acting like men (50% and 47%, respectively).

Pathologizing masculinity may even undermine support for feminism. Fewer than a third of American women now describe themselves as a feminist.[25] In 2018, YouGov polled those women who did not identify as feminist for their views on feminism. Almost half (48%) said that "feminists are too extreme" and that "the current wave of feminism does not represent true feminism" (47%). One in four (24%) said that "feminists are anti-men."[26] These findings should give progressives some pause. In the rush to condemn the dark side of masculine traits, they are in grave danger of pathologizing the traits themselves. Many women are uncomfortable with this trend. And to the boy or man who feels lusty or restless, the message, implicit or explicit, is all too often, *there is something wrong with you.* But there is not. Masculinity is not a pathology. As I showed in chapter 7, it is, quite literally, a fact of life.

BLAMING THE VICTIM

The second big flaw in progressive thinking on men and masculinity is individualism. Usually, progressives are reluctant to ascribe too much responsibility to individuals for their problems. If someone is obese, or commits a crime, or is out of employment, the progressive default is to look first to structural, external causes. This is a valuable instinct. It is all too easy to blame individuals for structural challenges. But there is one group that progressives do seem willing to blame for their plight: men. YouTuber Natalie Wynn describes the stance well: "We say 'look, toxic masculinity is the reason you don't have room to express your feelings and the reason you feel lonely and inadequate.' . . . We kind of just tell men, 'you're lonely and suicidal because you're toxic. Stop it!'"[27]

Carol Harrington believes that the term toxic masculinity plays an important role here, since it naturally focuses attention on the character flaws of individual men, rather than structural problems. If men are depressed, it is because they won't express their feelings. If they get sick, it is because they won't go to the doctor. If they fail at school, it is because they lack commitment. If they die early, it is because they drink and smoke too much and eat the wrong things. For those on the political Left, then, victim-blaming is permitted when it comes to men.

The pandemic illustrated this individualistic tendency well. Men are considerably more vulnerable to COVID-19. Globally, men were around 50% more likely than women to die after contracting the virus.[28] In the U.S., about 85,000 more men than women had died from COVID by the end of 2021. For every 100 deaths among women aged 45–64, there were 184 male deaths.[29] The result was to cut 2 years off the average predicted life spans for American men, the largest drop since World War II, compared to a decline of 1 year for women.[30] In the UK, the death rate among working-age men was twice as high as for women of the same age.[31] These differences appear not to have made any impression on public health officials or policymakers, however, even when they were aware of them.[32]

The higher male death rate also received almost no attention from health institutions or media. When it was acknowledged, the main explanations provided were that men were either more vulnerable because of preexisting conditions related to "lifestyle" factors, such as smoking or alcohol, or to a lack of responsibility with regard to safety measures, for example, mask wearing.[33] In short, if men were dying, it was their own fault. But this was not true. The gap in mortality is not explained by sex differences in rates of infection, or in preexisting conditions.[34] The difference is biological.

The sex differences in Covid mortality make it clear that we need more of what feminist health care advocates have been urging for decades: more gender-specific medicine, including clinical trials that break down the results and side effects by gender. "Over the past two decades, we've radically revised how we conduct medical research and take care of our female patients," writes Marianne J. Legato. "I now believe that . . . it's time to focus on the unique problems of men just the way we have learned to do with women."[35] A good first step would be to establish an Office of Men's Health in the Department of Health and Human Services, to mirror the excellent one that already exists for women, and with equivalent funding of $35 million.[36] The Affordable Care Act should also be expanded to provide men with the same coverage that allows women to get a free annual health checkup. Given the disparate impact of COVID-19, we do have to ask, if not now, when?

When it comes to masculinity, both the Left and the Right fall into the individualistic trap, but from different perspectives. For conservatives, masculinity is the solution; for progressives, masculinity is the problem. But they do both agree that the problem lies at the level of the *individual*, and therefore in the realm of psychology, rather than economics, anthropology, or sociology. This is a profound intellectual error. Given the scale of the cultural shifts of recent decades, simply lecturing boys and men to get with the program is not a good approach. "There's a contradiction in a discourse that on the one hand claims that male privilege, entitlement and the patriarchy are the most powerful forces of oppression humanity has ever created," writes the *Guardian* commentator Luke Turner, "and on the other would (understandably) like men to process this quickly, and without fuss."[37]

SCIENCE IS REAL

One of the rallying cries of the modern political Left is that "science is real." While conservatives succumb to myth and misinformation, progressives carry the enlightenment torch of reason. At least, that is how they see things. The truth is that there are science deniers on both sides. Many conservatives deny the environmental science of climate change. But many progressives deny the neuroscience of sex differences. This is the third major weakness in the progressive position.

There is strong evidence for a biological basis for some differences of psychology and preferences between the sexes, as I showed in chapter 7. The genetic psychologist Kathryn Paige Harden writes, "Genetic differences in human life are a scientific fact, like climate change. . . . That genetic and environmental factors are braided together is simply a description of reality."[38] But for many progressives, it is now axiomatic that sex differences in any outcomes or behaviors are wholly the result of socialization. When it comes to masculinity, the main message from the political Left is that men are acculturated into certain ways of behaving (generally bad ways, of course, in this version), which can therefore be socialized out of them. But this is simply false. Men do not have a higher sex drive just because society valorizes male sexuality, even if it does. They have more testosterone. Likewise aggression. Remember, boys under the age of 2 are five times more likely to be aggressive than girls.[39] This is surely not because 1-year-olds have picked up gender cues from around them.

To be fair, there are some reasonable concerns about how this science will be used. The philosopher Kate Manne worries that "naturalizing" any inequalities between men and women can have the effect of "making them seem inevitable, or portraying people trying to resist them as fighting a losing battle."[40] She is right in principle about this danger. Natural differences between men and women have often been used to justify sexism. This is mostly an outdated fear. In recent years, most of the scientists identifying natural differences have, if anything, tended to stress the superiority of women.[41] But even careful scientists who continue to argue for a role for biology are caricatured as being "reductive" or engaging in "sex essentialism."

One way around this problem is to adopt the approach taken by Melvin Konner in *Women After All*, and conclude that while biology matters a great deal, it is only in a way that favors females. In fact, there is some evidence that people in general are more comfortable with the

idea of natural differences if women come out ahead in the comparison.[42] Alice Eagly and Antonio Mladinic call this the "WoW (women-
are-wonderful) effect."[43] With regard to sex drive, for example, Konner
is able to write that "to think that these differences result merely from
cultural arrangements is naive in the extreme." But this blunt, true
statement follows the moralizing claim that "regardless of how natural
men's [sexual] needs may be, I can't see that those divergent preferences
are equally admirable."[44]

The appeal of this approach is obvious. It allows for a discussion of
biological differences but in a way that underlines the pathologies of
men, thereby ensuring a warmer reception among liberal scholars and
reviewers. But in some ways this is the most dangerous message of all:
men are naturally different than women, but only in ways that are bad.
Konner's apparent disdain for higher male sex drive, for example, veers
dangerously close to puritan ideas of sexual sin. It is not helpful to claim
that either men or women are somehow naturally better than the other.
We are just, on average, different in some ways that can be either negative or positive depending on the circumstances and the way the differences are expressed.

ONE-WAY INEQUALITY

The fourth major failure of the political Left is an inability to recognize that gender inequalities can—and increasingly do—run in both
directions. In 2021, President Biden created a White House Gender
Policy Council, a successor to the previous Council on Women and
Girls, which had been abolished by Donald Trump. But while the name
changed, the mission did not. The formal charge of the new Council is
"to guide and coordinate government policy that impacts women and
girls."[45] In October 2021, the Council published a National Strategy on
Gender Equity and Equality, the first in U.S. history.[46]

The strategy is entirely asymmetric. No gender inequalities related
to boys or men are addressed. The fact that women now outnumber
men in college is noted, but only in order to highlight the fact that
women hold more student debt than men. This is absurd. It is like com-

plaining that men pay more income tax because they earn more. There is no mention at all in the strategy of the sizable gender gaps in favor of girls in K–12 education. The need for reform of school discipline policies to help Black girls is emphasized, but there is no mention of the specific challenges of Black boys (even though they are twice as likely as Black girls to be suspended or expelled).[47] The goal of increasing access to health insurance for women is highlighted, but nothing is said about the fact that men are at a higher risk of being uninsured than women (15% v. 11%).[48]

I could go on, but you get the picture. You might wonder how much this lack of even-handedness matters, especially if you are skeptical about the impact of White House strategy papers. But this one will drive policy. The strategy directs all government departments and agencies to "establish and prioritize at least three goals that will serve to advance the objectives identified in this strategy, and detail the plans and resources needed to achieve them in an implementation plan." Flawed thinking makes for bad policy.

Introducing its new strategy, the White House declared that "the COVID-19 pandemic has fueled a health crisis, an economic crisis, and a caregiving crisis that have magnified the challenges that women and girls . . . have long faced."[49] This was in line with an almost universal tendency to emphasize the negative implications of the pandemic for women, while ignoring those for men. The main gender story has been the catastrophic impact on women's progress. "One of the most striking effects of the coronavirus will be to send many couples back to the 1950s," wrote Helen Lewis, in *The Atlantic* in March 2020, adding, "Across the world, women's independence will be a silent victim of the pandemic."[50] The headline on a gloomy *Washington Post* article by Alicia Sasser Modestino was "Coronavirus Child-Care Crisis Will Set Women Back a Generation."[51] In December 2020, the Aspen Institute Forum on Women and Girls declared that "COVID-19 has eroded the little progress we have made on gender equality."[52]

Almost every major think tank and international organization in the world produced reports on the negative impact of the pandemic on women, many written in a hyperbolic tone. By comparison, the much higher risk of death from COVID-19 for men warranted barely a mention. Nor the sharp drop in male college enrollment. Of course, the pandemic was mostly just bad all around. But it was bad for women in some ways, and bad for men in other ways. We can hold two thoughts in our head at the same time.

The assumption that gender gaps run only one way even gets embedded in inequality measures. Every 2 years, the World Economic Forum (WEF) produces its Global Gender Gap Report. It is the most influential international study of progress toward gender equality, but like the White House strategy, it is distorted by asymmetric thinking. To compile the report, a gender equality score is calculated for each nation, between 0 (complete inequality) and 1 (complete equality). The score is based on fourteen variables across four domains—economics, education, health, and politics. (Each variable in the index is also calculated on a 0–1 range.) In 2021, the U.S. scored 0.76 on the scale and placed thirtieth in the world. Iceland, in first place, scored 0.89.[53]

But crucially, no account is taken of domains where women are doing better than men. As WEF's number-crunchers explain, "The index assigns the same score to a country that has reached parity between women and men and one where women have surpassed men." Across the fourteen measures, U.S. women are now doing as well or better than men on six. In higher education, for example, the actual gender parity score is 1.36, reflecting the large lead that women have over men on this front. But the number factored into the index to generate the overall U.S. score is not 1.36. It is 1. The idea that gender inequality only counts in one direction is baked into WEF's methodology. But this assumption is untenable, especially in advanced economies. My colleague Fariha Haque and I have recalculated the WEF rankings, taking into account gender inequalities in both directions.[54] We also removed one of the fourteen variables, a subjective survey of the pay gap of dubious quality, and weighted all the domains equally (WEF gives more weight to variables with the widest gaps). Our two-way approach pushed the U.S. score up to 0.84 and Iceland's up to 0.97. As our paper shows, it also changed the country rankings, in some cases quite significantly.

The point here is not to devalue the work done by the Gender Policy Council, or WEF, or any of the other organizations aiming to improve the position of women. Closing the gaps where girls and women are behind remains an important policy goal. But given the huge progress made by women in recent decades and the significant challenges now faced by many boys and men, it makes no sense to treat gender inequality as a one-way street. On a practical level, it leads to a lack of policy attention to the problems of boys and men. But ignoring glaring gender gaps that run in the other direction, I believe, also robs these efforts of the moral force of egalitarianism. "There is now wide consensus that gender inequalities are unfair, and lead to wasted human potential," says Francisco Ferreira, Amartya Sen Chair in Inequality Studies at the London School of Economics, commenting on education gaps. "That remains true when the disadvantaged are boys, as well as girls."[55]

What is required here is a simple change in mindset, recognizing that gender inequalities can go in both directions. I said simple, not easy. The fight for gender equality has historically been synonymous with the fight for and by girls and women, and for good reason. But we have reached a point where gender inequalities affecting boys and men have to be treated seriously. Many people on the political Left seem to fear that even acknowledging the problems of boys and men will somehow weaken efforts for women and girls. This is the progressive version of zero-sum thinking. Anything extra for boys and men must mean less for girls and women. This is entirely false as a matter of practice, and creates a dangerous political dynamic. There are real problems facing many boys and men, which need to be addressed, and if progressives ignore them others will be sure to pick them up.

Our politics are now so poisoned that it has become almost impossible for people on the Left to even discuss the problems of boys and men, let alone devise solutions. This is a missed opportunity. We need the strongest advocates for gender equality, many of whom are on the liberal side of the political spectrum, to take a more balanced view. Otherwise, the danger is that boys and men will look elsewhere. "Thousands of years of history don't reverse themselves without a lot of pain," says Hanna Rosin. "That is why we are going through this together."[56] Rosin is right about the pain. But she is wrong about facing it together. We are in fact tearing ourselves apart over gender issues, with the result that the problems of boys and men are left untreated.

CHAPTER 9

SEEING RED

The Political Right Wants to Turn Back the Clock

On November 1, 2021, Senator Josh Hawley gave a speech to the National Conservatism Conference. The audience was ready for his standard fare: economic nationalism, patriotism, the power of the free market, and so on. But Hawley surprised them. He focused solely on the problems of men, highlighting some of the challenges I have described here, including in education, employment, and family life. For Hawley, however, these problems are not by-products of social and economic change. They are the result of a targeted political assault from the Left. Hawley described the "Left's attempt to give us a world beyond men," and declared that "the attack on men has been the tip of the spear of the Left's broader attack on America."[1] He went on: "The Left want to define traditional masculinity as toxic. They want to define the traditional masculine virtues . . . as a danger to society. . . . Can we be surprised that after years of being told they are the problem, that their manhood is the problem, more and more men are withdrawing into the enclave of idleness and pornography and video games?"

Senator Hawley argued that boys and men are struggling because the Left hates them. This is a powerful political message, because the first part is true, and the second part can be made to sound plausible given the tendency of many on the Left to pathologize masculinity. He got plenty of attention for the speech. But when it came to solutions, Hawley came up largely empty-handed. The best he could offer was a vague promise to restore manufacturing jobs, and a marriage bonus in the tax code. He did, however, score a small political victory a few weeks later, leading an eleventh-hour move to strike down a provision in the National Defense Authorization Act that would have made women eligible for the military draft. "It is wrong to force our daughters, mothers, wives and sisters to fight our wars," he said.[2] By implication, Sen. Hawley does not see it as wrong to force our sons, fathers, husbands, and brothers to do so.

Conservatives have paid more attention than progressives to the growing problems faced by boys and men. But their agenda turns out to be equally unhelpful. There are three big weaknesses in their approach. First, many conservatives fuel male grievances for political gain, which simply creates more anger and discontent. Second, they overweight the importance of biological sex differences for gender roles (a mirror image of the progressive tendency to dismiss them altogether). Third, they see the solution to men's problems as lying in the past rather than the future, in the form of a restoration of traditional economic relations between male providers and female carers. Rather than helping men adapt to the new world, conservatives beguile them with promises of the old. This may provide some temporary psychological relief. But we don't need painkillers. We need a cure.

GRIEVANCE POLITICS

Donald Trump secured the presidency of the United States in 2016 with a 24-point lead among men, the widest gender gap in the half-century history of exit polling.[3] Among white men, who make up a third of the electorate, Trump's margin was 30 percentage points (62% to 32%).[4] Women tilted toward the Democrats, but only to about the same degree as in previous elections. "The gender gap widened this year for the same reason Trump took the White House," reported the *Washington Post*. "Men, especially white men, surged right."[5] In the same year, male votes Brexited the UK out of the European Union.[6]

The anger fueling populism is about all kinds of things—demographic change, secularization, trade, labor market shocks, and so on. But it is also about gender. Note that even as he lost in 2020, Trump still won most of the male votes, and actually increased his support among Black and Latino men. When Trump said that it was "a very scary time for young men in America," he was scorned by progressives.[7] But it likely resonated with many men and at least some parents. Trump's appeal was a nostalgic one: Make America Great *Again*. And he found a big political market. The majority of his voters believed that life has gotten worse since the 1950s and gender plays an important role here.[8] Implicit in the invocation of the past are traditional ideas of femininity and masculinity. One of the most popular T-shirts on sale at his rallies declared, "I support Donald Trump. I love freedom. I drink beer. I turn wrenches. I protect my family. I eat meat & I own guns. If you don't like it, MOVE."[9] This is about as good a description of the identity of the Trump Army as you will find, a pure expression of what Pankaj Mishra described as a form of "rear-guard machismo."[10]

But this is not just found in the U.S. It is an international phenomenon. Across the world, men have been more likely than women to support right-wing or protest parties.[11] In Sweden, for example, one in four men supported the far-right Sweden Democrats in a 2015 poll, twice the level of support among women.[12] In Germany, especially in the east, men have swung sharply to the political right. In 2017, a third of Saxon men voted for the far-right Alternative for Germany Party. "We have a crisis of masculinity in the East and it is feeding the far right," says Petra Köpping, minister for integration in Saxony.[13] In South Korea, young men are also swinging hard right, fueled by antifeminist sentiment. In the Seoul mayoral election of April 2021, 73% of men in their 20s voted for the conservative candidate, compared to 41% of women in the same age group.[14] The overwhelming support of young men also helped to propel conservative presidential candidate Yoon Suk-yeol to a narrow victory in March 2022.[15] Yoon has promised to abolish the Department of Gender Equality and Family. India's prime minister, Narendra Modi, boasts of his 56-inch chest. There was alpha male Imran Khan in Pakistan ("feminism has completely degraded the role of a mother"), antifeminist Recep Tayyip Erdoğan ("women are not equal to men") in Turkey, and straight-out misogynist

Rodrigo Duterte in the Philippines ("as long as there are many beautiful women, there will be more rape cases").[16] These politicians do not
have a thoughtful understanding of male dislocation, or any positive
remedies. They are simply exploiting it for political purposes. As former
Trump adviser Stephen Bannon wrote, "These guys, these rootless,
white males, have monster power."[17]

Some conservatives go as far as to claim that there is a "war on
men" or a "war on boys."[18] This language validates and fuels a sense
of victimhood. South Korean men in their 20s are now twice as
likely to believe there is more severe discrimination against men
than against women.[19] In the U.S., a third of men of all political per-
suasions believe that they are discriminated against, and among Republicans, the number is rising.[20] This is false. While the problems
of boys and men are real, they are the result of structural changes in
the economy and broader culture, and the failings of our education
system, rather than of any deliberate discrimination. But on the political Right as on the Left, attitudes on gender issues float free of the
facts.

The conservative goal here is to whip up the partisan base in op-
position to what Senator Hawley described as the attempt by the Left
to "deconstruct America" through "an assault on the very idea of gender." One of the data points he used to justify this claim was the inclusion of trans women in competitive female sports. Invoking the threat
of transgender rights has now become a standard part of the conservative playbook. Even the question of which bathrooms people use has
become a political football. (To his credit, Donald Trump answered a
question on the bathroom issue in 2016 by saying that trans people
should simply "use the bathroom that they feel is appropriate.")[21] Even
though the numbers involved in any of these controversies are tiny—
after all, trans people account for just 0.6% of the population—it is an
issue that can be weaponized in defense of traditional ideas of sex and
gender.[22]

Conservative activists see the trans issue as a way to turn the headlights onto what they see as a radical gender ideology, which seeks to

entirely erase all biologically based sex differences. Their concern is not really about whether trans people can serve in the military or use the bathroom of their choice. It is about the very idea of clear and separate masculine and feminine categories and characteristics, grounded in biology. But they protest too much. The overwhelming majority of people, at least 99%, are cis, identifying themselves as male or female in line with their natal sex. That some people do not fit into simple binary categories is no threat to the categories themselves. Trans people are rather the exceptions that prove the rule, and both the rule and the exceptions are okay.

The good news here is that the general trend is still toward greater inclusion and protection for trans people, especially the landmark Supreme Court decision in June 2021 to secure protection for LGBT people from workplace discrimination under Title VII of the Civil Rights Act. Trump appointee Neil Gorsuch wrote the majority opinion, which was crystal clear: "An employer who fires an individual merely for being gay or transgender defies the law."[23] A third gender option (an "X") has now been added for U.S. passports.[24] Twenty-one states and DC have done the same for driver's licenses.[25] But it seems clear that many conservatives will likely continue to use the issue of trans rights as a weapon in the broader culture war over sex and gender.

Disenchanted men, following the Pied Piper of the internet search algorithm, can be led deeper and deeper into what has been labeled the "manosphere," a world of pickup artists, incels, and even some male separatists—MGTOWs (Men Going Their Own Way). This is where men who have taken the *red pill* go to commiserate, organize, and generally hate on feminists. The term red pill, adopted from *The Matrix*, refers to a choice to see the world as it really is. Here, it means to see that, far from being an oppressive patriarchy, our society is actually dominated by feminists, seeking to entrap and exploit men. In the more sensible parts of the manosphere, there are debates about real issues facing boys and men, like school discipline, overdiagnosis of ADHD (attention deficit hyperactivity disorder), suicide rates, occupational injury and death, and so on. But it is easy for the disgruntled young man to click to the next video, and the next. In her book *Men Who Hate Women*, feminist activist Laura Bates describes "the boys who are lost, who fall through the cracks of our society's stereotypes and straight into the arms of the communities ready to recruit them, greedy to indoctrinate them with fears of threats to their manhood, their livelihood."[26] A legitimate worry or normal anxiety metastasizes into misogyny. Women might come to be seen as psychological prey, to be manipulated into providing sex; this is what it means to be a pickup artist. For the most extreme, the incels, even having to go to the lengths of tricking women into sex seems unfair. Men have a right to sex, they claim, and women have a responsibility to give it to them. The misogyny can seep out of the chat rooms onto social media, and ultimately even to physical violence.

By contrast, MGTOWs don't want to pick up women or harass them online. They want to get away from them altogether. One of the big fears stoked in this community is of a false rape accusation; better to stay away. There is a helpful hierarchy of MGTOWs, eerily similar to the levels you might find in a computer game. Once a man has taken the red pill and chosen the MGTOW route, the steps are to reject long-term relationships (level 1); disavow any sexual relationship or "go monk" (level 2); disconnect from the economy, making only enough to support themselves (level 3); and finally, completely disengage from society, or "go ghost" (level 4). Many young men dip their toes into some of these waters at some point. It might even have become something of a rite of passage. Some find a genuine sense of community, which may be lacking in their offline life. But the overwhelming majority grow out of it; very few end up acting out in one terrible way or another. Underneath it all is a deep well of confusion and disorientation, which, as always, somebody is willing to exploit. I am not saying that Hawley or other populist conservatives are to blame for the rise of these online manosphere movements. If anything, progressives have more to answer for here, by either neglecting male issues altogether or by blaming them on toxic masculinity. But what Hawley shares with these communities is a reactionary worldview, a belief that the only way to help men is by restoring traditional gender roles and relationships. They want the old world back, one in which men and women know their place. But our solutions are not to be found in the past.

LOBSTERS AGAINST EQUALITY

In 2016, just as Donald Trump was defying almost every political prediction to win the 2016 election, a Canadian psychologist broke out of academic obscurity to become, according to George Mason economist and podcaster Tyler Cowen, "the most influential public intellectual in the Western world right now."[27] Respected among scholars for his work on personality traits, Jordan Peterson came to fame for refusing to use the preferred pronouns of a transgender student, in protest of new Canadian laws on trans rights. His 2018 book, *12 Rules for Life*, based on a Quora post and accompanied by a global speaking tour, sold more than 5 million copies.[28] For anyone serious about understanding what is happening with young men, Peterson's appeal is an important datapoint. By Peterson's own reckoning, they account for 80% of his audience. Men flock to him because, unlike so many, he does not mock or patronize them. He makes them feel heard. Peterson stumbled across a gigantic reservoir of unmet human need. His genuine compassion for the plight of young men marks him out from the people of the Left who want to excoriate them and the people on the Right who want to exploit them. He's a genuine intellectual wrestling with real and important issues.

But like many conservatives, he also sets too much store by biology. Like all successful modern public intellectuals, Peterson has an online merch store, selling not only books but stickers, socks, and framed art. There is also a special lobster section, featuring T-shirts and hoodies covered with small red images of Peterson's favorite crustacean— including, now, of course, a lobster-dotted face mask. Among Peterson fans, the lobster has become a sign of tribal loyalty. You are probably wondering why. "Lobsters exist in hierarchies," he explains. "They have a nervous system attuned to the hierarchy. And that nervous system runs on serotonin, just like our nervous systems do. And the nervous system of the lobster and of the human being is so similar that antidepressants work on lobsters."[29] One of the main planks of Peterson's philosophy is that social hierarchies are part of the natural order. Mammals are wired to know their place.

But the science here is not very good. Lobsters don't actually have brains, it turns out. For what it's worth, I think his use of lobsters is better seen as simply part of his storytelling style. I see Peterson as the latest incarnation of the "mytho-poetical" strand of the men's movement, which uses allegory (in his case, of lobster societies) to evoke an older, deeper form of masculinity. Robert Bly's *Iron John*, a bestseller in 1990, offered a similar prospectus, arguing that men had been over-domesticated into "soft men" and needed to rediscover the "hairy man" within.[30] In his 1996 book *Transforming Men*, British sociologist Geoff Dench casts men as frogs making their way through forests in search of a princess.[31] Dench, Bly, and Peterson all write a lot about witches and whales and castles and towers and kings. This should not be a surprise. Bly was a poet, and Peterson's earlier book, *Maps of Meaning*, is a dense, well-regarded academic study of mythology.

If it was just the lobsters, Peterson's overweighting of biology would not matter too much. Unfortunately, it also distorts his views on gender. He points out that women are more agreeable and conscientious than men, more into people, and more nurturing. Men are more aggressive, status conscious, driven by sex. This is all true. The real question is how far these differences can be relied on to explain gender inequalities in current societies. For Peterson, it seems, a great deal.

While progressives make the mistake of denying any biological basis for sex differences, conservatives like Peterson—and he is quite representative in this regard—make the opposite error of explaining away current gender inequalities with an appeal to nature. They end up justifying disparities that are much too wide to be attributed to natural causes. The question of occupational choice is a good example. In an interview, Peterson said that "men and women won't sort themselves into the same categories if you leave them to do it of their own accord." So far, so good. But he then went on to say that ratios of "20 to 1" of men to women in engineering, and the other way around in nursing, are "a consequence of the free choice of men and women. . . . Those are ineradicable differences."[32] When Petersonian conservatives see that only 15% of engineers are women and only 9% of nurses are men, they see nothing more than a reflection of natural sex differences (these are much higher proportions, after all, than 1 in 20). But remember that study by Su and Rounds that I cited in chapter 7, showing that if occupational choices actually matched underlying preferences, there would be at least twice as many female engineers and male nurses. There is also a danger that sex differences in nurturing behavior are used to justify a traditional division of labor in terms of family life: Peterson has urged that we "stop teaching 19-year-old girls that their primary destiny is a career."[33]

Things become trickier still when it comes to specific policies. Conservative scholar Charles Murray describes the evidence on sex differences between men and women in his book *Human Diversity*. It is a thorough, mostly balanced, summary. The problem comes when he uses these data to justify sexist policies. Laws governing child custody are a good case in point. Murray argues that "by any measure of which sex is better at nurturing young children, there is a big effect size favoring females and an overwhelming evolutionary case that the female advantage is grounded in biology."[34] He argues that courts should therefore default to maternal custody of young children, instead of the current legal default to consider the "best interests" of children on a case-by-case basis.

As Murray writes, "Where judges . . . are faced with no clear evidentiary basis for favoring one parent over another and a helpless third party's welfare is at stake, a principled liberal position can acknowledge an important innate difference between men and women." This is wrong. If a judge really has "no clear evidentiary basis" of a difference in the parenting abilities of two separating parents, granting custody to one of them solely based on their sex is arbitrary and unfair. Murray marshals evidence for a real *average* difference in *some* aspects of parenting abilities to argue for the incorporation of a sexist principle into family law. Fathers are struggling to retain their role as it is, and Murray's proposal would make matters worse. He makes similar arguments with regard to women serving in military combat roles, and was no doubt pleased by Senator Hawley's success in preventing women being added to the draft.

The broader problem here is that conservatives justify gender inequalities with biological explanations that are not *wrong*, just too thin to bear the weight they put on them. Of course, conservative arguments for the importance of biology in human behavior seem more reasonable when their opponents deny their existence altogether. It is hard to see how much someone is exaggerating the truth when their principal antagonists deny the truth altogether. This is one of the most unfortunate dynamics in the culture wars over sex and biology. The more fervently the Left denies any innate sex differences, the more strongly many on the Right feel the need to insist on their importance, and vice versa. The room for nuance becomes smaller.

FORWARD TO THE PAST

The final and most serious mistake made by conservatives is their assumption that the only way to help boys and men is to restore traditional gender roles, which means reversing some of the gains made by women in terms of economic independence. In this zero-sum world, if women are doing better, that must be why men are doing worse. This is not a fringe opinion. Almost two out of five Republican men (38%) agree with the statement that "the gains women have made in society have come at the expense of men."[35]

In a fascinating study conducted before the 2016 election, Dan Cassino, a professor at Fairleigh Dickinson University, added an unusual question to a survey of voting intentions: "Do you earn more, less, or about the same as your spouse?" Half the respondents got the question early in the survey, before being asked about voting, and the other half got it after declaring their voting intention. The question was intended to prime men "to think about potential threats to their gender roles," Cassino writes.[36] The results were striking. Men asked the question about spousal earnings early in the survey were much more likely to say they would vote for Donald Trump than Hillary Clinton. This was a small poll of around seven hundred registered voters. But Cassino's experiment hints at the potential for politicians to activate and exploit male anxiety about the loss of status.

The argument made by many conservative intellectuals is that if men lose their traditional role, they will become detached from society, or start to act out. The "monster power" Bannon observed gets channeled into antisocial behavior. This is not a new concern. Conservatives have been worrying about the dangers posed to men by the women's movement for decades. In his 1992 book, *Men and Marriage* (an update of his 1973 book *Sexual Suicide*), conservative intellectual George Gilder argued that feminism would render men redundant.[37] Once women were able to be "both provider and procreator," he warned, the need for marriage to a man would decline, leaving them as either "outlaws" or "exiles." Younger readers may be unfamiliar with Gilder's work. But among feminists of a certain age, his name provokes a strong reaction. Gilder went on to influence Ronald Reagan's economic policies and was proud to have been named Male Chauvinist Pig of the Year by both *Time* magazine and the National Organization of Women.[38] There is much to dislike about Gilder's worldview. But here's the thing. He wasn't completely wrong.

Like most of the anthropologists I cited back in chapter 7 (including Margaret Mead, Melvin Konner, David Gilmore, and Sherry Ortner), Gilder saw the fragility of the male role. "Unlike a woman, a man has no civilized role or agenda inscribed in his body," he wrote. "The man's role in the family is thus reversible; the woman's is unimpeachable and continues even if the man departs. . . . A man without a woman has a deep inner sense of dispensability."[39] Writing along similar lines, Geoff Dench identified the "fundamental weakness of feminist analysis" as a failure "to see that men may need the status of the main provider role to give them a sufficient reason to become fully involved, and stay involved, in the longer-term draggy business of family life."[40]

Conservatives are right to worry about the dangers of anomie and detachment among men stripped of their traditional role. But they are wrong to think that the solution is to somehow turn back the clock, making women dependent again in order to resupply men with purpose. For all the hankering after an imagined past, fewer than one in five Americans (18%) said in 2012 that "women should return to their traditional roles in society," down from 30% in 1987, according to Pew's social values survey—and on this question there are, unusually, no major differences here by sex, age, political inclination, or race.[41]

The conservative claim is that feminism has upended the natural order of things, and we are all—but men, especially—paying the price. The restoration of traditional families and roles is the answer. This analysis is wrong. Feminism has upended patriarchy, a *specific* social order that had the fatal flaw of being grossly unequal. The resulting disruption is real and must be taken seriously. Men do need help. But we can help men without hindering women or trying to turn back the clock. Fatherhood in particular can be reinvented for a more egalitarian world.

"The key to the recovery of masculinity does not lie in any wistful hope of humiliating the aggressive female and restoring the old masculine supremacy," wrote Arthur Schlesinger Jr. in a 1958 essay titled "The Crisis of American Masculinity." "Masculine supremacy, like white supremacy, was the neurosis of an immature society. It is good for men as well as for women that women have been set free. In any case, the process is irreversible; that particular genie can never be put back into the bottle."[42]

If that was true in 1958, it is obviously dramatically more so today. That is why it is so unhelpful to suggest that we can turn back the tide. Rather than helping boys and men in the difficult task of adapting to the new world of equality, conservatives encourage them to resist women's progress. Resistance may feel good, at least for a while, better perhaps than the demanding task of adaptation. But it is also futile and pointless.

CENTRIFUGAL GENDER POLITICS

"Roles are changing for both men and women. Women are being pressured . . . to believe that their past status was brought about by male oppression," writes one astute cultural observer. "At the same time men . . . are being accused of being oppressors—and angry oppressors at that. The whole process of change is taking place in an atmosphere of the greatest bad temper, and a tremendous amount of secondary hostility is being generated that in itself poses a threat to a good outcome."

That was Margaret Mead—in 1975.[43] The hostility remains, despite the extraordinary successes of the women's movement. Our politicians must shoulder much of the blame here. The failure of both Left and Right to respond to the growing problems of boys and men has created a dangerous vacuum in our political life. In the centrifugal dynamic of culture-war politics, the more the Right goes to one extreme, the more the Left must go to the other, and vice versa. The Left dismisses biology, the Right leans too heavily on it. The Left see a war on girls and women; the Right see a war on boys and men. The Left pathologizes masculinity; the Right pathologizes feminism.

Meanwhile, far away from the frontlines of the culture war, the real-world problems of boys and men go largely unaddressed. And the stakes here are high. As Daniel Schwammenthal, director of the American Jewish Committee's Transatlantic Institute, says, "The iron rule of politics is that if there are real problems in society and responsible parties don't deal with them, the irresponsible parties will jump on them."[44]

PART V

WHAT TO DO

CHAPTER 10

REDSHIRT THE BOYS

Boys Need an Extra Year in the Classroom

My wife and I were torn. Our middle son, Bryce, was about to start elementary school. But he just didn't seem ready, socially or intellectually. His pre-K teachers agreed. So we decided to hold him back a few months, enrolling him in our local school in January, rather than September. At the time I thought we had gone too far, and that the 4-month delay was a mistake. Now I think we did not go far enough. We should have waited a full year. Bryce struggled throughout his school years, especially in high school, in no small part because of undiagnosed sleep apnea (yes, it turns out kids can have it too). He managed, just barely, to leave high school with a diploma. At his graduation ceremony, as most of the parents around me swapped notes on which college their child was headed to, tears streamed down my face, tears of joy and of such fierce pride that despite everything, my boy had made it through high school.

Bryce's educational experience was not that unusual, especially for boys. Among many of the parents we know, a shorthand explanation has developed to explain the struggles of an adolescent child to stay on track, especially academically, but also in terms of life in general: "He's a boy." One night, the 15-year-old son of one of our friends climbed up a ten-story crane and posted a picture of himself at the top on Snapchat with the message "Hi, Mom!" (The police were waiting for him when he descended.) It's that prefrontal cortex, and that risk appetite.

"True equality between groups that are different in any way can be attained only by providing for the differences." That's Margaret Mead again, in 1974.[1] Mead's idea of true equality might now be labeled equity. When there are differences in starting conditions, treating people the same (i.e., equally) is not the same as treating them equitably. A common visual illustration is of three children of different heights, who want to look over a fence. To get them to the same level, you need to give taller boxes to the shorter children. The switch from a mindset of equality to one of equity has been powerful in considerations of racial justice, especially in the U.S. But there are gender implications here too. An equitable education system, for example, will be one that recognizes natural sex differences, especially the fact that boys are at a developmental disadvantage to girls at critical points in their schooling.

This chapter sets out proposals for a more male-friendly education system. Specifically, I argue for three main reforms: giving boys an extra year of pre-K before starting them in school; a recruitment drive of male teachers into classrooms; and significant investments in vocational education, including more technical high schools. I am aware that parts of this agenda may seem radical. But if we are serious about gender equality, some radicalism is required.

THE GIFT OF TIME

Starting school a year later has been dubbed "redshirting." This is a term borrowed from a practice in collegiate athletics in which a player is held out of regular competition for a season. The idea got a burst of popular attention in 2008, when Malcolm Gladwell presented evidence in his book *Outliers* that children older than their classmates do better on academic tests, and in life generally. He argued that being either old or young within a class cohort leads "children into patterns of achievement and underachievement, encouragement and discouragement, that stretch on and on for years."[2]

It is worth noting that redshirting is reasonably common. In a 2021 survey by Morning Consult and EdChoice, 12% of parents of school-age children said they had delayed kindergarten entry for at least one of their children, compared to 6% of those whose children are now over 18.[3] The top three reasons given for delay were that the child was too young, not emotionally ready, or not academically ready. Interestingly, among *teachers* with school-age children, the share of redshirters was a little higher, at 15%.[4] These numbers are higher than the official figures for the 2010/2011 school year (the last for which data are publicly available), when 7% of boys and 5% of girls had a delayed entry into kindergarten.[5] (The pandemic could of course be a factor here.)

But some children are much more likely to be redshirted than others. Children with affluent parents are twice as likely to have a delayed school start as those from a low-income home. There is a similar gap between white and Black children. Boys are more likely to be redshirted than girls, especially by parents who are teachers.[6] Children who are young for their school year are also more likely to be held back a year. When these factors are combined, the rate gets quite high. Among summer-born boys with BA-educated parents (the kind of folks who read *Outliers*), the redshirting rate is 20%, according to an analysis of the 2010/11 data by the Northwestern University economist Diane Whitmore Schanzenbach and Stephanie Howard Larson.[7] Anecdotally, it also seems that redshirting is more common at private schools. And far from being those at most educational disadvantage, children who are redshirted have slightly above average literacy and math scores when the decision is made.[8] In other words, the boys who will benefit least are the ones most likely to be redshirted.

I propose that all boys be redshirted by default. Introducing a 1-year chronological age gap would reduce the *developmental* age gap between boys and girls. In other words, it would be more equitable. I have shown in chapter 1 that the gender gaps in learning open up early, but that the biggest differences, in terms of brain development, occur in adolescence. The main reason for starting boys later is not so that they will be a year older in kindergarten. It is so they will be a year older when they get to middle and high school.

WILL REDSHIRTING WORK?

Would a delayed start for boys narrow the gender gap? I don't know for sure. Such a significant change in education policy is hard to evaluate in advance. But the evidence from studies of redshirting makes me hopeful that it could help quite a lot. A raft of studies of redshirted boys have shown dramatic reductions in hyperactivity and inattention through the elementary school years, higher levels of life satisfaction, lower chances of being held back a grade later, and higher test scores.[9]

Schanzenbach is the scholar who has conducted the most recent high-quality study of redshirting, along with Elizabeth Cascio of Dartmouth College, using data from Tennessee. The children in their sample were disproportionately lower income and racially diverse. Half were getting free or reduced-price lunch in kindergarten. A third were Black. Overall, Schanzenbach and Cascio find that being a year older had a positive impact on test scores in eighth grade, reduced the risks of repeating a grade before high school, and improved the chances of taking the SAT or ACT at the end of high school. But the benefits for boys were at least twice as big as for girls on all the outcome measures through 8th grade, and by high school only boys were seeing any gains. Cascio and Schanzenbach also find the biggest gains for lower-income students, which as they note, "stands in contrast to the observed patterns in which higher-income children are substantially more likely to be redshirted."[10] Lastly, they find no negative effects on the younger classmates of redshirted children. If anything, they say, there are modestly positive "spillover" effects.

So redshirting provides a long-term positive benefit for boys in particular, especially those from poorer backgrounds, with no adverse effects on their classmates. Importantly, these results were driven not by a *relative* age effect but an *absolute* age effect—which is what my redshirting policy is intended to deliver. One of the most encouraging findings from the study was a big reduction in the risk of being held back a grade later on. Grade retention is massively unequal by race, gender, and economic background: one in four Black boys (26%) have repeated at least one grade before they leave high school.[11] By redshirting boys from the outset, we can reduce their risk of being held back a year later on.

Cascio and Schanzenbach's findings are consistent with another study by Philip Cook and Songman Kang, using data from North Carolina.[12] Their analysis shows that redshirted children are doing significantly better in both reading and math by the end of third grade. Looking at gender gaps within racial groups, they find that the 10% redshirting rate among white boys reduced the overall gender gap among white students in third grade reading by 11%.

There is some qualitative evidence here too. An in-depth study by Suzanne Stateler Jones of Collin College found a much higher level of life satisfaction among summer-born adolescent boys who had been redshirted, compared to their peers.[13] Among those who started school at the prescribed age, she said a common refrain was, "I'm always trying to keep up." But she says the overall message from the older boys was, "They loved it, liked being older, no problem with it, can't think of any way it's hurt, it's only helped." Jones also interviewed parents and asked them what they would do if they had another summer-born son. "Automatically (they said): 'We would redshirt.'" It is worth noting, however, that this small group was largely white and affluent, simply because this is the group currently most likely to redshirt their children.

Taken together, these results point to potentially big benefits from starting all boys a year later. The largest gains would be for those who are least likely to be redshirted right now, especially boys from lower-income families and Black boys. I also expect the gains would be even bigger on other outcome measures, such as GPA, which existing studies have been unable to assess. High school grades, for example, are related to executive functioning skills—one likely reason why girls have higher grades.[14] An extra year of development is unlikely to completely close the gap on these skills, but it would surely help.

OBJECTIONS TO REDSHIRTING

There are of course some good arguments against my proposal. I will address five here. First, delaying school entry could put pressure on parents to provide childcare for another year; this is likely to be one reason why lower-income parents are already much less likely to red-shirt their children. This is a real concern. My proposal is to enroll boys in a universal pre-K program at the same age as girls but give them an extra year before they move on. In other words, boys would get a double dose of pre-K. So as far as parents are concerned, the policy should be neutral with regard to childcare costs.

Second, there is a concern that boys who start school later will be more likely to drop out of high school, because they will legally be able to leave formal education some time before their high school educa-tion is complete. It is hard to know how big a problem this would be. Data analyzed by the education economists David Deming and Susan Dynarski do not show much impact on high school graduation rates among those who start school a year later, though they do show a delay.[15] But as we have seen, this group is hardly representative; today's red-shirted children are from more advantaged backgrounds and so much less likely to drop out of high school in any case. One thing that would help here is to raise the legal age for leaving school to 18—which about half of U.S. states have already done.[16]

Third, a related objection is that boys will lose a year in the labor market once they become men, potentially reducing their lifetime earn-ings. This is one of the main concerns of Deming and Dynarski. "Hold-ing constant retirement age, a person who starts school a year later spends one less year in the labor force," they point out. "The financial losses from starting one year later consist of one year of labor market earnings, as well as the lifetime return to that lost year of labor mar-ket experience."[17] Again, this is a reasonable fear. But it is one that ap-plies to *any* policy that increases the number of years spent in school, at whatever age. You might spend 2 years in community college, for ex-ample, and leave without any kind of credential. The truth is that right now few young men are hitting the labor market at full stride out of secondary education. Almost one in five don't finish high school on time.[18] Of those who start community college, fewer than one in three have gained a qualification three years later.[19] More than one in ten young men, aged between 16 and 24, are "disconnected" (i.e., neither in paid work nor in education).[20] My point is simply that we should not assume that the extra year of learning will mean a lost year of earnings. If it helps to improve outcomes for boys, as I believe it will, it should improve labor market prospects.

Fourth, there is a question of how to phase in the reform. If we were to suddenly hold a whole cohort of boys back for a year, there would be a single, female-only cohort going through the education system, which would be distinctly odd, especially for them. My suggestion is to phase the policy in over a few years, starting with the youngest boys and gradually expanding the age range each year until all boys are covered by the policy. Perhaps a third of the boys could be redshirted in the first year, two-thirds in the second year, and all of them only in year three, for example. (This would also create a natural experiment for social scientists to evaluate the benefits of redshirting for boys of different ages.)

Last but not least, would it be legal? Let us imagine that a school district or state adopts my plan. Some legal challenge would likely be mounted, perhaps by the ACLU. They would cite Title VII on the Civil Rights Act of 1964, which prohibits discrimination on the basis of sex, and possibly the Equal Protection Clause in the 14th Amendment.[21] The defense would be that girls and boys are different in terms of their development, and that such differences can be taken into account in education policy without breaching Title VII. A famous case of the Virginia Military Institute, an all-boys school, would surely be cited. In 1996, the Supreme Court forced the institute to open its doors fully to women. Justice Ruth Bader Ginsburg penned the majority opinion.[22] Importantly, the court did not dispute the claim that there are differences on average in the way boys and girls learn. As Ginsburg wrote, this however did not provide a justification for excluding girls "whose talent and capacity place them outside the average description" (i.e., who learn more like a typical boy). Today, around 12% of students at the institute are women.[23]

The court ruled that in order to exclude one sex entirely from a public educational institution, the state must provide an "exceedingly persuasive justification."[24] But my proposal is not to *exclude* either sex from any institution, merely to slightly stagger the default age at which boys and girls move on from preschool to kindergarten, on the grounds of their different developmental trajectories. Parents would be at liberty to override the default, to either hold back their daughter or accelerate their son, just as they are in the current system. All this said, there are clear legal challenges to explicitly basing a policy on sex differences, which need to be considered in design and implementation.

So I think there are reasonable answers to these reasonable concerns with my redshirt-the-boys plan. The only way to find out for sure is to do it, initially in the form of some pilot programs, perhaps in a selection of school districts in a range of settings. I expect these would show good results in terms of reducing the gender gap in education, and a good return on investment. But of course, I could be wrong. That is why evaluation studies are so important. Let's find out.

MORE MEN TEACHING BOYS

Right now, boys and school don't mix too well. Around the world, boys are twice as likely as girls to say that school is "a waste of time," according to a survey commissioned by the OECD in 2015.[25] In the U.S., boys are three times as likely as girls to be expelled from school and twice as likely to be suspended.[26] There are a number of reforms that might improve the school environment for boys, including more physical education, a later school start time, and better food. Exercise, food, sleep: all in all, the education system needs to do a much better job of recognizing that students are flesh and blood, not just brains on a stick. Of course, these reforms would benefit girls too.

But one school reform would dwarf all of these: more men at the front of our classrooms. In the U.S, the proportion of male teachers is low, and falling. The male share of K–12 teachers is now 24%, down from 33% at the beginning of the 1980s.[27] Male teachers are especially scarce in elementary and middle schools, as figure 10-1 shows. Similar trends can be observed in other nations, including the UK and South Korea.[28]

FIGURE 10-1   Not enough Misters
Gender of teachers, by school level

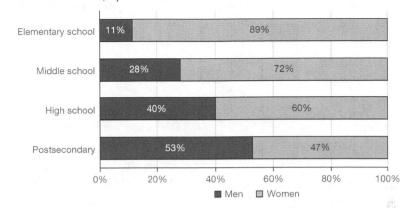

Note: For postsecondary, figures shown are for full-time faculty in degree-granting institutions.
Source: National Center for Education Statistics (IPEDS, March 2021): K-12 figures are for 2017–2018; postsecondary figures are for 2017, 2018 and 2019.

"If the trend continues, we may see a day when 8 of 10 teachers [in the U.S.] will be female," write Richard Ingersoll and his colleagues in a 2018 report from the University of Pennsylvania. They add that "an increasing percentage of elementary schools will have no male teachers. . . . Given the importance of teachers as role models, and even as surrogate parents for some students, certainly some will see this trend as a problem and a policy concern."[29] Honestly, I don't know how anyone could *not* see this trend as a problem. But it is important to spell out why. For one thing, if children grow up seeing care or education as women's work, this reinforces gender stereotypes across generations. As Gloria Steinem said in 1995, "The way we get divided into our false notions of masculine and feminine is what we see as children."[30]

There is also solid evidence that male teachers boost academic outcomes for boys, especially in certain subject areas like English. The potential upsides here are quite large. Education researcher Thomas Dee estimates that if half the English teachers from sixth to eighth grade were male, "the achievement gap in reading [between girls and boys] would fall by approximately a third by the end of middle school."[31] (Notably, the performance of girls in English seemed not to be affected by teacher gender.) A separate study in Chicago found that in classes with a male teacher, the gender gap in ninth-grade GPA was almost halved.[32]

When the share of men teaching in Finnish primary schools was boosted by a 40% quota for training courses, both boys and girls did better in school.[33] The quota was scrapped in 1989, and the share of men entering primary teaching halved. The policy ended because of a sex discrimination law passed in 1987. But in 2005, the Finnish government instituted a legal requirement on every state-owned company to have at least 40% women on their board.[34] I will admit to a lack of expertise on the intricacies of the Finnish legal system, but surely something is awry here.

But I digress. While the evidence that male teachers matter is strong, the precise mechanisms are not well understood. Attitudes may be one factor. Female teachers are more likely than male teachers to see the boys in their class as disruptive, while male teachers tend to have a more positive view of boys and their capabilities.[35] There may also be a role model effect. It is worth mentioning here that the race of teachers is important too, and that teaching skews even more white than it does female. But it seems that Black boys benefit most from having a Black teacher.[36] "Having both male and female teachers is likely good for students for many of the same reasons that they benefit from a racially and ethnically diverse teacher workforce," writes Lisette Partelow, an education scholar at the progressive Center for American Progress.[37]

What is required here is a massive, urgent recruitment effort. In an ideal world, we would have similar numbers of male and female teachers, all the way from pre-K classrooms to PhD seminars. Huge progress has been made on college campuses, where women now make up almost half of full-time faculty (47%), as figure 10-1 shows.[38] Women also account for over half the heads of university and college departments, 40% of deans, and 30% of college presidents.[39] The American Council on Education has set the goal of reaching complete gender parity in college leadership by 2030. Given the recent upward trend, and the fact that half of current college presidents say they plan to leave their position in the next 5 years, this ambitious goal looks achievable.[40] The Council calls it the Moving the Needle initiative. In higher education, then, we have seen real progress toward gender balance at all levels, and the setting of clear goals for the future. Meanwhile, in K–12 we are moving further away from gender parity with every passing year, and no goals have been set. Surely, moving the needle here is at least as important. As an initial step, we should set the target of reaching 30% male representation in K–12 teaching. School districts could be asked to pledge to reach the goal.

Specific efforts are also needed to recruit more men into early years education, more Black men, and more male English teachers. Early years education is close to being an all-female environment. It ought to be a source of national shame that only 3% of pre-K and kindergarten teachers are men.[41] There are now twice as many women flying U.S. military planes as there are men teaching kindergarten (as a share of the professions).[42] The barriers to male recruitment in this field are high, according to an in-depth study of 46 male educators working in pre-K and kindergarten classrooms in New York by Kirsten Cole of Manhattan Community College and her colleagues.[43] Stigma is one major challenge. Many of the men had been advised to make sure they were never alone with a child, and to be wary of any physical contact. (Just as I was writing this chapter, my son called to say he had been turned down for a childcare job because the parents were uncomfortable leaving their children with a man. "At least they were honest about it," he said.)

On the upside, many of these educators said they felt proud that they were providing positive male role models for young children, and reported many parents being delighted that their children would have a male teacher. Cole and her coauthors urge concerted policy efforts to attract and retain more men in early education. "Because of their current scarcity in the field," they write, "male educators may also require intentional supports that address the particular circumstances they face related to bias and isolation." They propose targeted recruitment of men into the field, modeled on programs like NYC Teaching Fellows, which supports professionals making career transitions into teaching in high-need subject areas, such as math, science, and special needs in underserved New York schools. Philanthropic foundations serious about gender equity should be flooding the education market with generous college scholarships for men who want to pursue a career in early years education, just as they have supported girls interested in STEM careers.

The second priority is to recruit more Black men into teaching. "As a black male teacher, sometimes I feel like a unicorn," says Charles Jean-Pierre, a D.C. Public Schools art and French teacher.[44] This is not surprising. Black men account for just 2% of teachers in the U.S.[45] As I have already mentioned, Black boys in particular seem to benefit from having a Black teacher. There are now a range of initiatives, mostly at the city level, to boost the number of Black male teachers, including NYC Men Teach, the National Association of Black Male Educators, The Male Teacher of Color Initiative, the Black Male Educators Convening, and so on. But many of these are operating on shoestring budgets and in urgent need of support.

In Columbia, South Carolina, school superintendent Baron Davis has set the explicit goal of hiring an extra 100 male teachers of color (with a particular focus on Black men), which would bring their representation up to 10% in his district. This is the kind of intentionality and specificity we need for a nationwide affirmative action program for male teachers. "You can't keep saying there's not enough Black men in education," says Davis. The question is, he says, "What are you going to do about it?"[46] I think the same can now be said of men in education generally.

The third recruitment priority is to get more men teaching English. Literacy and verbal skills are where boys lag furthest behind girls, and these skills matter a lot to later educational prospects. One study finds that moving U.S. students up by a single letter grade in ninth-grade English increases the probability of college enrollment by 10 percentage points.[47] The extra year that boys would gain from redshirting would certainly help here. But so would more male teachers in the appropriate subjects, especially English. Remember that having a male English teacher improved results for boys, with no negative impact for girls. So the more men teaching English, the better. Currently, men account for 12% of the English teachers in middle school, and 23% of those in high school.[48] Most policy efforts in terms of teacher recruitment are currently focused on attracting more teachers, male or female, into STEM subjects. This is important, of course. But I would say that there is now an equally urgent need to get more men teaching English. One option is to borrow an idea from the STEM field and provide college students majoring in English the opportunity to gain their teacher accreditation at the same time, reducing the years of study. Obviously, this might be attractive to both men and women.

LESS TALK, MORE SHOP

The third major policy reform I propose is a massive investment in male-friendly vocational education and training. Our educational system is tilted toward the standard academic track, up to and including a 4-year college degree. I have written a fair amount about college in earlier chapters. But many people do just fine without a 4-year college degree. In fact, 16% of people with a high school diploma and 28% of those with an associate's degree make more money across their working life than the median person with a bachelor's degree, according to a study by Georgetown's Anthony Carnevale and his coauthors.[49] As they observe, "The simple advice to high school students to 'go to college' no longer suffices." Carnevale says we need more career counselors in high schools, with the skills and information to help students see a range of options. Sometimes the job title is "College and Career Counselor," but it is usually the former that gets the most attention. (We should strive for more gender balance here too: right now, only one in four guidance counselors is a man.)[50]

The singular focus on the traditional college route sends a strong signal that some skills are more valuable than others, specifically the ones that make you "college ready." There is a lot I could say here about the classism and the "cult of smart" that underpins a lot of thinking and policy in this area.[51] But one upshot has been a persistent undervaluing of vocational learning. This has been harmful in general, but especially for boys and men. On average, male students seem to do better with a more "hands on" and practical approach to learning and

so benefit most from a more vocational approach.[52] But there has been
a precipitous decline in career and technical education (CTE) in American schools, a result of the go-to-college obsession and a residual fear
of "tracking" some students away from more academic classes. Between
1992 and 2013 (the last year for which data are available), the number
of CTE credits earned by U.S. high school students dropped by 17%.[53]
Federal spending has declined in the last few decades.[54]

High school curricula need more "hands-on" elements. This does
not mean sending all the boys into shop class to learn a trade while the
girls polish their college application essays. But it does mean incorpo-
rating more practical and more vocational elements (i.e., CTE) into the
general curriculum, and especially creating more stand-alone technical schools. The broader goal here is more of what philosopher Joseph
Fishkin calls "opportunity pluralism."[55] Rather than a single narrow
path in what he calls a "unitary opportunity structure," there should
be many different routes to success.

How much can CTE help boys in particular? The evidence base
here is not very broad, but what there is looks encouraging. A few high-
quality studies stand out. The first examined the impact of career
academies, which are small, vocationally oriented high schools. There
are an estimated 7,000 of these academies across the nation, although
they vary greatly in their approach.[56] The evaluation study by MDRC
looked at nine academies in New York. On traditional education metrics, such as grades, test scores, and college entry, they were a failure.
But male students from these schools, mostly Hispanic and Black, saw
a 17% earnings boost, equivalent to an extra $30,000, over the eight
years of the follow-up study.[57] This wage bump is similar to the one for
students completing 2 years of community college. Strikingly, for young
women graduating from the academies, there was no apparent benefit
on any measured outcome, an exception to the rule of educational interventions overall that I described in chapter 6—and further evidence
that CTE is a particularly male-friendly educational approach.

A second study examined the impact of a statewide system of sixteen CTE schools in Connecticut, which collectively educate around
11,000 students, 7% of those in the school system.[58] Male students at

these schools had a graduation rate 10 percentage points higher than in traditional schools, and their wages were 33–35% higher by the age of 23. Again, there were no apparent gains for female students. These U.S. studies echo similar findings from a study in Norway, where a new vocational track in high school boosted earnings for male participants. As the authors Marianne Bertrand, Magne Mogstad, and Jack Mountjoy write, "Considerations related to differential benefits by gender should be an integral part of the policy conversation surrounding vocational education."[59]

In recent years, there have in fact been some welcome signs that policymakers are warming to investments in CTE. A number of states have boosted funding. Nevada, for example, tripled CTE investment.[60] In 2018 the Carl D. Perkins Career and Technical Education Act was reauthorized, providing an annual $1.3 billion to states to support funding for CTE.[61] This is good, as far as it goes. But compared to the $150 billion supporting college education, it does not go very far.[62]

Another problem is that almost all the investment in CTE goes to within-school courses, even though the best evidence on the benefits of CTE is from whole-school approaches. We need more CTE in every school, for sure. But more importantly, we need more CTE schools. By my estimates, there are currently around 1,600 technical high schools in the country, accounting for about 7% of all public high schools.[63] These are clustered in larger urban or suburban school districts in the Northeast.[64] Overall, only 12% of school districts have a CTE school. We should aim to add at least 1,000 new technical high schools across the nation by 2030. If the federal government offered states a subsidy of $5,000 per student for these schools, this goal could be achieved for around $4 billion a year.[65] These new schools would of course be open to boys and girls. But given the results of the evaluation studies, it would make sense to market them to male students.

Beyond high school, there is a strong case for expanding apprenticeships. The National Apprenticeship Act, which passed in the House of Representatives in 2021, would invest $3.5 billion over the 5 years, to create nearly a million new apprenticeships.[66] This kind of investment is urgently needed; let's hope the Senate thinks so too. Despite some recent growth, the U.S. remains stuck right at the bottom of the international table for the number of adults taking apprenticeships, at about 636,000.[67] Community colleges also offer vocational courses leading to higher employment and earnings, especially those in health, business, and STEM. These colleges are also the most common postsecondary destination for young adults in the U.S. (By comparison, an associate's degree in a liberal arts subject is not a great investment, in terms of labor market outcomes.)[68] At least $20 billion a year should be diverted toward community colleges through a new federal grant program, along with more incentives to ensure that the students complete their studies, especially in subjects leading to the best job prospects.[69]

All of these reforms will take time. As Oren Cass, head of the center-right think tank American Compass, writes, "Refocusing education reform from an obsession with college to a respect for the other pathways that young people can follow into the labor market will be a long, slow process."[70] So we had better get started.

I've focused here on vocation routes, but I'll make just one plea on colleges. I would like to see more countries, or U.S. states, following the lead of Scotland, which as part of its Gender Action Plan has set the goal of reducing the gender gap in undergraduate enrollment to 5 percentage points. This will be a challenge, given that the difference is currently 17 percentage points.[71] But the Scottish government stands out for clearly stating that gender inequalities in *both* directions matter, and for setting specific targets to address them.

Finally, I should probably mention one policy proposal that I do not endorse: more single-sex schooling. This solution comes up quite a lot in discussions of how to help boys. There are a few studies showing impressive effects, including one from twenty schools in Trinidad and Tobago.[72] But overall, the research does not suggest much benefit to either boys or girls from separate schooling.[73] It may be that single-sex education provides particular benefits for certain groups, including Black boys; there just isn't strong evidence either way on this specific question. It is certainly true that as Michael Gurian puts it in the title of his book, *Boys and Girls Learn Differently*.[74] But this difference is better addressed by revising teacher education courses to include some of the scientific evidence on sex differences, as Gurian urges. (Currently, they do not.)

Many of the differences between boys and girls in today's classrooms are because the girls are just much "older," developmentally speaking. We can send boys to the same schools as girls, just a year later.

CHAPTER 11

MEN CAN HEAL

Getting Men into the Jobs of the Future

Cameron was about 6 when I was driving him home after seeing the doctor. "Dad," he said, "I didn't know that men could be doctors." I was perplexed for a moment. Then I realized that the two or three doctors he had previously encountered happened to have been women, which was not that odd given that more than half of the primary care doctors in the UK are female. Having encountered only women working as doctors, it was reasonable for him to wonder if men could do that job. I reassured him that men could indeed be doctors, but I was careful to add, "and nurses, of course." The elementary school our sons attended had an all-female staff too, so it also took a while to convince them that men could also be teachers.

In an attempt at balance, we deliberately tried to hire men to provide childcare for our sons. This wasn't always easy, of course, since men account for such a tiny proportion of childcare workers. One in particular, "Michael the Australian," was a particular hit. He would pitch tents as "homework camps" and make the boys run after a rugby ball between assignments. Michael instinctively knew how to make doing homework less like a prison sentence and more like playing a game. (I sometimes wonder if this is one reason that Bryce ended up working in the childcare and education field.)

In chapter 10, I offered some solutions to the structural problems facing boys in the education system. Here I turn to the problems of men in the world of work. As I showed in chapter 2, there has been a hemorrhaging of decently paid jobs in traditionally male sectors, such as manufacturing and heavy industry. The new middle class jobs are in fields that are often labeled "pink collar" because they are overwhelmingly occupied by women. While women have moved decisively into many previously male-dominated occupations, including pharmacy, law and accountancy, there has been nothing like the same movement in the other direction. The gender desegregation of the labor market has been almost entirely one way.[1] In particular, the share of men in HEAL occupations—health, education, administration, and literacy—remains stubbornly low. "Women are always saying, 'We can do anything that men can do,'" observed Gloria Steinem. "But men are not saying, 'We can do anything that women can do.'"[2] More men can certainly do HEAL jobs. And given the trends in the labor market, they must.

Here I first describe and define HEAL occupations. Then I make the case for getting more men into HEAL occupations, which has three main components. First, given the decline in traditional male occupations, it is imperative that men look to these sectors for jobs. Second, diversifying these professions would also help to meet their growing demand for labor. Third, it would make it more likely that boys and men could find male providers of these services. So getting men into HEAL occupations would be good for men, good for the professions, and good for clients—a win-win-win.

I then make some policy proposals for getting more men into HEAL, drawing on some of the lessons from the successful efforts to get more women into STEM. The three main elements of my Men Can HEAL plan are to build a pipeline in the education system, provide financial incentives, and reduce the social stigma faced by men working in these fields.

STEM AND HEAL

Never doubt the power of a good acronym. Two decades ago, Judith A. Ramaley, assistant director for education and human resources at the National Science Foundation, was tasked with promoting science,

mathematics, engineering, and technology. The acronym she inherited
for the work was SMET. She "didn't like the sound of that word" and
started using STEM instead.[3] By 2005 there was a STEM caucus in
Congress, and the term has since passed into regular use. From the
outset, the STEM drive was motivated by concerns about economic
growth and national security. But in recent years the goal has moved
to gender equality, and specifically the importance of getting more
women into male-dominated STEM occupations—with considerable
success.

In broad terms, HEAL occupations can be seen as the opposite of
STEM. They are more focused on people, rather than things, and they
tend to require more literacy than numeracy skills; hence the L in place
of the M. There may only be around 120,000 prime age workers (25 to
54 years) with job titles such as mathematician or statistician, but there
are many more jobs where math skills are important.[4] Likewise, there
are roughly 150,000 authors, writers, and editors, but many more jobs
where literacy and communication skills are important. In the HEAL
category, I include some broad occupational categories, such as education (e.g., teachers, librarians), health care (e.g., nurses, doctors, dental
hygienists), and health care support (e.g., home health aides, medical
assistants).[5] In addition, some specific jobs are included, such as social
workers, mental health counselors, training and development managers
and specialists, education and child care administrators, editors, court
clerks, and so on. In 2020, STEM jobs accounted for 9% of U.S. employment among prime-age workers, while HEAL jobs accounted for
23%. Health care and education are very large sectors, between them
accounting for around 15% of all jobs.

In recent decades, there has been an increase in female representation in STEM jobs. Women now account for almost half (45%) of the
life scientists and physical scientists working in the U.S., for example,
up from fewer than one in five in 1980.[6] Among engineers, the proportion of women has risen from 4% to 15%. The tech industry has seen
much smaller gains in recent decades, with women's representation
stuck at about 25%. Overall, women now account for 27% of STEM
workers, up from 13% in 1980, as figure 11-1 shows. But the trend has

FIGURE 11-1 Women Rise in STEM, Men Fall in HEAL

Share of workers in STEM and HEAL occupations by gender, 1980 and 2019

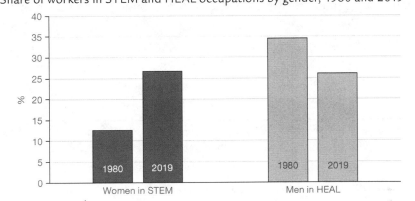

Note: Full-time, year-round, civilian, employed workers ages 25–54 with positive earnings. HEAL and STEM are categorized using 1990 occupational codes.
Source: Steven Ruggles and others, *IPUMS USA*: Version 11.0, 2021.

been the other way in terms of male representation in HEAL jobs. In 2019, 26% were held by men, down from 35% in 1980. (I should note again here that all my figures are for full-time workers aged between 25 and 54.)

WHY WE NEED MORE MEN IN HEAL

Does it matter if women continue to dominate HEAL jobs? After all, given the natural sex differences between men and women, we should not be surprised if more women than men are attracted to these occupations. The question, however, is how many more. As I have been at some pains to point out, the distributions of male and female natural preferences and interests greatly overlap. Just as the current underrepresentation of women in engineering or in leadership roles cannot be plausibly attributed to natural causes, it is equally absurd to think that the 18% male share of social workers is an authentic representation of the true level of interest in the job among men, especially since it has halved since 1980.[7] If certain occupations are seen as no-go zones for men, their choices are constrained, just as much as for women in the reverse case.

HEAL sectors are where the jobs are coming from. To improve men's employment prospects, we need to get more of them into these kinds of jobs. Harvard's David Deming calculates that between 1980 and 2012, "jobs requiring high levels of social interaction grew by nearly 12 percentage points as a share of the U.S. labor force." Meanwhile "math-intensive but less social jobs . . . shrank by 3.3 percentage points over the same period."[8] It is true that STEM professions are more often described as the jobs of the future. The glossy photos of bright young people in lab coats certainly add to that sense. But in terms of raw job creation, HEAL is outpacing STEM; by my calculations, for every new STEM job created by 2030 there will be more than three new HEAL jobs.[9]

It is true that on average, STEM jobs pay better than HEAL ones. This reflects the fact that some of the largest HEAL occupations have low wage rates. There are around 610,000 home health and personal care aides, for example (working full time and aged 25–54), earning a median annual wage of $26,000. But there are also plenty of HEAL jobs with relatively high pay levels, such as nurse practitioners ($100,000), medical and health services managers ($71,000), education and child care administrators ($70,000), or occupational therapists ($72,000).[10] Many HEAL jobs also offer a high degree of job security even in an economic downturn; we still need nurses and teachers in a recession.

The second reason to get more men into HEAL jobs is to help meet the growing demand for labor in occupations like nursing and teaching. Almost half of all registered nurses are now over the age of 50. This means many are likely to retire over the next 15 years, especially if they are under greater stress at work.[11] Meanwhile the number of nurses and nurse practitioners needed is expected to increase by about 400,000 by 2030.[12] Even before COVID-19, nurse burnout was seen as a growing problem.[13] "Hospitals were having difficulty finding nurses to fill positions before the pandemic," says Kendra McMillan, senior policy adviser to the American Nurses Association. "The pandemic's demand on the healthcare system has further exacerbated a long-standing projection that has burdened our nursing workforce."[14] In September 2021, the American Nursing Association urged the federal government to declare a "national nurse staffing crisis."[15] In a survey conducted at the end of 2021 by the Chartis Center for Rural Health, 99% of rural hospitals reported staffing shortages, with 96% saying that recruiting and retaining nurses were their biggest challenges. One in four hospitals said that a lack of nurses had forced them to suspend certain services, including newborn delivery, chemotherapy, and colonoscopies.[16] A number of solutions have been suggested to meet this demand, including higher pay, more flexible hours, hiring bonuses, better workplace culture, and expanded nurse education.[17] All good ideas. But one solution is almost never mentioned: get more men into nursing.

The teaching profession faces similar challenges. Two-thirds of school districts reported teacher shortages, in a survey of 1,200 school and district leaders conducted in 2021 by Frontline Education.[18] Again, rural areas are suffering most. The main sources of the problem, according to education leaders, are a lack of qualified teachers and low pay relative to other jobs. Overall, it is a "grim picture" according to the survey authors.

In 2014, public opinion on teaching passed an ominous milestone. For the first time ever, a majority of parents answered "No" to the following survey question, "Would you like your child to become a public school teacher?" (54%, up from 28% in 2009).[19] Enrollment rates in teacher training programs declined by more than a third between 2000 and 2018, and the fall was larger for men than for women.[20] The pandemic made matters worse, and drastic action is being taken in some places. New Mexico has drafted National Guard soldiers as substitute teachers; a Minneapolis school district asked for parent volunteers to get a substitute teacher license; and Polk County, Florida, flew in sixty teachers from eight foreign countries, all with J-1 visas.[21] But when longer-term solutions are discussed, again almost nothing is said about the possibility of attracting more men to the profession.

We face labor shortages in two of the largest and most important sectors of our economy—health care and education. But we are trying to solve them with only half the workforce.

The third and final argument for getting more men into HEAL jobs is to improve the gender match between providers and users of many

FIGURE 11-2   Not enough men in caring professions
Male share, select HEAL occupations

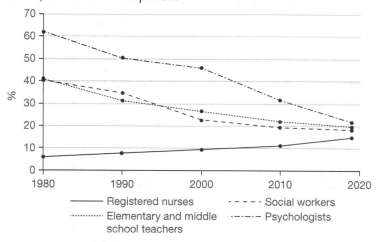

Note: Full-time, year-round, civilian, employed workers ages 25–54 with positive earnings. Occupations categorized using 1990 occupational codes.
Source: Steven Ruggles and others, IPUMS USA: Version 11.0, 2021.

critical services, especially in caring professions. In chapter 10, I described the continuing fall in the proportion of male teachers, now down to fewer than one in four, as well as the shocking lack of men in early education. But there has also been a striking drop in the share of men in mental health and related caring professions. Men account for the minority of social workers (18%) and psychologists (22%), for example, and the gender imbalance is growing, as figure 11-2 shows. Like teaching, these professions are ones where a big gender gap really matters. Seeking help can be difficult for many people, and it often seems to be even harder for men.[22] We know that men are less likely, for example, to seek mental health counseling.[23]

There might be something of a vicious circle at work here. Men might be more reluctant to open up to a female counselor or therapist, especially if they are struggling with issues related to aggression, risky behavior, addiction, or sex.[24] There are no good data on this, so we cannot know for sure. (I will say, based on my own N of 1, that I did much better with a male therapist.) But I'll go out on a limb here and simply state that it is not ideal if most substance abuse counselors are women (76%) when most substance abusers are men (67%), or that most special education teachers are women (84%) when most students being referred to special education are male (64%).[25] I'm not saying we need to aim for perfect gender parity in these occupations. But it is reasonable to aim for a closer match between clients and providers.

ONE BILLION DOLLARS FOR MEN IN HEAL

As a nation, we should set the twin goals of reaching 30% female representation in STEM jobs, and 30% male representation in HEAL ones by 2030. Achieving this "30 by 30" goal means getting more than 3 million more men into HEAL jobs. This will take money, like the efforts to increase the number of women in STEM.

In 2019, Melinda French Gates pledged $1 billion to promote women's opportunities in the U.S. One of her three main focus areas is improving female representation in STEM careers, and this was a welcome boost to the already strong women-into-STEM movement in the U.S.[26] In 2019, Congress passed the Building Blocks of STEM Act, which instructs the National Science Foundation to direct more of its K–12 STEM funding, of around $160 million a year, toward elementary and pre-K education and toward girls, for example through "gender-inclusive computer science enrichment programs."[27] In 2021, the National Science Foundation announced that $29 million of grant funding was available in 2021 and 2022 under its program Organizational Change for Gender Equity in STEM Academic Professions, which supports initiatives to increase the share of women faculty in STEM subjects.[28]

Getting a good estimate of how much is being spent overall on getting more women into STEM jobs is impossible, not least because so many institutions are involved. But to give one specific example, the Society of Women Engineers has a headquarters staff of 36, about $19 million in assets, and an annual expenditure of $12 million.[29] The society does an amazing job of providing speaker programs, financial support to students through scholarships, professional development opportunities, as well as effective advocacy and lobbying. By contrast, the men-into-HEAL movement is essentially nonexistent. There are a handful of organizations trying to get more Black and Hispanic men into teaching, all with a shoestring budget. In nursing there is just the American Association for the Advancement of Men in Nursing, which has no employees, $40,000 in assets, and an annual income of $183,000.[30]

As a society, we recognized the need to get more women into STEM jobs, and invested accordingly. Now the same is true of men and HEAL. I propose at least a $1 billion national investment, over the next decade, in service of this goal. This money, from both government and philanthropy, should be spent in three ways. First, creating a pipeline of future male HEAL workers in schools and colleges. Second, providing financial support to male students and workers in HEAL. Third, running social marketing campaigns to make these career choices more appealing to boys and men.

A PIPELINE FULL OF MEN

First, the pipeline. We need to get more boys and young men thinking about HEAL careers early. One of the lessons of successful STEM initiatives is that the pipeline really matters. That is why there is a "She Can STEM" campaign aimed at middle-schoolers, with learning resources, online concerts, and active social media channels. How about a similar "He Can HEAL" campaign? In high schools, we need more service-learning opportunities for boys interested in HEAL occupations, such as early childhood education, as well as school-based initiatives to raise awareness of men working in these jobs. A great model here is the National Girls Collaborative Project, which deploys minigrants (781 to date) to build a network to "create the tipping point for gender equity in STEM."[31] (The collaborative has National Science Foundation funding of over $4 million.[32]) Another model is the Million Girls Moonshot, with a mission to "reimagine who can be an engineer; who can build; who can make, by engaging one million more girls in STEM learning opportunities through afterschool and summer programs over the next 5 years."[33] Again, great stuff. But we also need a million boys engaged in HEAL opportunities.

These kinds of initiatives should increase the number of men choosing HEAL courses in college. As things stand, men account for only 16% of the bachelor's degrees awarded in health care fields, and 12% of those in registered nursing.[34] They are also poorly represented in teaching, accounting for 18% of education degrees and just 8% of those in elementary school teaching. It simply does not occur to many boys and young men that these jobs might be for them. Twenty percent of high school girls expect to be working in health care at the age of 30, compared to just 4% of boys.[35] Only one in ten male social workers said they considered entering the profession before going to college. This is hardly surprising given that these occupations are now so female dominated. You have to see it to be it.

There are also many HEAL jobs that do not require a 4-year degree, so opening up vocational training opportunities to boys and men is important too. Three times as many women as men pursue a health science qualification, for example. In a 2017 report, the National Coalition for Women and Girls in Education noted that "men may be . . . discouraged from taking nontraditional courses, including courses in relatively high-growth, high-wage fields such as nursing and paralegal work."[36] The coalition goes on to urge the use of financial incentives to boost the number of female trainees in male-oriented CTE (career and technical education) courses. Okay, but what about the other way around too? To be fair, the coalition is doing the job implied by its name. It would be up to the National Coalition for Men and Boys in Education to argue the other side of the case. But there is no such organization.

Another important step is to get more men teaching these subjects in universities and colleges. It is inevitably tougher to persuade young men that nursing is a career for them when 94% of the professors are women.[37] There is some evidence that women taking STEM classes by a female professor get better grades and are more likely to take more

STEM courses in later years and to graduate with a STEM degree.[38] I know of no similar studies on male professors in HEAL subjects, but there is no reason to imagine it wouldn't work the other way around as well, especially given the research on male teachers in secondary schools.

We need to break the cycle of professions taught by women for women. Some robust affirmative action is justified here. I suggest that among candidates for teaching posts in health and education, a 2:1 preference should be given to male applicants. Before you report me to the Equal Employment Opportunity Commission, you should know that I didn't pluck that number out of thin air. It is in fact the same preference that is currently given to female tenure-track professors in STEM fields, according to a study by Wendy Williams and Stephen Ceci. As they observe, "These results suggest it is a propitious time for women launching careers in academic science."[39] This is great news. But we need a similar boost for men launching academic careers in HEAL.

MONEY TALKS

Sometimes it is a good idea to throw money at a problem. That is why there are hundreds of college scholarships available to women pursuing STEM studies, provided by a range of foundations, community groups, and postsecondary institutions themselves. As the website scholarships.com, the leading aggregator of information on postsecondary scholarships puts it, "If you happen to be a woman who excels at and is interested in a scientific major or concentration, this could be a great opportunity for you."[40] The Marie Curie Scholarship, for example, offers $80,000 to young women studying biology, chemistry, or mathematics at the College of Saint Mary, a private Catholic women's college in Omaha, Nebraska. This scholarship is also supported by the National Science Foundation, which has so far invested about half a million dollars in it.[41] A skeptic might question this spending; after all, women now account for a large share of the bachelor's degrees awarded nationally in the subjects covered by the Marie Curie Scholarship: biology (64%), chemistry (50%), and mathematics (43%).[42] But my argument is not that we should be doing less to attract women into

STEM; it is that we should be doing as much to encourage men into HEAL. Two thoughts at once.

Despite the fact that women have overtaken men in post-secondary education, there are almost no scholarships for men, and virtually none aimed at encouraging them into HEAL. The American Association for Men in Nursing offers five scholarships, with a combined value of just over $10,000, and these are mostly for men who have already embarked on a nursing career. There are also a handful of scholarships for Black and Hispanic men seeking a career in teaching, notably through the Call Me MISTER program. Originating in South Carolina, this initiative now has participating schools of education in Georgia and Texas, offering financial and academic support. But it is not just Black male teachers we need. We also need more Hispanic men in our classrooms. Latina women make up the fastest-growing group of K–12 teachers except for white women, especially in states like California. And teaching is now the profession of choice among college-educated Latinas, according to Chicago sociologist Glenda Flores.[43] But there has been no equivalent upturn among Latino men. We now need a much broader campaign, building on the success of programs like Call Me MISTER, but for men of all races and ethnicities.

Funds should also be made available to HEAL employers to encourage them to hire more men. Again, we can learn here from the women-into-STEM movement. There is already a good policy framework in place, the Workforce Innovation and Opportunity Act (WIOA). This allocates funds toward workforce development programs, particularly in order to help displaced or less skilled workers find employment in the fast-growing sectors of the economy.[44] In 2021, $5.5 billion was spent.[45] A number of programs to support women, including in STEM fields, are funded through this legislation. The Texas Workforce Commission, for example, highlights its use of WIOA funds for a Women Empowered Summit, which "empowered, motivated, and inspired attendees and enriched their professional lives," as well as Camp Code, "to focus on increasing middle school girls' interest in computer coding and computer science through participation in summer camps."[46] Again, good. But I have not been able to find any

WIOA programs to help men into HEAL occupations. This is a serious policy blind spot.

Some dedicated funds should also be allocated to this effort. Here, a good model is provided by the STEM RESTART Act, reintroduced on a bipartisan basis into Congress in 2021.[47] RESTART stands for Restoring Employment Skills through Targeted Assistance, Re-entry, and Training. (I think they *really* wanted that acronym.) The act would amend WOIA and provide an additional $50 million a year for "returnships," or midcareer internships, for workers who have either left the STEM workforce or who want to transition into the field. The grants awarded would support 10-week programs, with access to mentorship and training and with a specific focus on "underrepresented populations," especially women and racial minorities. I love this idea. But I would also like to amend the bill just a bit, renaming it the STEM and HEAL RESTART Act, and allocating an additional $50 million to help underrepresented workers, especially men, to transition into HEAL jobs.

There is also a strong case for increasing pay levels in some of these critical occupations, including social work, counseling, and teaching. Higher wages are likely to attract more men into these roles, but would also help the women working in them already. The pay of K–12 teachers is the same today as it was at the beginning of the century.[48] Following a series of teacher strikes, President Joe Biden told teachers in 2021, "You deserve a raise, not just praise."[49] He wants to spend an extra $20 billion annually through the Title I program, which provides resources to schools serving poorer students. For $15 billion, we could give a $10,000 pay raise to every teacher in a high-poverty school.[50] That just seems like a no-brainer to me.

PICTURE A NURSE

In 2000, Rachel Kranton and George Akerlof created a new scholarly field of "identity economics." They showed that individual decisions are shaped not just by the hard numbers of a cost–benefit analysis but by the more personal aspects of human identity. "In a world of social difference, one of the most important economic decisions that an individual makes may be the type of person to be," they wrote. "Limits on this choice would also be critical determinants of economic behavior, opportunity, and well-being."[51] Breaking prescribed gender identity norms, for example, comes at a cost to an individual. This acts as a deterrent. An equilibrium is created that maintains the norm, and thus the cost of breaking it. Or as they put it, "$I_j = I_j(\mathbf{a}_j, a\_ j; c_j, e_j, P)$."

Kranton and Akerlof applied their model to segregation in the labor market, as well as unpaid work at home. They argued that feminism reduced the "identity loss" for women choosing to work in traditionally male jobs, and to men working in pink-collar jobs or in the home. But so far only the first of these has been true. The same year that Kranton and Akerlof published their paper, the comedy film *Meet the Parents* hit the screen. One of the main themes of the movie is that the main character, played by Ben Stiller, is a nurse. "That's great to give something back like that," says another character to him, "I'd love to find time to do volunteer work."

Two decades later, the proportion of nurses who are men has nudged up slightly, from 10 to 15%.[52] But men working in nursing report stigmatization and stereotyping on a regular basis. "They ask, why are you a nurse, or why didn't you go to medical school," says Shawn Rodgers, a nurse in Denver, Colorado.[53] His experience is typical. Male nurses are also often stereotyped as effeminate or homosexual, or simply as failed doctors.[54] Florence Nightingale set the tone right from the beginning, when she effectively founded modern nursing in the nineteenth century, opposing men in the profession on the grounds that with their "hard and horny hands" they were not suited to "touch, bathe and dress wounded limbs, however gentle their hearts may be."[55]

Men working in teaching, especially with younger children, can face even worse stigmatization. One D.C. kindergarten teacher says, "Some people assume if you're a man teaching young kids that you're somehow a pedophile or weirdo pervert or something."[56] There is also more widespread gender bias among employers against hiring men into predominantly female jobs than the other way around, as a 2019 study by Jill Yavorsky finds.[57]

HEAL occupations remain highly gendered in popular culture, with TV shows and advertisements underlining the link between certain professions and being female. One study finds that gender roles in TV advertisements are most unbalanced when it comes to the portrayal of people in jobs.[58] We have to reduce what Claudia Goldin calls "the 'auras of gender'" that attach to certain occupations—and especially, now, the female-dominated ones.[59] But how?

Role models are crucial here. You can't be what you can't see. Popular culture has an important part to play here. Decisions made in Hollywood and New York about the TV shows, adverts, and movies consumed by millions can influence behavior more than any laws passed in Washington, DC. *Will and Grace* helped pave the way for marriage equality.[60] MTV's *16 and Pregnant* significantly reduced teenage pregnancy rates.[61] A stronger representation of men in HEAL roles in shows and ads could help to reduce the identity loss for boys and men who might pursue these professions.

National social marketing campaigns to encourage boys and men into HEAL should also be undertaken, especially in places and fields with particularly low numbers of male workers.[62] The goal here is to create "norm cascades" or "behavior contagion," in the terms of the legal scholar Cass Sunstein and economist Robert Frank.[63] It is possible for norms and stereotypes to alter quickly once enough cultural momentum has been achieved. Women in STEM is one I have been focused on here for obvious reasons. But you might think too of the changes in public attitudes about LGBTQ people and marriage.

HEAL employers should also ensure that men are prominent in recruitment campaigns. Back in 2003, the Oregon Center for Nursing produced a striking recruitment poster, which asked, ARE YOU MAN ENOUGH . . . TO BE A NURSE? The ad featured nine nurses who, as the Center's Deborah Burton, explained, "embody male characteristics in our society." Among them were a former Navy SEAL, a biker, a karate champion, a rugby player, a snowboarder, and an ex-firefighter. The campaign generated media attention. It was certainly a bold effort with precisely the right intent. But it didn't seem to move the dial in terms of the rate of recruitment of men in the state.[64] It also seems like the ad might have overdone the contrast between stereotypes of nursing and stereotypes of men. Subsequent studies suggest that this approach can backfire, by highlighting what psychologists call the "role incongruity" between ideas of masculinity and those of nursing.[65] An in-depth study of marketing materials aimed at attracting men to nursing in the U.S. by Marci Cottingham, a behavioral scientist at the University of Amsterdam, found that a more common approach was to combine some elements likely to appeal to traditional masculine norms, such as images of men playing sport or using technical equipment, and a strong emphasis on economic rewards, but alongside other images emphasizing the nurturing, people-centered nature of the work.[66]

Jennifer Bosson, a University of South Florida psychologist who has studied men's attitudes toward traditionally female jobs, told NPR's Shankar Vedantam, "You could spin nursing as a very masculine occupation. It's dangerous. It's physically grueling. Our stereotype of the nurse—you know, you could modify that stereotype and turn nursing into a profession that does seem masculine or male appropriate."[67] I think "male appropriate" is the right way to think about it. The goal is not to make professions like nursing, social work, mental health, or teaching seem like masculine rather than feminine ones, but to emphasize a range of opportunities that they can provide for both men and women. We don't need to make men feel like being a nurse will somehow bolster their masculinity, just that it will not diminish it.[68]

All the proposals I have made here will require institutional support. Some can be public. Just as the National Science Foundation supports a range of initiatives for women into STEM, the Department of Health and Human Services could do the same for men into nursing, and the Department of Education for men into teaching. But we also need philanthropic foundations committed to gender equality to devote some of their resources to the cause of men in HEAL (how about it, Melinda?). We need companies to sponsor conferences, mentoring programs, and marketing campaigns. We need new, well-resourced nonprofit and advocacy organizations, like those that have been so suc-cessful at getting more women into STEM.

We need, in short, a national effort. As I have argued here, getting more men into HEAL jobs is important for their own economic pros-pects, given the decline of many traditional male jobs. But I also hope to have persuaded you that it would be good for society too. Men can HEAL.

CHAPTER 12

NEW DADS

Fatherhood as an Independent
Social Institution

When the number on your phone is your child's elementary school, it doesn't matter what you are doing, you pick up. On multiple occasions, in order to take one of these calls, my wife had to step out of a business meeting in Paris or New York. Told that one of our sons was sick or injured and needed to be picked up, she would politely remind the caller that her husband was listed as the first parent to call on such occasions. I was, after all, the stay-at-home parent, and just a mile away from the school. (Actually, by the third or fourth time this happened, the politeness might have been wearing off.) Eventually the school got it. But it was a reminder that for all the distance we've traveled, we have much further to go in updating our model of fatherhood. "The working mother is now the norm," observes Hanna Rosin. "The stay-at-home father is still a front-page anomaly."[1]

In chapters 10 and 11, I offered some solutions to the structural problems faced by boys at school and by men in the labor market. Now I turn to the biggest challenge of all, which is to reconstruct the role of men in the family. Throughout this book, I have tried to resist the temptations of hyperbole. In general I think that claims of a "crisis" are almost always overblown, and usually invoked in the service of a partisan goal. But I do think that the loss of the traditional male role in the family has been a massive cultural shock, and one that has left many men reeling. The old model of fatherhood, narrowly based on economic provision, is unfit for a world of gender equality. It has to be replaced with a much more expansive role for fathers, one that includes a much bigger caring element and is on an equal footing with that of mothers.

This of course does not mean that fathers no longer have a responsibility to provide in a material way. It just means that the responsibility is shared with mothers. The same, however, is true of providing care to children: this can, and should, be shared too. So while there is a huge challenge here, there is also a huge opportunity to broaden the very definition of what it means to be a father.

Unfortunately, rather than being a subject of serious cultural attention, fatherhood has become another victim of the culture wars. Progressives resist the idea that fathers have a distinct role to play, afraid that this will somehow undermine mothers or belittle same-sex couples. So they recoil from any proposal that might smack of "fathers' rights." Conservatives meanwhile lament an epidemic of fatherlessness but simply want to restore traditional marriage, with clear and separate roles for men and women.

Even the idea of fathers as carers seems to be threatening to some on the political right. Witness the attack from Fox News host Tucker Carlson in October 2021 on Pete Buttigieg, the secretary of transportation, for taking "paternity leave, they call it."[2] Piers Morgan made a similar jab at Daniel Craig, when the James Bond actor was photographed carrying his baby, tweeting, "Oh 007. . not you as well?!!! #papoose #emasculatedBond."[3]

Contrast Ruth Bader Ginsburg's more evolved vision for an equal society. In 1975 she successfully argued the case of *Weinberger v. Wiesenfeld* before the Supreme Court. In a unanimous decision, the court declared it unconstitutional to give Social Security benefits to widows caring for children while refusing them to widowers. Ginsburg said that this was the case she was most proud to have argued, because it provided an opportunity to promote "the care of two loving parents, rather than just one."[4] As far as Justice Ginsburg was concerned, to be a feminist meant supporting equal rights for fathers.

In this chapter I set out the evidence that fathers matter to children, including in some ways that are distinct from those of mothers. I then describe a new family model, one where the relationship between fathers and children is independent of the one between fathers and mothers: direct dads. Finally, I outline a policy agenda to support direct fatherhood, including equal and independent parental leave; a modernized child support system; and father-friendly employment opportunities.

These policies are intended to support the development of a new model of fatherhood, suited to a world where mothers don't need men, but children still need their dads.

DADS MATTER

Fathers really came into their own about half a million years ago, when human brains had a growth spurt. The need for food, especially meat, to nourish new mothers and their babies increased dramatically. From this point on, as anthropologist Sarah Blaffer Hrdy points out, it took about 13 million calories to rear a human from birth to nutritional independence. "This is far more than a woman could provide by herself," she says.[5] If fathers wanted their children to survive, they had to stick around and provide for them. So they did. Fatherhood is a product of evolutionary selection. As such, writes Anna Machin, anthropologist and author of *The Life of Dad*, "Fathers are not mere adjuncts to mothers, occasional babysitters or bag-carriers. They are the consequence of half a million years of evolution and they remain a vital part of the human story."[6] Machin observes that while fathers and mothers can do many of the same things, Dads are wired to make two distinct contributions, "protection and teaching." Of course, their expression will vary by social context. To "protect" your child means something very different in twenty-first-century New York than on the savanna half a million years ago.

Fathers matter for their children's welfare in ways that are different from, but equal to, those of mothers.[7] Engaged fatherhood has been linked to a whole range of outcomes, from mental health, high school graduation, social skills, and literacy to lower risks of teen pregnancy, delinquency, and drug use.[8] Three-year-olds with involved, supportive dads score more highly on tests of cognitive development.[9] A study in the state of Georgia found that infant mortality rates were twice as high among children whose fathers were not listed on their birth certificate (a proxy for paternal involvement) after taking account of differences in health conditions and socioeconomic background.[10] It is hard to pin down direct causal effects here: we can hardly remove or add fathers at random to children's lives in the name of social science. But as Harvard scholars Marc Grau-Grau and Hannah Riley Bowles write, "The importance of engaged fatherhood is now undismissable in ways it was not in earlier decades."[11]

A 2016 overview of research on fathering relationships and outcomes, conducted by education scholar William Jeynes, concludes that "the role of fathers in raising children is unique and can be distinguished in kind from the role of mothers in child rearing."[12] This is not breaking news to most of us. According to a Pew Research Center survey, most people (64%) think that men and women have a different approach to parenting, and almost all of those (89%) think this is either a good or neutral thing.[13] I am reminded of Pauline Hunt's classic ethnographic study of domestic work in an English village in the 1970s, where she found that without exception, men washed the windows outside, while women washed them inside.[14] There was a sharp but equal division of labor, and perhaps a degree of specialization in the tasks. But in the end what mattered was that the windows got clean.

. . . ESPECIALLY TO TEENS

Many of us think of adolescence as a period to be survived, by both adolescents and parents. But there is now a growing recognition that the teen years are in fact a vitally important period of development. As the National Academies of Sciences, Engineering, and Medicine note in their 2019 report, "The adaptive plasticity of adolescence marks it as a window of opportunity for change through which mechanisms of resilience, recovery, and development are possible."[15]

Fathers have an especially important role to play in this period. In contrast to the early years, when nurture and attachment are key, adolescence is a time when children are finding their own feet, testing boundaries, and starting to go their own way. Rob Palkovitz, professor of human development and family studies at the University of Delaware, suggests that fathers "play a particularly important role in stimulating children's openness to the world . . . encouraging them to take risks and to stand up for themselves."[16]

Fathers who are engaged with their teenagers help to reduce harmful forms of risk-taking behavior, for example. Delinquency rates are lower among the adolescent children of involved fathers.[17] These effects seem to last too. Sixteen-year-old girls who are close to their fathers have better mental health at the age of 33.[18] Father involvement predicts stronger academic outcomes in adolescence too.[19] The teaching role of fathers really seems to kick in strongly during these years. Machin writes that "many dads in the West really step into their role during late childhood and adolescence, particularly when the time comes to teach their children. It's that all-important role in preparing children to step into the big wide world."[20]

Overall, as the sociologist Kevin Shafer writes in his book *So Close, Yet So Far: Fathering in Canada and the United States*, there are "substantial benefits associated with father involvement from birth to adolescence."[21] An important question here, of course, is the extent to which the contribution of fathers is distinct from that of mothers, or indeed a second parent of any gender. The sociologist David Eggebeen tackled this question using the National Longitudinal Study of Adolescent to Adult Health, a representative survey of 20,000 young adults in the U.S. He examined how fathers' and mothers' engagement affects mental health, delinquency, and civil engagement in their teenage children. A quarter of the parental inputs had no impact. The other parental contributions were additive, redundant, or unique. Additive inputs were those where the contributions of each parent were positive, and identical: 42% fell into this category. Redundancies, with no additional benefit from the input of the second parent, accounted for 12%. The remaining 22% were unique, with positive contributions *only* from the father or the mother. Specifically, Eggebeen concluded that "fathers appear to especially make unique contributions to the well-being of their children through their human capital while mothers make unique contributions through their availability and closeness to their children."[22] Dads teach, moms tend. Eggebeen's results are convincing. He shows that there is considerable overlap in the contributions made by parents to their adolescents' well-being, and that two is often better than one. But he also shows that both mothers and fathers also bring something unique to the parenting enterprise.

It is important to note here that in all these studies, it is the quality of the relationship between parent and child that is being measured: time, engagement, involvement, closeness, and so on. It doesn't make much sense, from this perspective, to divide fathers into a binary of "present" or "absent," as if their role could be captured by simply taking attendance. What matters is the relationship between parent and child.[23] The whole idea of an "absent" father becomes even more complicated if, as the masculinity scholars William Marsiglio and Joseph H. Pleck suggest, "one broadens the concept from physical to psychological absence."[24] One study finds that adolescents close to their nonresident fathers do better than those with *resident* fathers with whom they are not close, as measured by higher self-esteem, delinquency rates, and mental health.[25] There is no residency requirement for good fatherhood. The relationship is what matters.

DIRECT DADS

Fathers matter to their children whether or not they are in a relationship with their mother. The goal then is to bolster the role of fathers as direct providers of care to their children, whether or not they are married to or even living with the mother. There is a role for policy here, and I'll get to that in a moment. But there's clearly a big cultural shift required, on the part of both men and women.

Kathryn Edin and Tim Nelson spent 7 years interviewing 110 fathers, mostly unmarried, in low-income neighborhoods in Philadelphia and Camden, New Jersey. In their 2013 book, *Doing the Best I Can: Fatherhood in the Inner City*, they show that most fathers want involvement in their children's lives but are stymied by their own problems—poverty, mental illness, crime—as well as legal and child support systems that seek primarily to extract money, and mothers who act as a "gatekeeper" to their children.[26] In many ways, Black fathers are leading the way here. They are currently more likely to be classified as nonresidential fathers (44% compared to 21% of white fathers).[27] But they are also more likely than nonresident white fathers to be involved in their children's lives in various ways, including helping with homework, taking them to activities, and checking in with them on their day.[28] As one study concludes, "Black nonresident fathers . . . shared responsibilities more frequently and displayed more effective coparenting than Hispanic and White [nonresident] fathers."[29]

As I showed in chapter 3, there is a huge disconnect between obsolete mental models of fatherhood based on traditional family roles, and the reality of modern societies and economies. Fatherhood matters just as much as ever in a world of women's economic independence, but necessarily in a reinvented form. The good news is that fathers can potentially have an even more fulfilling role, with a much closer relationship with their children. The bad news is that in much of our society, men are a very long way from being able to occupy this role as new dads.

A policy agenda to support the new direct model of fatherhood will have three key elements. First, equal and independent paid leave eligibility. Second, a reformed child support system. Third, father-friendly employment opportunities. I describe each in turn.

PAID LEAVE FOR DADS

Fathers and mothers should be legally entitled to six months of paid leave for each child. Ideally this leave would offer 100% wage replacement up to median earnings, paid for by higher Social Security contributions from employers and employees. I have been arguing for equal leave for mothers and fathers my whole career, but the specific proposal made here closely matches the one made by scholars Janet Gornick and Marcia Meyers in their 2009 essay "Institutions That Support Gender Equality in Parenthood and Employment." Gornick and Meyers's aim was to create a set of institutions that would allow parents to spend real time caring for their children, while also promoting gender equality.

Their goal was a "dual-earner / dual-caregiver" society, including "symmetrical contribution from mothers and fathers at home."[30] I share these aspirations.

This will seem like a radical proposal for three reasons. First, 6 months may seem a long period of paid parental leave, equivalent to the provision in only a few European countries. Second, replacing wages at or close to 100% is unusually generous. Third, the granting of 6 months "use it or lose it" leave specifically for fathers (i.e., not transferable between parents) goes beyond anything offered by any nation thus far. I will briefly defend each of these features.

Six months of leave is necessary to allow parents to spend meaningful time with their children without losing all connection to the labor market. Given that dual-earner couples are now the norm, I honestly think 6 months is a modest proposal. Our labor market has been fundamentally altered by women's dramatic entry into the workforce, but our welfare system trundles along almost as if nothing has happened. As the economist Heather Boushey writes, "The world of work and the needs of families always seem to be in conflict—and it's been this way for decades."[31]

Generous wage replacement is also needed if both parents are to be able to actually take the time off. The most common reason parents give for not taking paid leave is that they cannot afford a drop in income.[32] Parents with the fewest economic resources face the most financial pressure to return to work when they often want to be caring for their child. There are some encouraging moves at the state level: Oregon's new twelve-week paid leave plan, for example, provides 100% wage replacement for workers earning up to two-thirds of the state average.[33] It is also worth noting that fifteen OECD nations now offer 90% replacement rates or higher for father-only leave, although for much shorter durations than the 6 months I propose here.[34]

Finally, granting nontransferable parental leave to fathers will encourage and allow men to become equal partners on the home front. To support a more direct model of fatherhood, we need to think of parental leave as an individual benefit rather than a family one. The evidence suggests that providing father-only "use it or lose it" leave policies significantly increases take-up rates among dads.[35] But it is important to be honest about the trade-offs here. Making the full leave available only if both parents take it involves what Norwegian sociologist Arnlaug Leira calls "mild structural coercion."[36] An alternative proposal would be to grant 12 months of paid leave and allow parents to share it between them as they choose. A compromise position would be to give fathers a shorter period of dedicated leave than mothers, which is the approach taken in countries like Norway, as well as Quebec in Canada. I have changed my mind on this issue twice already over the course of my career, so I am acutely aware of the arguments on both sides. One specific fear is that families where fathers have little or no contact with their children will only be able to access 6 months of leave, and these are mostly lower-income families.

But I now believe that if we are serious about expanding the role of fathers, equal leave is essential. The signal policymakers need to send is that paternal care matters as much as maternal care. Anything short of full equality blunts that message. I also believe that until and unless fathers begin to take more time out of the labor market, progress on closing the gender pay gap will be achingly slow.[37] There is no getting around it: if we want equality at work, we need equality at home.

But this equality does not have to be measured every day, or even every year. When you have young children, people say "they'll be grown before you know it." No offense to my sons, whom I love dearly, but that is not how it felt to me. Sometimes it felt like time had stopped altogether. Parenting is a really long road. The average couple has two children, with a gap of 2 or 3 years between them. That means it takes about two decades to get them from birth to adulthood. One modification I would therefore make to the Gornick and Meyers plan is to make paid leave available to parents up until their child's 18th birthday, not up to the age of 8 as they propose. This is partly because of the evidence I have already summarized on the importance of adolescence as a critical developmental phase, a period that too often gets short shrift in public policy. Discussions of paid leave or flexible working too often assume that the main work of parenting is over by the time children start school.

I agree with Gornick and Meyers that the goal is a "symmetrical contribution from mothers and fathers at home." But it is important that this symmetry can be achieved over a couple decades, rather than a couple years—asynchronous symmetry, if you like. Jules Pieri, cofounder and former CEO of The Grommet, describes family life as a "ballet," and that she and her husband "alternated who took the lead."[38] That is how my wife and I did it too (though I will say it rarely felt balletic). Even with equal access to paid leave, it is likely that mothers will choose to do more of the care in the very early years. Even after the huge rise in women's employment over recent decades, most mothers with children under the age of 3 are either out of the labor market or working part-time.[39] By and large, this seems to be by choice; over half of mothers working part-time (54%) say that this is their preference at this point in their life, and 14% say they would prefer not to be in paid work at all.[40] (The remaining 33% would rather be in a full-time job.)

My observation is that moms are rarely annoyed at dads for doing less than half of the direct parenting when their children are very young, so long as he is working just as hard in other ways. When they get really irritated is when he is still doing less than his fair share many years later. Just because moms are better at breastfeeding a 3-month-old does not mean they are better at making dentist appointments for a 13-year-old. The feminist writer Mary Daly politely calls this "gender politics of family time."[41] I have presented evidence that fathers may in fact have some unique strengths when it comes to raising adolescents, and I can imagine a social norm developing where mothers and fathers contribute broadly equally to the care of their children, just not at the same time. Tots for Moms, teens for Dads?

CHILD SUPPORT—CASH, CUSTODY, CARE

"Virtually every legal and institutional arrangement governing these fathers' lives tells them that they are a paycheck and nothing more," write Kathryn Edin and Timothy Nelson in *Doing the Best I Can*. "At every turn an unmarried man who seeks to be a father, not just a daddy, is rebuffed by a system that pushes him aside with one hand while reaching into his pocket with the other."[42]

The laws governing family life have simply failed to keep pace with society. When parents are married, their rights and responsibilities to their children are clearly defined. If they divorce, there is a legal apparatus in place to determine custody arrangements, visitation rights, and financial obligations. Of course there is often conflict between divorcing couples, but at least they each have legal standing with regard to their children. And in recent decades, family laws have shifted in a more egalitarian direction toward divorce. Courts are now obliged to treat mothers and fathers fairly in determining custody, and the usual legal standard is now the best interests of the child or children. As a result, there has been a dramatic shift toward joint custody arrangements. In a study of cases in Wisconsin, Maria Cancian and others show a decline in the proportion of mothers being awarded sole physical custody from 80% in 1986 to 42% in 2008. The share of equal custody arrangements, with children spending the same amount of time with each parent, rose from 5% to 27%. As Cancian and her coauthors write, "The trend away from mother-sole custody and toward shared custody is dramatic."[43] Nationally, fathers now get about a third of the time with children after separation or divorce.[44] These trends are extremely positive. The legal default ought to be shared custody, with children wherever possible spending equal time with each of their parents.

The problem is that there are no similar laws for unmarried parents. In every U.S. state, an unmarried mother is the presumed sole custodial parent. Unmarried fathers must first prove paternity (in married couples this is assumed), and then petition for visitation and custody. For many fathers this can prove a difficult process. In the meantime, the mother can choose to bar all access. Regardless of visitation rights, however, unmarried fathers will typically be obliged to pay child support, often at levels that low-income fathers in particular struggle to meet.[45]

Divorcing couples typically work out their arrangements as part of a single process. But for unmarried parents, child support payments are adjudicated entirely separately from custody and visitation rights. Married fathers are seen as three-dimensional beings. Unmarried fathers are seen as walking ATMs. In 2020, $38 billion was collected in child support, and an estimated $115 billion was owed in arrears.[46] Some of the money collected from fathers doesn't even go to provide for their children. It goes to the government to help offset welfare costs, specifically, Temporary Assistance for Needy Families, which undermines support for the whole system. In three states—Colorado, Minnesota, and Vermont—all child support now goes to the family, rather than to the government. Time for the other states to follow suit.[47] As one struggling father tells Timothy Nelson, "Whatever I produce, I give up. I try to be the best dad I can, afford the best things that I can, even at the sacrifice of myself. [I] pray and hope things change [but I'm] tired of being at the bottom so long that you can't see the top no more."[48]

Child support payments should be set with greater sensitivity to a father's ability to pay, and considering their nonmonetary contributions, including the direct provision of care for their children. Oregon, for example, has a "parenting time credit" that reduces child support payments made by a noncustodial parent if they spend more time caring for their children.[49] The long run goal ought to be to integrate child support decisions for unmarried parents into the legal process for determining custody and visitation arrangements. "If we truly believe in gender equity," write Edin and Nelson, "we must find a way to honor fathers' attempts to build relationships with their children just as we do mothers'—to assign fathers rights along with their responsibilities."[50]

FATHER-FRIENDLY JOBS

In their 1973 book *The Symmetrical Family*, sociologists Peter Willmott and Michael Young (famous for inventing the term *meritocracy*) wrote: "By the next century—with the pioneers of 1970 already at the front of the column—society will have moved from (a) one demanding job for the wife and one for the husband, through (b) two demanding jobs for the wife and one for the husband, to (c) two demanding jobs for the wife and two for the husband. The symmetry will be complete."[51]

Well, sort of. I think a lot of women would argue that a couple decades into the twenty-first century we have gotten stuck at step (b). In part this is because labor market institutions have not adapted to a world without wives—stay-at-home wives, that is. It is worth noting that in Young and Willmott's symmetrical utopia, the standard work week will have been cut to just 3 days, leaving 4 days for family and leisure. You have probably noticed that this hasn't happened. In the U.S., average working hours have in fact barely declined in the last half century.[52] In two-thirds of families, both parents are in paid work.[53]

Whether we like it or not, the family is now a labor market institution, and the labor market is a family institution. But so far, only the family has changed. Men, children, and women are all bending their lives and schedules to fit the largely unaltered demands of market work, to the "standard" workday and the typical career path. I support efforts to increase access to childcare and provide after-school clubs and so on.[54] But I do worry that the goal of public policy often seems to be to create work-friendly families, rather than family-friendly work. "We've reached an unprecedented era of equality between men and women economically," writes Claudia Goldin, "but . . . our work and care structures are relics of a past when only men had both careers and families."[55]

Mothers are caught most painfully in this trap right now. But we should not assume that fathers are okay with the trade-offs. Twice as many fathers as mothers say they spend too little time with their children (46% v. 23%).[56] My proposals for paid leave are a step toward lessening these tensions. But jobs must change too. More options to work flexibly, or part-time, or from home, can at least ease the trade-offs between earning and caring. The wholesale shift to remote work during the pandemic represents an unprecedented opportunity to modernize work; it remains to be seen if it will be seized upon. I hope so, not least for the sake of dads; two-thirds of fathers say that the pandemic brought them closer to their children.[57] Surprisingly, the opportunities for flexible working seemed to benefit men more than women during the pandemic, according to one study.[58]

As well as more flexibility in the day-to-day nature of jobs, career ladders need to be modernized. For many parents, scaling back on paid work doesn't just mean a temporary dip in income, it can also result in permanent damage to career prospects. This problem is worse in what Goldin calls "greedy jobs," which offer big financial rewards for putting in long and unpredictable hours. Law, finance, and management consulting are good examples.[59] If you want to move up, you cannot take time out. In these circumstances, it makes sense for one parent to stay on the ladder and maximize income, while the other steps back to do more on the home front. Usually that is dad and mom, respectively. The career structure of these occupations doesn't just incentivize a sharp division of labor between parents, it virtually imposes it. It should be no surprise, then, that these are also the professions with the widest gender pay gaps. Women working in law and finance earn just 77 cents on the male finance dollar. Fifteen years after graduating from the University of Michigan with a law degree, four out of five men are working at least 45 hours a week, compared to only half the women. Almost one in four of the women were working part time, compared to just 2% of men.[60]

But it doesn't have to be this way. There are nongreedy professions that still pay high wages, including engineering, technology, and pharmacy. These are also, not coincidentally, occupations with much smaller gender pay gaps. Taking account of hours worked, female pharmacists make 94 cents on the male dollar.[61] So what has pharmacy done right that law and finance continue to do wrong? The key change has been to make it easier for one pharmacist to substitute for another. How many of us care if we see the same pharmacist when we go to pick up our prescription? We likely feel differently about our lawyer or financial adviser. But it is important to remember that pharmacies used to be like that too, and had the gender pay gaps to match. A combination of corporate consolidation and technological advances has made it possible for information to be transferred from one pharmacist to the next when they change shifts. Crucially, this means that there is almost no hourly wage penalty for part-time work in pharmacy. Earnings rise with hours in a virtually linear fashion. This is why Goldin calls pharmacy "a most egalitarian profession."[62]

Can law, finance, and consultancy follow the pharmacy path? Technology helps, by dramatically reducing the cost of transferring information between client-facing staff. Some financial firms, consultancies, and legal companies have made some modest moves in the right direction, such as cutting back on weekend hours, insisting staff take their vacation allowance, and allowing more part-time options, such as a 4-day week.[63] In 2016, Amazon announced the creation of teams where all members, including leaders, could work 30 hours a week for 75% of their current salary.[64] The option to work part time at the same rate of pay is important here—but it will be critical to ensure that opportunities for development and promotion are not lost. Somewhere between "greedy jobs" and the "mommy track," there is a way of working—let's call it the "normal people track"—that allows flexibility for family responsibilities at various points along the career track, without losing out on major opportunities in the future.

But I think we should be realistic about what it will take to bring about change in these family-hostile professions, which is for talented workers to vote with their feet. Major employers are finding that, especially among younger workers, expectations of a better work/life balance are rising rapidly, ranked second only to salary in many surveys.[65] The loss of female talent from the pipeline has prompted some remedial action. But as long as men continue to be willing to put in long and often unpredictable hours, the prospects for structural reform remain dim. There is a lot of discussion of the need for "culture change" in the workplace. This is important for sure. Most American men say there is an "unspoken rule" in their workplace that fathers should not take their full entitlement to paternity leave.[66]

But the greedy-job professions need more than a new ethos. They need to be reengineered. I have described these changes as promoting "father-friendly" employment. It would of course be more accurate to describe them as parent-friendly. In the short run, they may in fact be most helpful to mothers. But I have chosen the label deliberately. A job that requires a man to work long hours to make good money is not father-friendly, at least not in the way I think fatherhood must now be defined. Even if it enables a man to fulfill a breadwinning role, it does so at the price of his parenting role. As Anne-Marie Slaughter, head of the New America Foundation, warns, progress will be slow if we continue to define the "care problem" as "women's problem."[67]

To those of us blessed to be dads, fatherhood is a core component of our identity. I have argued here that it now needs to be a bigger social role too, one that is different from, but equal to, motherhood. Prosocial masculinity no longer means having to get married or having to be the main breadwinner. But it does require stepping fully into the role of father.

EPILOGUE

When you mention to somebody that you're writing a book, they will usually ask what it's about. Sometimes you can see them regretting the question as you describe the project. (This happened to me quite often, I'm sorry to say, when I talked with great enthusiasm about my biography of the nineteenth-century philosopher John Stuart Mill.) But it did not happen with this book. Not even once. I often barely had time to describe my overall argument before my interlocutor would begin to share their own experiences and opinions—and anxieties. I found that many people are *really* worried about boys and men, including the ones in their own life. Wives are concerned that their husbands won't find decent work. Mothers of teenage sons are forming informal support groups to help each other through the trying time of high school. Young women are frustrated by the rudderless men on the dating market.

I was especially surprised that even the staunchest feminists I spoke with seemed much more concerned about their sons than their daughters. I wondered if this was a general pattern. In 2020, I was able to add some questions to the American Family Survey, a 3,000-strong annual poll, to find out. It is. Parents are generally more worried about their sons "growing up to be successful adults" than they are about their daughters.[1] But it is liberal parents who are the most worried about their sons. There is a deep well of private anxiety about boys and men that has yet to find a productive public outlet, and one of my goals in this book has been to try and bridge the gap between private and public. We are right to be worried about boys and men, because they're facing real challenges as learners, as workers, and as fathers. Just as parents want all their children to flourish, so we want all of our fellow citizens to flourish.

Doing more for boys and men does not require an abandonment of the ideal of gender equality. In fact, it is a natural extension of it. The problem with feminism, as a liberation movement, is not that it has "gone too far." It is that it has not gone far enough. Women's lives have been recast. Men's lives have not. We need, as I said in the introduction, a positive vision of masculinity for a postfeminist world. We also need to be grown up enough as a culture to recognize that big changes, even positive ones, have repercussions. Dealing with these is not only possible, but necessary; that is simply the nature of progress. In this case, it means reforming an education system that no longer works well for boys, and helping men adjust to the genuine dislocation caused by the loss of traditional male roles. We must tackle gender-specific challenges and inequalities in both directions.

Right now, there is a distinct lack of responsible leadership on this front. Politics has become like trench warfare, both sides fearing even the slightest loss of any ground. While moms and dads worry about their kids, our leaders are trapped in their partisan positions. Progressives see any move to provide more help to boys and men as a distraction from the fight for girls and women. Conservatives see any move to provide more help to girls and women as motivated by a desire to put men down. My hope is that away from the heat and noise of tribal politics, we can come to a shared recognition that many of our boys and men are in real trouble, not of their own making, and need help.

ACKNOWLEDGMENTS

The conversations and arguments that have informed this book have been going on for decades, and they have involved countless friends, relatives, and colleagues. I am not going to list all their names here. It would be a long list, and they know who they are. I am likewise grateful to the dozens of scholars who have answered my queries, read sections of the book, or even all of it, and given me their feedback. Again, you know who you are. Thank you. I must, however, give a couple of special mentions. First to Peter Blair, who was simply the perfect reviewer—constructively critical, substantively helpful, and as bluntly honest as every scholar should aspire to be. Second to Belle Sawhill, who brought me into the Brookings fold in the first place and has been a true friend and colleague ever since. I also want to express my gratitude to several researchers at the Brookings Institution, who have toiled alongside me without complaint and with grace and professionalism: Beyond Deng, Coura Fall, Tiffany Ford, Ariel Gelrud Shiro, Fariha Haque, Ashleigh Maciolek, Christopher Pulliam, Hannah Van Drie, Morgan Welch, and, especially, Ember Smith. Thanks also to the Smith Richardson Foundation, for helping me to carve out some time to write this book.

Above all, I can't say enough to express my love and appreciation for Erica Hauver, my partner and wife of 23 years. It's a cliché, I know, but you really do make me a better man. You've also made this a much better book. Thank you.

NOTES

PREFACE

1. Our work is available at www.aibm.org. Visit the site to learn more, support our work, or sign up for our newsletter.
2. *The Ezra Klein Show*, "The Men—and Boys—Are Not Alright," March 10, 2023.
3. Centers for Disease Control and Prevention, "Provisional COVID-19 Deaths by Sex and Age," accessed November 11, 2023. According to the CDC, the total number of deaths was 113,000 men aged 25–54, compared to 67,000 women of the same age.
4. Richard Reeves and Will Secker, "Male Suicide: Patterns and Recent Trends," American Institute for Boys and Men, November 17, 2023.
5. Josh Hawley, *Manhood: The Masculine Virtues America Needs* (Washington, DC: Regnery, 2023), p. 140.
6. U.S. Department of Education, National Center for Education Statistics, "Number and Percentage Distribution of Teachers in Public and Private Elementary and Secondary Schools, by Selected Teacher Characteristics: Selected School Years, 1987–88 through 2020–21," *Digest of Education Statistics*, Table 209.10. For the trend, see Richard M. Ingersoll et al., "Seven Trends: The Transformation of the Teaching Force—Updated October 2018," University of Pennsylvania, CPRE Research Reports, 2018.
7. Brian Kennedy, Richard Fry, and Cary Funk, "6 Facts about America's STEM Workforce and Those Training for It," Pew Research Center, April 14, 2021.
8. Richard Reeves, "How to Solve the Education Crisis for Boys and Men," TED Conference, Vancouver, April 2023.
9. U.S. Department of Labor, Bureau of Labor Statistics, *The Economics Daily*, "Median Earnings for Women in 2022 Were 83.0 Percent of the Median for Men," accessed November 11, 2023.
10. U.S. Department of Education, National Center for Education Statistics, "Degrees Conferred by Postsecondary Institutions, by Level of Degree and Sex of Student: Selected Years, 1869–70 through 2030–31," *Digest of Education Statistics*, Table 318.10.
11. Cordelia Fine, "The Evolved Gender Constructivist?" Presentation to The Big Conversation: Sex/Gender Differences, Sante Fe, New Mexico, September 30–October 1, 2023 (available online).

12. Sarah A. Donovan and David H. Bradley, *Real Wage Trends, 1979 to 2019* (Washington, DC: Congressional Research Service, 2020).

13. Lindsay M. Monte, "'Solo' Dads and 'Absent' Dads Not as Different as They Seem," U.S. Census Bureau, November 5, 2019.

14. Joint Economic Committee, *Long-Term Trends in Deaths of Despair*, Social Capital Project Report 4–19 (September 2019). See data appendices.

15. Donovan and Bradley, *Real Wage Trends, 1979 to 2019*.

16. "Men Adrift: Badly Educated Men in Rich Countries Have Not Adapted Well to Trade, Technology or Feminism," *The Economist*, May 28, 2015.

17. Camille Busette, "A New Deal for Poor African-American and Native-American Boys," Brookings Institution, March 14, 2018. Note that she includes Native American boys and men, while I focus here on Black boys and men.

18. Sherry N. Mong and V. J. Roscigno, "African American Men and the Experience of Employment Discrimination," *Qualitative Sociology* 3, no. 1 (March 2010), pp. 1–21.

19. Susan Faludi, *Stiffed: The Betrayal of the American Man* (New York: HarperCollins, 1999), p. 40.

20. Timothy J. Bartik, Bard J. Hershbein, and Marta Lachowska, "The Merits of Universal Scholarships: Benefit-Cost Evidence from the Kalamazoo Promise," *Journal of Benefit-Cost Analysis* (2016), p. 406; Timothy J. Bartik, Bard J. Hershbein, and Marta Lachowska, "The Effects of the Kalamazoo Promise Scholarship on College Enrollment, Persistence, and Completion," Upjohn Institute Working Paper 15–229 (December 2017), p. 51.

21. According to Gallup polling conducted in 2020. See Jeffrey M. Jones, "LGBT Identification Rises to 5.6% in Latest U.S. Estimate," Gallup, February 24, 2021.

22. Simone de Beauvoir, *The Second Sex* [1949], trans. H. M. Parshley (New York: Alfred A. Knopf, 1953), p. 3.

1. GIRLS RULE

1. Carol Frances, "The Status of Women in American Higher Education," *Sociology and Anthropology* (September 2018), pp. 696 and 698.

2. "The Weaker Sex," *The Economist*, May 7, 2015.

3. Hanna Rosin, *The End of Men: And the Rise of Women* (New York: Penguin, 2012), p. 149.

4. National Center for Education Statistics, Digest of Education Statistics 1990, p. 232.

5. National Center for Education Statistics, "Degrees Conferred by Postsecondary Institutions, by Level of Degree and Sex of Student: Selected Years, 1869–70 through 2029–30," *Digest of Education Statistics*, Table 318.10.

6. National Student Clearinghouse Research Center, "Current Enrollment Term Estimates: Fall 2021," January 13, 2022.

7. Stephanie Riegg Cellini, "How Does Virtual Learning Impact Students in Higher Education?," Brookings Institution, August 13, 2021.

8. John F. Helliwell and others, *World Happiness Report 2021* (New York: Sustainable Development Solutions Network, 2021).

9. OECD, "Finland: Student Performance (PISA 2018)," Education GPS, 2018.

10. OECD, "Are Boys and Girls Ready for the Digital Age?," *PISA in Focus* 12 (January 2012).

11. "Men Adrift: Badly Educated Men in Rich Countries Have Not Adapted Well to Trade, Technology or Feminism," *The Economist*, May 28, 2015.

12. Julia B. Isaacs, "Starting School at a Disadvantage: The School Readiness of Poor Children," Brookings Institution, March 2012, fig. 7, p. 9. A Norwegian study also finds that by the age of 5, over half of girls have mastered writing words while among boys, the same milestone is passed at 6. Ragnhild E. Brandlistuen and others, "Gender Gaps in Preschool Age: A Study of Behavior, Neurodevelopment and Pre-academic Skills," *Scandinavian Journal of Public Health* (July 2021).

13. National Center for Education Statistics, "Percentage of Students at or above Selected National Assessment of Educational Progress (NAEP) Reading Achievement Levels, by Grade and Selected Student Characteristics: Selected Years, 2005 through 2019," *Digest of Education Statistics*, Table 221.20.

14. National Center for Education Statistics, "Average National Assessment of Educational Progress (NAEP) Mathematics Scale Score, by Sex, Race/Ethnicity, and Grade: Selected Years, 1990 through 2017," Table 222.10.

15. Sean F. Reardon and others, "Gender Achievement Gaps in U.S. School Districts," *American Educational Research Journal* (December 2019), p. 26.

16. Nicole M. Fortin, Philip Oreopoulus, and Shelley Phipps, "Leaving Boys Behind: Gender Disparities in High Academic Achievement," Working Paper 19331 (Cambridge, MA: National Bureau of Economic Research, August 2013).

17. National Center for Education Statistics, "Number and Percentage of Public High School Graduates Taking Dual Credit, Advanced Placement (AP), and International Baccalaureate (IB) Courses in High School and Average Credits Earned, by Selected Student and School Characteristics: 2000, 2005, and 2009," 2009 High School Transcript Study (HSTS), U.S. Department of Education.

18. J. Q. Easton, Esperanza Johnson, and Lauren Sartain, *The Predictive Power of Ninth-Grade GPA* (University of Chicago Consortium on School Research, September 2017), p. 1.

19. For the SAT see College Board, *2021 Suite of Assessments Annual Reports*. For the ACT see *The ACT Profile Report—National* (2020).

20. *New York Times* editorial contest organizers, personal communication.

21. Richard V. Reeves, Eliana Buckner, and Ember Smith, "The Unreported Gender Gap in High School Graduation Rates," Brookings Institution, January 12, 2021.

22. Civic and Everyone Graduates Center, *2019 Building a Grad Nation: Progress and Challenge in Raising High School Graduation Rates* (Johns Hopkins University School of Education, 2019), p. 15.

23. Nicole M. Fortin, Philip Oreopoulus, and Shelley Phipps, "Leaving Boys Behind: Gender Disparities in High Academic Achievement," *Journal of Human Resources* (Summer 2015).

24. U.S. Department of Education, National Center for Education Statistics, "Number and Percentage Distribution of Teachers in Public Elementary and Secondary Schools, by Instructional Level and Selected Teacher and School Characteristics: 1999–2000, 2015–16, and 2017–18," *Digest of Education Statistics*, Table 2019.22.

25. Benjamin Zablotsky and others, "Prevalence and Trends of Developmental Disabilities among Children in the United States: 2009–2017," *Pediatrics* (October 2019).

26. Laurence Steinberg, *Age of Opportunity: Lessons from the New Science of Adolescence* (New York: Houghton Mifflin Harcourt, 2014), p. 77.

27. Robert M. Sapolsky, *Behave: The Biology of Humans at Our Best and Worst* (London: Penguin Publishing Group, 2017), p. 164.

28. Louann Brizendine, *The Female Brain* (New York: Harmony Books, 2017), p. 65. See also Elizabeth Vargas and Alan B. Goldberg, "The Truth behind Women's Brains," ABC News, October 5, 2006.

29. Gokcen Akyurek, "Executive Functions and Neurology in Children and Adolescents," in *Occupational Therapy: Therapeutic and Creative Use of Activity*, ed. Meral Huri (London: IntechOpen, 2018), p. 38.

30. M. A. J. van Tetering and others, "Sex Differences in Self-Regulation in Early, Middle and Late Adolescence: A Large-Scale Cross-Sectional Study," *PLoS ONE* (January 2020). See also Theodore D. Satterthwaite and others, "Sex Differences in the Effect of Puberty on Hippocampal Morphology," *Journal of the American Academy of Child and Adolescent Psychiatry* (March 2014).

31. Sol Lim and others, "Preferential Detachment during Human Brain Development: Age- and Sex-Specific Structural Connectivity in Diffusion Tensor Imaging (DTI) Data," *Cerebral Cortex* (June 2015).

32. Krystnell Storr, "Science Explains Why Women Are Faster to Mature Than Men," *Mic*, February 24, 2015.

33. Liz Griffin, "The Developing Teenage Brain," *The School Superintendents Association*, interview with Frances Jensen, chair of the department of neurology at the University of Pennsylvania's Perelman School of Medicine, September 2017. See also Frances Jenson, *The Teenage Brain* (New York: HarperCollins, 2015): "Organization requires brain connectivity and integration, not just raw intelligence and synaptic power. Myelination plays a huge part in this, and as we have said earlier, it requires the better part of the first three decades of life to be fully completed. The time of greatest gender disparity in this process occurs during adolescence," pp. 232–33.

34. "Because college preparation and applications must be done by teenagers, small differences in development can lead to large disparities in college outcomes," write Claudia Goldin, Lawrence F. Katz, and Ilyana Kuziemko, in "The Homecoming of American College Women: The Reversal of the College Gender Gap," Working Paper 12139 (Cambridge, MA: National Bureau of Economic Research, March 2006), p. 3. In a cross-cultural review of personality development,

Marleen De Bolle and her coauthors also find that "adolescent girls consistently score higher than boys on personality traits that are found to facilitate academic achievement, at least within the current school climate. Stated differently, the current school environment might be in general more attuned to feminine-typed personalities, which makes it—in general—easier for girls to achieve better grades at school." Marleen De Bolle and others, "The Emergence of Sex Differences in Personality Traits in Early Adolescence: A Cross-Sectional, Cross-Cultural Study," *Journal of Personality and Social Psychology* (January 2015). See also Tony Cox, "Brain Maturity Extends Well Beyond Teen Years," NPR, October 10, 2011.

35. National Academies of Sciences, Engineering, and Medicine, *The Promise of Adolescence: Realizing Opportunity for All Youth* (Washington, DC: The National Academies Press, 2019), p. 40.

36. "As the playing field was leveled, developmental differences between boys and girls become more salient in explaining differences in educational attainment." Goldin, Katz, and Kuziemko, "The Homecoming of American College Women," p. 4.

37. National Center for Education Statistics, "Degrees Conferred by Postsecondary Institutions, by Level of Degree and Sex of Student: Selected Years, 1869–70 through 2029–30," *Digest of Education Statistics*, Table 318.10. See also National Center for Education Statistics, "Degrees in Business Conferred by Postsecondary Institutions, by Level of Degree and Sex of Student: Selected Years, 1955–56 through 2017–18," Table 325.25.

38. National Center for Education Statistics, "Number of Postsecondary Institutions Conferring Doctor's Degrees in Dentistry, Medicine, and Law, and Number of Such Degrees Conferred, by Sex of Student: Selected Years, 1949–50 through 2018–19." See also Higher Education General Information Survey (HEGIS), "'Degrees and Other Formal Awards Conferred' Surveys from 1965–66 through 1985–86 and IPEDS Fall 2019 Completions Component," July 2020.

39. National Center for Education Statistics, "Degrees Conferred by Degree-Granting Institutions, by Level of Degree and Sex of Student." Note that for reference years 1970–1971 to 1978–1979, I use the 2005 edition of Table 246; for years 1979–1980 onward I use the 2020 edition.

40. National Center for Education Statistics, "Degrees Conferred by Degree-Granting Institutions, by Level of Degree and Sex of Student," Table 318.20, July 2020.

41. Author's calculation from National Center for Education Statistics, "Number of Postsecondary Institutions Conferring Doctor's Degrees in Dentistry, Medicine, and Law, and Number of Such Degrees Conferred, by Sex of Student: Selected Years, 1949–50 through 2018–19."

42. Jay Reeves, "Women Are Law Review Editors at Top 16 Law Schools," Lawyers Mutual, *Byte of Prevention* (blog), April 17, 2020.

43. Nick Hillman and Nicholas Robinson, *Boys to Men: The Underachievement of Young Men in Higher Education—and How to Start Tackling It*" (Oxford, UK: Higher Education Policy Institute, 2016). For the 2018/2019 school year, see Higher

Education Student Statistics: UK, 2018/2019, Table 1. Women were awarded 244,535 degrees out of 424,540.

44. "Widening Access and Participation," in *UCAS End of Cycle Report 2019* (Cheltenham, UK: UCAS, 2019), chap. 6.

45. Jon Marcus, "The Degrees of Separation between the Genders in College Keep Growing," *Washington Post*, October 27, 2019.

46. Rosamond Hutt, "These 10 Countries Are Closest to Achieving Gender Equality," World Economic Forum, December 19, 2019.

47. Marcus, "The Degrees of Separation."

48. Scottish Funding Council, *Gender Action Plan: Annual Progress Report*, February 6, 2019.

49. For overall STEM, see U.S. Department of Education, National Center for Education Statistics, "Number and Percentage Distribution of Science, Technology, Engineering, and Mathematics (STEM) Degrees/Certificates Conferred by Postsecondary Institutions, by Race/Ethnicity, Level of Degree/Certificate, and Sex of Student: 2009–10 through 2018–19," Table 318.45, February 2021. For math and physical sciences, see U.S. Department of Education, National Center for Education Statistics, "Bachelor's, Master's, and Doctor's Degrees Conferred by Postsecondary Institutions, by Sex of Student and Discipline Division: 2017–18," May 2021.

50. OECD, "Educational Attainment and Labour-Force Status: ELS - Population Who Attained Tertiary Education, by Sex and Age Group." Data extracted on March 10, 2022, most estimates from 2020.

51. Brown University, "Students by Gender," 2020–2021; Columbia University, "Enrollment by School and Gender," Fall 2020; Cornell University, "Composition Dashboard Fall 2019"; Dartmouth College, "Class Profile & Testing," Class of 2025 Enrollment; Jessica M. Wang and Brian P. Yu, "Makeup of the Class," *Harvard Crimson*, 2021; University of Pennsylvania, "Penn Diversity Facts and Figures," Fall 2020; Princeton University, "Diversity: Gender," 2020 Degree-Seeking Students; Yale University, "By the Numbers," Fall 2020.

52. Jennifer Delahunty Britz, "To All the Girls I've Rejected," *New York Times*, March 23, 2006.

53. Dave Bergman, "Gender in College Admissions—Do Men or Women Have an Edge?," *College Transitions*, May 21, 2021.

54. Vassar College, "Common Data Set 2020/21," Institutional Research.

55. Integrated Postsecondary Education Data System (IPEDS), "Kenyon College: Enrollment by Gender, Student Level, and Full- and Part-Time Status: Fall 2020," 2019–2020.

56. Hanna Rosin, *The End of Men: And the Rise of Women* (New York: Riverhead Books, September 2012), p. 148.

57. Rosin, p. 148–9.

58. Douglas Belkin, "A Generation of American Men Give Up on College: 'I Just Feel Lost,'" *Wall Street Journal*, September 6, 2021.

59. Dylan Conger and Mark C. Long, "Why Are Men Falling Behind? Gender Gaps in College Performance and Persistence," *Annals of the American Academy of Political and Social Science* (January 2010).

60. Esteban Aucejo and Jonathan James, "The Path to College Education: The Role of Math and Verbal Skills," *Journal of Political Economy* (October 2021).

61. National Center for Education Statistics, "Graduation Rate from First Institution Attended for First-Time, Full-Time Bachelor's Degree-Seeking Students at 4-Year Postsecondary Institutions, by Race/Ethnicity, Time to Completion, Sex, Control of Institution, and Percentage of Applications Accepted: Selected Cohort Entry Years, 1996 through 2012," *Digest of Education Statistics*, Table 326.10.

62. David Leonhardt and Sahil Chinoy, "The College Dropout Crisis," *New York Times*, May 23, 2019.

63. This is my back-of-the-envelope estimate based on data provided to me by Matthew Chingos.

64. Siwei Cheng and others, "Heterogeneous Returns to College over the Life Course," *Science Advances* (December 2021).

65. David Autor and Melanie Wasserman, *Wayward Sons: The Emerging Gender Gap in Labor Markets and Education* (Washington, DC: Third Way, 2013).

66. School League Tables Team, "School League Tables: Boys behind Girls for Three Decades," BBC News, February 6, 2020.

67. Claudia Goldin, Lawrence F. Katz, and Ilyana Kuziemko, "The Homecoming of American College Women: The Reversal of the College Gender Gap," *Journal of Economic Perspectives* (Fall 2006).

68. Catherine E. Freeman, "Trends in Educational Equity of Girls & Women: 2004," National Center for Education Statistics, Institute of Education Sciences, November 2004, p. 66. For later figures see National Center for Education Statistics, High School Longitudinal Study of 2009 (HSLS).

69. Rosin, *The End of Men*, p. 263.

70. School League Tables Team, "School League Tables: Boys behind Girls for Three Decades."

2. WORKING MAN BLUES

1. "Emerging Labor Market and Education Trends: Reshaping Pathways to the Middle Class," Federal Reserve Bank of Chicago, YouTube channel (video), July 19, 2019 (quote at 1:03).

2. Susan Faludi, *Backlash: The Undeclared War against American Women* (New York: Crown, 2006), p. 41.

3. David Autor and Melanie Wasserman, *Wayward Sons: The Emerging Gender Gap in Labor Markets and Education* (Washington DC: Third Way, 2013), p. 7.

4. These figures are for prime-age males, from Q1 1970 to Q4 2019, seasonally adjusted. Source: U.S. Bureau of Labor Statistics. Series ID: LNS11300061Q.

5. U.S. Bureau of Labor Statistics, "Labor Force Participation Rate—High School Graduates, No College, 25 Yrs. & over, Men." Series ID: LNU01327676Q.

6. In Q4 2019, there were about 21.4 million men in the civilian labor force 25 years and older who completed high school but did not attend college. Data retrieved from FRED, Federal Reserve Bank of St. Louis on February 4, 2022. A labor force participation rate of 68% (see previous note) implies there were about 10 million men not in the labor force 25 years and older who completed high school but did not attend college. The People's Liberation Army has about 2 million active personnel: see Cathleen Campbell, "China's Military: The People's Liberation Army" (Congressional Research Service, June 2021).

7. Richard V. Reeves and Eleanor Krause, "Why Are Young, Educated Men Working Less?," Brookings Institution, February 23, 2018.

8. Gray Kimbrough, "Xboxes and Ex-workers? Gaming and Labor Supply of Young Adults in the U.S." (American University, 2020), p. 9.

9. Betsey Stevenson, *Women, Work, and Families: Recovering from the Pandemic-Induced Recession*, (Brookings Institution, September 2021), figure 1, p. 2.

10. Stefania Albanesi and Jiyeon Kim, "Effects of the COVID-19 Recession on the US Labor Market: Occupation, Family, and Gender," *Journal of Economic Perspectives* (August 2021). Stephanie Aaronson and Francisca Alba also find "modest" negative effects on maternal employment from school closures during the pandemic: see "The Relationship between School Closures and Female Labor Force Participation during the Pandemic," Brookings Institution, November 2021.

11. Stevenson, "Women, Work, and Families," p. 1.

12. Jason Furman and Wilson Powell III, "US Makes Solid Job Gains in October but Millions Are Still on the Sidelines," Peterson Institute for International Economics (November 2021).

13. Vanessa Fuhrmans and Lauren Weber, "Burned Out and Restless from the Pandemic, Women Redefine Their Career Ambitions," *Wall Street Journal*, September 27, 2021.

14. Mark Muro and others, *Automation and Artificial Intelligence*, (Brookings Institution, January 2019, p. 44.

15. Sarah O'Connor, "The Robot-Proof Skills That Give Women an Edge in the Age of AI," *Financial Times*, February 12, 2019.

16. Guido Matias Cortes, Nir Jaimovich, and Henry Siu, "The 'End of Men' and Rise of Women in the High-Skilled Labor Market," Working Paper 24274 (Cambridge, MA: National Bureau of Economic Research, November 2018).

17. Marcus Casey and Sarah Nzau, "The Differing Impact of Automation on Men and Women's Work," Brookings Institution, September 11, 2019.

18. U.S. Bureau of Labor Statistics, "Occupational Requirements Survey: Sedentary Strength Requirements" (2018).

19. Elizabeth Fain and Cara Weatherford, "Comparative Study of Millennials' (Age 20–34 Years) Grip and Lateral Pinch with the Norms," *Journal of Hand Therapy* (October 2016).

20. U.S. Bureau of Labor Statistics, *Occupational Outlook Handbook.*

21. For a discussion, see Katherine G. Abraham and Melissa S. Kearney, "Explaining the Decline in the US Employment-to-Population Ratio: A Review of the Evidence," *Journal of Economic Literature* (September 2020).

22. Richard V. Reeves, "With Respect: How Liberal Societies Flourish," Brookings Institution, February 12, 2019.

23. Fatih Guvenen and others, "Lifetime Earnings in the United States over Six Decades," Becker Friedman Institute, Working Paper 2021–60 (University of Chicago, 2021). I have reported here their main results using the PCE deflator. See also Stephen J. Rose and Heidi I. Hartmann, *Still a Man's Labor Market* (Institute for Women's Policy Research, 2018).

24. BLS Reports "Highlights of Women's Earnings in 2020," US Bureau of Labor Statistics (September 2021), p. 5.

25. Hans Rosling, *Factfulness: Ten Reasons We're Wrong about the World—and Why Things Are Better Than You Think* (New York: Flatiron Books, 2018), p. 38.

26. U.S. Bureau of Labor Statistics, *Highlights of Women's Earnings in 2020*, BLS Reports, September 2021.

27. Claudia Goldin, "A Grand Gender Convergence: Its Last Chapter," *American Economic Review* (April 2014).

28. Toni Van Pelt, "The Paycheck Fairness Act Would Help Close the Gender Wage Gap. Why Won't the Senate Pass it?," *Fortune*, August 26, 2019.

29. Christina Hoff Sommers, "No, Women Don't Make Less Money Than Men," *Daily Beast*, May 29, 2019.

30. Kerri Anne Renzulli, "46% of American Men Think the Gender Pay Gap Is 'Made Up to Serve a Political Purpose,'" CNBC, April 4, 2019.

31. Francine D. Blau and Lawrence M. Kahn, "The Gender Wage Gap: Extent, Trends, and Explanations," *Journal of Economic Literature* (September 2017). See also *2022 State of the Gender Pay Gap Report* (PayScale, 2022). For international comparisons, see Gabriele Ciminelli and Cyrille Schwellnus, "Sticky Floors or Glass Ceilings? The Role of Human Capital, Working Time Flexibility and Discrimination in the Gender Wage Gap," VoxEU CEPR (May 16, 2021).

32. CONSAD Research Corporation, *An Analysis of the Reasons for the Disparity in Wages between Men and Women*, report prepared for the U.S. Department of Labor Employment Standards Administration (January 2009), p. 2.

33. John Iceland and Ilana Redstone, "The Declining Earnings Gap between Young Women and Men in the United States, 1979–2018," *Social Science Research* (November 1, 2020). See also Press Association, "Women in Their 20s Earn More Than Men of the Same Age, Study Finds," *The Guardian*, August 28, 2015; and Sarah Kliff, "A Stunning Chart Shows the True Cause of the Gender Wage Gap," Vox, February 19, 2018.

34. Heather Long, "80 Nations Set Quotas for Female Leaders. Should the U.S. Be Next?," *Washington Post*, November 3, 2021.

35. Michelle J. Budig, "The Fatherhood Bonus and the Motherhood Penalty: Parenthood and the Gender Gap in Pay," Third Way, September 2, 2014. The fact that adoptive mothers see a similar dent in earnings as birth mothers underscores the point that this is more about maternal care than female biology. See also Henrik Kleven, Camille Landais, and Jakob Egholt Søgaard, "Does Biology Drive Child Penalties? Evidence from Biological and Adoptive Families," *American Economic Review: Insights* (June 2021). They conclude that "most of the remaining gender inequality in high-income countries can be attributed to the unequal impacts of children on men and women," p. 183.

36. Yoon Kyung Chung and others, "The Parental Gender Earnings Gap in the United States," Working Paper CES 17-68 (U.S. Census Bureau, November 2017). See also Danielle Sandler and Nichole Szembrot, "Maternal Labor Dynamics: Participation, Earnings, and Employer Changes," Working Paper CES 19-33 (U.S. Census Bureau, December 2019).

37. Ylva Moberg, "Does the Gender Composition in Couples Matter for the Division of Labor After Childbirth?," Working Paper 2016:8 (Institute for Evaluation of Labour Market and Education Policy, 2016). See also Martin Eckhoff Andresen and Emily Nix, "What Causes the Child Penalty? Evidence from Adopting and Same-Sex Couples," *Journal of Labor Economics* (accepted for publication).

38. Valentin Bolotnyy and Natalia Emanuel, "Why Do Women Earn Less Than Men? Evidence from Bus and Train Operators," *Journal of Labor Economics* (forthcoming). Available as a Working Paper, p. 34, https://scholar.harvard.edu/files/bolotnyy/files/be_gendergap.pdf.

39. Bolotnyy and Emanuel, "Why Do Women Earn Less than Men?," p. 34.

40. Claudia Goldin, *Career and Family: Women's Century-Long Journey toward Equity* (Princeton University Press, 2021), p. 149.

41. Marianne Bertrand, Claudia Goldin, and Lawrence F. Katz, "Dynamics of the Gender Gap for Young Professionals in the Financial and Corporate Sectors," *American Economic Journal: Applied Economics* (July 2010).

42. See Table 2 in BLS Reports, "Women in the Labor Force: A Databook," U.S. Bureau of Labor Statistics (April 2021).

43. Executive Office of the President Council of Economic Advisers, "The Economics of Family-Friendly Workplace Policies," in *Economic Report of the President 2015* (U.S. Government Publishing Office, February 2015), p. 157.

44. BLS Reports, "Women in the Labor Force."

45. BLS Reports, "Women in the Labor Force," Table 11.

46. Cynthia Grant Bowman, "Women in the Legal Profession from the 1920s to the 1970s: What Can We Learn from Their Experience about Law and Social Change?," *Cornell Law Faculty Publications*, Paper 12, 2009; U.S. Bureau of Labor Statistics, "Employed Full Time: Wage and Salary Workers: Lawyers Occupations: 16 Years and Over," Series LEU0254483400A, *Federal Reserve Bank of St. Louis*, November 19, 2021.

47. Goldin, *Career and Family*, p. 125.

48. Hanna Rosin, "New Data on the Rise of Women," TED talk (video), December 2010 (quote at 2:32).
49. Lisa O'Kelly, "Hanna Rosin: 'I Feel Miscast in the Gender Wars,'" *The Guardian*, September 29, 2019.
50. Courtney Connley, "A Record 41 Women Are Fortune 500 CEOs—and for the First Time Two Black Women Made the List," *CNBC Make It*, June 2, 2021. For the data on company directors, see "Women in the Workplace 2021," McKinsey & Company, September 27, 2021.
51. Kate Clark, "US VC Investment in Female Founders Hits All-Time High," TechCrunch, December 9, 2019.

3. DISLOCATED DADS

1. Adlai E. Stevenson, "A Purpose for Modern Woman," *Women's Home Companion* (September 1955), pp. 30–31. See also K. A. Cuordileone, *Manhood and American Political Culture in the Cold War* (London: Routledge, 2012), p. 261.
2. Gloria Steinem, "The Politics of Women," May 31, 1971, p. 6. Available from Smith College at www.alumnae.smith.edu/smithcms/1971/files/2015/08/Steinem-Commencement-Address.pdf.
3. Margaret Mead, *Some Personal Views* (New York: Walker, 1979), p. 50.
4. Claudia Goldin, Lawrence F. Katz, and Ilyana Kuziemko, "The Homecoming of American College Women: The Reversal of the College Gender Gap," Working Paper 12139 (Cambridge, MA: National Bureau of Economic Research, March 2006).
5. "Economic Diversity and Student Outcomes at America's Colleges and Universities: Find Your College," *New York Times*, January 18, 2017. Interactive drawing on data from Raj Chetty and others, "Mobility Report Cards: The Role of Colleges in Intergenerational Mobility," Working Paper 23618 (Cambridge, MA: National Bureau of Economic Research, December 2017).
6. David Gilmore, *Manhood in the Making: Cultural Concepts of Masculinity* (Yale University Press, 1991), pp. 222–23.
7. David Morgan, "Class and Masculinity," in *Handbook of Studies on Men & Masculinities*, ed. Michael S. Kimmel, Jeff Hearn, and R. W. Connell (Thousand Oaks, CA: Sage, 2005), p. 169. See also Stephen Nock, *Marriage in Men's Lives* (Oxford University Press, 1998) on the "universal trinity of roles that define adult men . . . fathers, providers and protectors," p. 132.
8. Geoff Dench, *Transforming Men: Changing Patterns of Dependency and Dominance in Gender Relations* (London: Routledge, 1998), p. 8.
9. Laura Tach, Ronald Mincy, and Kathryn Edin, "Parenting as a 'Package Deal': Relationships, Fertility, and Nonresident Father Involvement among Unmarried Parents," *Demography* (February 2010).

10. Gilmore, *Manhood in the Making*, p. 221.

11. John Stuart Mill, "The Subjection of Women" [1869], *Collected Works of John Stuart Mill*, vol. 21 (University of Toronto Press, 1984), p. 325. Gloria Steinem, "A New Egalitarian Life Style," *New York Times*, Aug 16, 1971.

12. See for example Clare Chambers, *Against Marriage: An Egalitarian Defence of the Marriage-Free State* (Oxford University Press, 2017), and Rebecca Traister, *All the Single Ladies: Unmarried Women and the Rise of an Independent Nation* (New York: Simon & Schuster, 2016).

13. Arthur Miller, *Death of a Salesman* [1949], (New York: Penguin Books, 1998), p. 11.

14. Irina Dunn, "A Woman Needs a Man Like a Fish Needs a Bicycle," (written in 1970), attributed to Dunn by Gloria Steinem in a letter to *Time* magazine, September 16, 2000.

15. Lorraine Ali, "The Secret Lives of Wives," *Newsweek*, July 11, 2004.

16. Sarah Jane Glynn, "Breadwinning Mothers Continue to Be the U.S. Norm," Center for American Progress, May 10, 2019.

17. U.S. Census Bureau, "Table F-22. Married-Couple Families with Wives' Earnings Greater Than Husbands' Earnings: 1981 to 2020," in Current Population Survey, 1982 to 2021 Annual Social and Economic Supplements.

18. Cheridan Christnacht and Briana Sullivan, "About Two-thirds of the 23.5 Million Working Women with Children Under 18 Worked Full-Time in 2018," United States Census Bureau, May 8, 2020. See also Pew Research Center, "Raising Kids and Running a Household: How Working Parents Share the Load," November 4, 2015.

19. David Willetts, *The Pinch: How the Baby Boomers Took Their Children's Future—and Why They Should Give it Back* (London: Atlantic Books, 2011), p. 53. See also Margaret Mead: "In modern industrialized societies . . . large numbers of children live in broken homes, supported by taxes levied on the males and working females of higher income brackets." Margaret Mead, *Male and Female* (New York: Harper Perennial, 2001), p. 191.

20. Vicki Larson and Beverly Willett, "Room for Debate: When Divorce Is a Family Affair," *New York Times*, February 13, 2013.

21. Social Capital Project, "Love, Marriage, and the Baby Carriage: The Rise in Unwed Childbearing," The United States Congress Joint Economic Committee, SCP Report 4-17 (December 11, 2017).

22. Social Capital Project, "Rising Unwed Pregnancy and Childbearing across Educational and Racial Groups," The United States Congress Joint Economic Committee, SCP Brief (February 14, 2018).

23. I have combined "strongly agree" and "agree" here. Data from GSS Data Explorer. The question is: "Working mom can have as good relationship with child as non-working mother (agree/disagree?)."

24. William J. Goode, "Why Men Resist," *Dissent* (Spring 1980).

25. Claire Cain Miller, "Why Men Don't Want the Jobs Done Mostly by Women," *New York Times*, January 4, 2017.

26. Kim Parker and Renee Stepler, "Men Seen as Financial Providers in U.S., Even as Women's Contributions Grow," Pew Research Center, September 20, 2017.

27. Shelly Lundberg, Robert A. Pollak, and Jenna Stearns, "Family Inequality: Diverging Patterns in Marriage, Cohabitation, and Childbearing," *Journal of Economic Perspectives* (Spring 2016).

28. Alexandra Killewald, "Money, Work and Marital Stability: Assessing Change in the Gendered Determinants of Divorce," *American Sociological Review* (August 2016), p. 696.

29. Marianne Bertrand, Emir Kamenica, and Jessica Pan, "Gender Identity and Relative Income within Households," *Quarterly Journal of Economics* (May 2015), p. 572.

30. Steven Ruggles, "Patriarchy, Power, and Pay: The Transformation of American Families, 1800–2015," *Demography* (December 2015), table 2, p. 1814.

31. Dench, *Transforming Men*, pp. 17 and 19.

32. David Blankenhorn, *Fatherless America: Confronting Our Most Urgent Social Problem* (New York: Harper Perennial, 1996), p. 18.

33. Andrew Cherlin, "Marriage Has Become a Trophy," *The Atlantic*, March 20, 2018.

34. Juliana Menasce Horowitz, Nikki Graf, and Gretchen Livingston, "Marriage and Cohabitation in the U.S," Pew Research Center, November 6, 2019.

35. Ariel J. Binder and John Bound, "The Declining Labor Market Prospects of Less-Educated Men," *Journal of Economic Perspectives* (Spring 2019), p. 181. They also write that "a decline in the formation of stable families . . . removes a labor supply incentive," p. 181.

36. Michèle Lamont, *The Dignity of Working Men: Morality and the Boundaries of Race, Class, and Immigration* (Harvard University Press, 2009), pp. 26 and 29.

37. For example, in the *Lancaster Intelligencer* on September 20, 1859, Vol. LX.

38. For health, see "Marriage and Men's Health," Harvard Health Publishing, June 5, 2019. For employment numbers, see "Labor Force Participation Rate—Never Married, Men," BLS Data Viewer, Series ID: LNU01300149Q. For social networks, see Daniel A. Cox, "Emerging Trends and Enduring Patterns in American Family Life," The Survey Center on American Life, American Enterprise Institute, February 9, 2022. See also Christopher J. Einolf and Deborah Philbrick, "Generous or Greedy Marriage? A Longitudinal Study of Volunteering and Charitable Giving," *Journal of Marriage and Family* (June 2014).

39. These figures are for prime-age men (25–54). Patrick T. Brown, "Opioids and the Unattached Male," *City Journal*, January 14, 2022.

40. Michael J. Rosenfeld, "Who Wants the Breakup? Gender and Breakup in Heterosexual Couples," in *Social Networks and the Life Course: Integrating the Development of Human Lives and Social Relational Networks*, ed. Duane F. Alwin, Diane Felmlee, and Derek Kreager (New York: Springer, 2018), pp. 221–243. See also

Daniel S. Felix, W. David Robinson, and Kimberly J. Jarzynka, "The Influence of Divorce on Men's Health," *Journal of Men's Health* (November 2013).

41. Mary Jo Murphy and Megan Thee-Brenan, "Poll Finds Most Voters Embrace Milestone for Women, If Not Hillary Clinton," *New York Times*, September 16, 2016.

42. "Where Americans Find Meaning in Life: Detailed Tables," Pew Research Center, November 20, 2018. For the gender breakdowns, see the detailed tables in the Appendix.

43. Janet Shibley Hyde, "Women, Men, Work, and Family: Expansionist Theory Updated," in *Gender and Couple Relationships*, ed. Susan M. McHale and others (New York: Springer, 2016), p. 102.

44. Maria Cotofan and others, "Work and Well-being during COVID-19: Impact, Inequalities, Resilience, and the Future of Work," in *World Happiness Report 2021*, ed. John F. Helliwell and others (New York: Sustainable Development Solutions Network, 2021).

45. Barack Obama, "Text of Obama's Fatherhood Speech," Politico, June 15, 2008.

46. Jacob E. Cheadle, Paul R. Amato, and Valarie King, "Patterns of Nonresident Father Contact," *Demography* (2010), appendix figure A1.

47. Gretchen Livingston and Kim Parker, "A Tale of Two Fathers: More Are Active, but More Are Absent," Pew Research Center, June 15, 2021.

48. Another 4.5% were living with a father only, up from 1%. See Paul Hemez and Channell Washington, "Percentage and Number of Children Living with Two Parents Has Dropped since 1968," U.S. Census Bureau, April 12, 2021.

49. Jill Daugherty and Casey Copen, "Trends in Attitudes about Marriage, Childbearing, and Sexual Behavior: United States, 2002, 2006–2010, and 2011–2013," *National Health Statistics Reports* (Hyattsville, MD: National Center for Health Statistics, 2016).

50. Patrick F. Fagan and Christina Hadford, "The Fifth Annual Index of Family Belonging and Rejection," Marriage and Religion Research Institute, February 12, 2015, table 1.

51. George F. Gilder, *Sexual Suicide* (New York: Quadrangle, 1973), p. 91.

4. DWIGHT'S GLASSES

1. Keith L. Alexander, "Trendy, Non-prescription Eyewear Latest in Criminal Defendant Strategic Attire," *Washington Post*, March 27, 2012.

2. Michael J. Brown, "Is Justice Blind or Just Visually Impaired? The Effects of Eyeglasses on Mock Juror Decisions," American Society of Trial Consultants, 2011.

3. Kimberlé Crenshaw, "Demarginalizing the Intersection of Race and Sex: A Black Feminist Critique of Antidiscrimination Doctrine, Feminist Theory and Anti-racist Politics," *University of Chicago Legal Forum* (1989), p. 166.

4. Tiffany N. Ford, "Exploring Complexity in Well-Being: A Mixed Methods Examination of the Black Women's Well-Being Paradox" forthcoming, p. 11. See also Lisa Bowleg and others, "'It's an Uphill Battle Everyday': Intersectionality, Low-Income Black Heterosexual Men, and Implications for HIV Prevention Research and Interventions," *Psychology of Men & Masculinity* (2013).

5. Evelyn M. Simien, "Doing Intersectionality Research: From Conceptual Issues to Practical Examples," *Politics & Gender* (June 2007).

6. Gene Demby, "The Truth behind the Lies of the Original 'Welfare Queen,'" NPR, December 20, 2013.

7. Colleen Flaherty, "Tommy Curry Discusses New Book on How Critical Theory Has Ignored Realities of Black Maleness," *Inside Higher Ed*, September 7, 2017.

8. Tommy Curry, *The Man-Not: Race, Class, Genre and the Dilemmas of Black Manhood* (Temple University Press, 2017), p. 17.

9. Sheryll Cashin, *White Space, Black Hood* (Boston: Beacon Press, 2021), p. 5.

10. Richard V. Reeves, "Boys to Men: Fathers, Family, and Opportunity," Brookings Institution, June 19, 2015.

11. Raj Chetty and others, "The Opportunity Atlas," Opportunity Insights, October 2018, www.opportunityatlas.org.

12. Maryland State Department of Education, "Belmont Elementary 2018–2019 School Report Card," Maryland Public Schools (2021).

13. It is important to note that the outcome measure being used here is *individual* income, not *household* income. Raj Chetty and others, "Race and Economic Opportunity in the United States: Executive Summary," The Equality of Opportunity Project, March 2018, p. 3.

14. Raj Chetty and others, "Race and Economic Opportunity in the United States: An Intergenerational Perspective," *Quarterly Journal of Economics* (May 2020), p. 747.

15. Scott Winship, Richard V. Reeves, and Katherine Guyot, "The Inheritance of Black Poverty: It's All about the Men," Brookings Institution, March 2018.

16. Daniel Patrick Moynihan, *The Negro Family: The Case for National Action* (Office of Policy Planning and Research, Department of Labor, 1965), chap. 4, "The Tangle of Pathology." See also Daniel Geary, "The Moynihan Report: An Annotated Edition," *The Atlantic*, September 14, 2015.

17. Jonathan Rothwell, "Housing Costs, Zoning, and Access to High-Scoring Schools," Brookings Institution, April 2012.

18. Jerlando F. L. Jackson and James L. Moore III, "African American Males in Education: Endangered or Ignored?," *Teachers College Record* (February 2006), p. 201.

19. National Center for Education Statistics, "Percentage of High School Dropouts among Persons 16 to 24 Years Old (Status Dropout Rate), by Sex and Race/Ethnicity: Selected Years, 1960 through 2017," U.S. Department of Education, November 2018. For college enrollment, see National Center for Education Statistics, "Percentage of 18- to 24-Year-Olds Enrolled in College, by Level of Institution and Sex and Race/Ethnicity of Student: 1970 through 2018," U.S. Department of Education, 2020. For postgraduate degree attainment see National Center for Education Statistics, "Percentage of Persons 25 to 29 Years Old with Selected Levels of Educational Attainment, by Race/Ethnicity and Sex: Selected Years, 1920 through 2020," U.S. Department of Education, October 2020.

20. National Center for Education Statistics, "Master's Degrees Conferred by Post-secondary Institutions, by Race/Ethnicity and Sex of Student: Selected Years, 1976–77 through 2018–19," U.S. Department of Education, June 2020.

21. Bart Shaw and others, *Ethnicity, Gender and Social Mobility, Social Mobility Commission* (London: Social Mobility Commission, December 2016).

22. Sherry N. Mong and Vincent J. Roscigno, "African American Men and the Experience of Employment Discrimination," *Qualitative Sociology* (2010).

23. Mitra Toossi and Leslie Joyner, "Blacks in the Labor Force," U.S. Bureau of Labor Statistics, February 2018.

24. Raj Chetty and others, "Race and Economic Opportunity in the United States: An Intergenerational Perspective," March 2018, www.equality-of-opportunity .org/assets/documents/race_paper.pdf. "The employment rates of black men with parents at the 75th percentile are comparable to those of white men with parents at the 9th percentile," p. 22. See especially figure VI F.

25. Sarah Jane Glynn, "Breadwinning Mothers Continue to Be the U.S. Norm," Center for American Progress, May 10, 2019.

26. Vincent J. Roscigno, *The Face of Discrimination: How Race and Gender Impact Work and Home Lives* (Lanham, MD: Rowman & Littlefield, 2007).

27. Emily Badger and others, "Extensive Data Shows Punishing Reach of Racism for Black Boys," *New York Times*, March 19, 2018.

28. Obama Foundation, "We Are Our Brothers' Keepers," My Brother's Keeper Alliance, 2014, www.obama.org/mbka.

29. "New Analysis Finds Little Evidence to Support the Focus on Boys and Young Men of Color in the White House My Brother's Keeper Initiative," Institute for Women's Policy Research, February 25, 2015.

30. Camille Busette, "A New Deal for Poor African-American and Native-American Boys," Brookings Institution, March 14, 2018.

31. Ta-Nehisi Coates, "The Black Family in the Age of Mass Incarceration," *The Atlantic*, September 14, 2015.

32. Coates, "The Black Family." Note that Black women are about as likely as white men to be seen as violent—while white women are very unlikely to be seen as violent.

33. Corrine McConnaughy and Ismail K. White, "Racial Politics Complicated: The Work of Gendered Race Cues in American Politics," paper prepared for the New Research on Gender in Political Psychology Conference, Rutgers University, March 4–5, 2011, fig. 1.

34. Moynihan, *The Negro Family*, chap. 3, "The Roots of the Problem."

35. Rashawn Ray, "Black People Don't Exercise in My Neighborhood: Perceived Racial Composition and Leisure-Time Physical Activity among Middle Class Blacks and Whites," *Social Science Research* (August 2017), p. 29.

36. Ibram X. Kendi, "Who Gets to Be Afraid in America?," *The Atlantic*, May 12, 2020.

37. Jonathan Rothwell, "Drug Offenders in American Prisons: The Critical Distinction between Stock and Flow," Brookings Institution, November 25, 2015.

38. Carroll Bogert and Lynnell Hancock, "Superpredator: The Media Myth That Demonized a Generation of Black Youth," The Marshall Project, November 20, 2020.

39. "Ta-Nehisi Coates: 'In America, It Is Traditional to Destroy the Black Body,'" *The Guardian*, September 20, 2015, book extract from his *Between the World and Me* (New York: Spiegel & Grau, 2015).

40. Jennifer L. Doleac and Benjamin Hansen, "The Unintended Consequences of 'Ban the Box': Statistical Discrimination and Employment Outcomes When Criminal Histories Are Hidden," *Journal of Labor Economics* (April 2020).

41. Christina Stacy and Mychal Cohen, "Ban the Box and Racial Discrimination," Urban Institute, February 2017.

42. Devah Pager, *Marked: Race, Crime, and Finding Work in an Era of Mass Incarceration* (University of Chicago Press, 2008). Quoted in Ta-Nehisi Coates, "The Black Family in the Age of Mass Incarceration."

43. Julie Bosman, "Obama Sharply Assails Absent Black Fathers," *New York Times*, June 16, 2008.

44. Jawanza Kunjufu, *Raising Black Boys* (Chicago: African American Images, 2007). See Lottie Joiner, "The Impact of Absent Fathers on the Mental Health of Black Boys," Center for Health Journalism, 2016.

45. Leila Morsy and Richard Rothstein, "Mass Incarceration and Children's Outcomes," Economic Policy Institute, December 2016.

46. "Daniel Beaty—Knock, Knock," YouTube (video), November 19, 2009.

47. Jo Jones and William D. Mosher, *Fathers' Involvement with Their Children: United States, 2006–2010*, National Health Statistics Reports, no. 71 (National Center for Health Statistics, 2013).

48. US Census Bureau, Annual Social and Economic Supplement (ASEC), "Table A3. Parents with Coresident Children under 18, by Living Arrangement, Sex, and Selected Characteristics: 2020," from *Current Population Survey, 1982 to 2021 Annual Social and Economic Supplements* (2021).

49. Elizabeth Wildsmith, Jennifer Manlove, and Elizabeth Cook, "Dramatic Increase in the Proportion of Births Outside of Marriage in the United States from 1990 to 2016," Child Trends, August 8, 2018.

50. R. Kelly Raley, Megan M. Sweeney, and Danielle Wondra, "The Growing Racial and Ethnic Divide in U.S. Marriage Patterns," *Future Child* (Fall 2015), p. 89.

51. William Julius Wilson, *The Truly Disadvantaged* (University of Chicago Press, 1990).

52. Pew Research Center, "Views on Importance of Being a Provider Differ along Key Demographic Lines," September 19, 2017.

53. Quoted in Coates, "The Black Family in the Age of Mass Incarceration."

54. Heather McGhee, *The Sum of Us: What Racism Costs Everyone and How We Can Prosper Together* (New York: OneWorld, 2021).

55. The Ferguson Commission, *Forward through Ferguson: A Path toward Racial Equity* (October 2015).

56. U.S. Commission on Civil Rights, Commission on the Social Status of Black Men and Boys, 2020.

57. Florida Office of the Attorney General, Florida Council on the Social Status of Black Men and Boys, 2006, www.cssbmb.com.

58. Congresswoman Frederica Wilson, "Wilson Passes the Commission on the Social Status of Black Men and Boys Act," July 27, 2020.

5. CLASS CEILING

1. Anne Case and Angus Deaton, "Mortality and Morbidity in the 21st Century," *BPEA* (Spring 2017), pp. 397–476; Anne Case and Angus Deaton, *Deaths of Despair and the Future of Capitalism* (Princeton University Press, 2020).

2. Case and Deaton, "Mortality and Morbidity," pp. 429 and 438.

3. Joint Economic Committee, *Long-Term Trends in Deaths of Despair*, Social Capital Project Report No. 4-19 (September 2019).

4. Sarah A. Donovan and David H. Bradley, *Real Wage Trends, 1979 to 2019*, report prepared for Members and Committees of Congress (Congressional Research Service, December 2020).

5. Nick Hillman and Nicholas Robinson, "Boys to Men: The Underachievement of Young Men in Higher Education—and How to Start Tackling It," Higher Education Policy Institute (2016), p. 12.

6. Donald Trump, "The Inaugural Address," January 20, 2017, trumpwhitehouse.archives.gov.

7. Shannon M. Monnat, *Deaths of Despair and Support for Trump in the 2016 Presidential Election*, Research Brief, Department of Agricultural Economics, Sociology, and Education (State College, PA: Pennsylvania State University, 2016).

8. Nicholas Kristof and Sheryl WuDunn, "Who Killed the Knapp Family?," *New York Times*, January 9, 2020. See also Nicholas Kristof and Sheryl WuDunn, *Tightrope: Americans Reaching for Hope* (New York: Knopf Doubleday, 2020), pp. 119–20.

9. Kaiser Family Foundation (KFF), "Opioid Overdose Deaths by Sex," March 16, 2021.

10. Alan B. Krueger, "Where Have All the Workers Gone? An Inquiry into the Decline of the U.S. Labor Force Participation Rate," Brookings Institution, September 7, 2017.

11. Katharine G. Abraham and Melissa S. Kearney, "Explaining the Decline in the US Employment-to-Population Ratio: A Review of the Evidence," *Journal of Economic Literature* (September 2020), p. 622.

12. A 2018 review of the evidence on opioid deaths in Canada concluded the following: "analysis of potential risk factors found the majority of opioid-related deaths occurred when the individual was alone, indoors in a private residence." See Belzak Lisa and Halverson Jessica, "Evidence Synthesis—the Opioid Crisis in Canada: A National Perspective," *Health Promotion and Chronic Disease Prevention in Canada* (June 2018), p. 231.

13. "Suicide Worldwide in 2019: Global Health Estimates," *World Health Organization*, 2021, figure 9, p. 10.

14. Rhys Owen-Williams, "Dataset: Leading Causes of Death, UK," UK Office for National Statistics, March 27, 2020, table 5.

15. National Center for Health Statistics, Data Brief 398, February 2021, figure 3.

16. Barrett Swanson, "Is There a Masculine Cure for Toxic Masculinity?," *Harper's Magazine*, November 2019.

17. F. L. Shand and others, "What Might Interrupt Men's Suicide? Results from an Online Survey of Men," *BMJ Open*, 2015.

18. Heather Boushey and Kavya Vaghul, "Women Have Made the Difference for Family Economic Security," Washington Center for Equitable Growth, April 2016, p. 5. I should note that there was a very small contribution from "earnings from other sources."

19. Arlie Hochschild with Anne Machung, *The Second Shift: Working Families and the Revolution at Home* (New York: Viking Penguin, 1989, reissued 1997 and 2012).

20. U.S. Census Bureau, Table C2, "Household Relationship and Living Arrangements of Children under 18 Years, by Age and Sex: 2020."

21. Kathryn Edin and Maria Kefalas, *Promises I Can Keep: Why Poor Women Put Motherhood before Marriage* (University of California Press, 2005).

22. Edin and Kefalas, *Promises I Can Keep*, p. 81.

23. Sarah Jane Glynn, "Breadwinning Mothers Continue to Be the U.S. Norm," Center for American Progress, May 10, 2019.

24. R. Kelly Raley, Megan M. Sweeney, and Danielle Wondra, "The Growing Racial and Ethnic Divide in U.S. Marriage Patterns," *The Future of Children* (Fall 2015), pp. 89–109.

25. David Autor and Melanie Wasserman, *Wayward Sons: The Emerging Gender Gap in Labor Markets and Education* (Washington, DC: Third Way, 2013), p. 27.

26. Edin and Kefalas, *Promises I Can Keep*.

27. Andrew Cherlin, "Marriage Has Become a Trophy," *The Atlantic*, March 20, 2018.

28. Richard V. Reeves and Christopher Pulliam, "Middle Class Marriage Is Declining, and Likely Deepening Inequality," Brookings Institution, March 11, 2020. See also Shelly Lundberg, Robert A. Pollak, and Jenna Steans, "Family Inequality: Diverging Patterns in Marriage, Cohabitation, and Childbearing," *Journal of Economic Perspectives* (Spring 2016).

29. Reeves and Pulliam, "Middle Class Marriage Is Declining."

30. Courtney C. Coile and Mark G. Duggan, "When Labor's Lost: Health, Family Life, Incarceration, and Education in a Time of Declining Economic Opportunity for Low-Skilled Men," *Journal of Economic Perspectives* (Spring 2019).

31. Isabel V. Sawhill, *Generation Unbound* (Brookings Institution Press, 2014), p. 76.

32. Elizabeth Wildsmith, Jennifer Manlove, and Elizabeth Cook, "Dramatic Increase in the Proportion of Births outside of Marriage in the United States from 1990 to 2016," *Child Trends*, August 8, 2018.

33. Andrew J. Cherlin, "Rising Nonmarital First Childbearing among College-Educated Women: Evidence from Three National Studies," *Proceedings of the National Academy of Sciences* (September 2021), p. 6.

34. "'Ms' Feminists Taken Aback as Their High Priestess Steinem Becomes a 'Mrs' at 66," *Irish Times*, September 8, 2000.

35. Richard V. Reeves, "How to Save Marriage in America," *The Atlantic*, February 13, 2014.

36. Marianne Bertrand, Claudia Goldin, and Lawrence F. Katz, "Dynamics of the Gender Gap for Young Professionals in the Financial and Corporate Sectors," *American Economic Journal: Applied Economics* (July 2010).

37. Shoshana Grossbard and others, "Spouses' Income Association and Inequality: A Non-linear Perspective," Working Paper 2019-076 (Chicago: University of Chicago, December 2019), p. 1.

38. Shelly Lundberg, Robert A. Pollak, and Jenna Stearns, "Family Inequality: Diverging Patterns in Marriage, Cohabitation, and Childbearing," *Journal of Economic Perspectives* (Spring 2016), p. 97.

39. David Morgan, "Class and Masculinity," in *Handbook of Studies on Men and Masculinities*, ed. Michael S. Kimmel, Jeff Hearn, and Robert W. Connell (Thousand Oaks, CA: Sage, 2004).

40. Kathryn Edin and others, "The Tenuous Attachments of Working-Class Men," *Journal of Economic Perspectives* (Spring 2019), p. 222.

41. Edin and others, "The Tenuous Attachments of Working-Class Men," p. 222.

42. Jennifer M. Silva, *We're Still Here: Pain and Politics in the Heart of America* (Oxford University Press, 2019), pp. 66, 48–9, 42–3.

43. Daniel Cox, "Yes, Having More Friends Is Better," Survey Center on American Life, August 9, 2021. See also Daniel Cox, "American Men Suffer a Friendship Recession," *National Review*, July 6, 2021.

44. Daniel Cox, "Men's Social Circles Are Shrinking," Survey Center on American Life, June 29, 2021.

45. Richard Fry, "For the First Time in Modern Era, Living with Parents Edges Out Other Living Arrangements for 18- to 34-Year-Olds," Pew Research Center, May 24, 2016.

46. Michael Kimmel, *Guyland: The Perilous World Where Boys Become Men* (New York: Harper Collins, 2018).

47. Cox, "American Men Suffer a Friendship Recession." See also Jacqueline Olds and Richard S. Schwartz, *The Lonely American: Drifting Apart in the Twenty-First Century* (Boston: Beacon Press, 2009). As they write: "Almost every father we spoke with explained that he had lost contact with most of his male friends," p. 116.

48. Matthew R. Wright and others, "The Roles of Marital Dissolution and Subsequent Repartnering on Loneliness in Later Life," *Journals of Gerontology: Series B, Psychological Sciences and Social Sciences* (October 2020).

49. Ernest Hemingway, *Men without Women* (New York: Scribner, 1927); Haruki Murakami, *Men without Women* (New York: Vintage, 2018).

50. John Steinbeck, *Of Mice and Men* (New York: Covici-Friede, 1937; New York: Penguin, 1993), pp. 72–3. Citation refers to the Penguin edition.

51. Shirley S. Wang, "The Fight to Save Japan's Young Shut-Ins," *Wall Street Journal*, January 25, 2015.

52. Nicolas Tajan, Hamasaki Yukiko, and Nancy Pionnié-Dax, "Hikikomori: The Japanese Cabinet Office's 2016 Survey of Acute Social Withdrawal," *Asia-Pacific Journal* (March 2017). See also Edd Gent, "The Plight of Japan's Modern Hermits," BBC, January 29, 2019.

53. Laurence Butet-Roch, "Pictures Reveal the Isolated Lives of Japan's Social Recluses," *National Geographic*, February 14, 2018.

54. Hikikomori Italia, Associazione Nazionale, www.hikikomoriitalia.it.

55. Alan R. Teo and others, "Development and Validation of the 25-Item Hikikomori Questionnaire (HQ-25)," *Psychiatry and Clinical Neurosciences* (June 2018).

56. Allie Conti, "When 'Going Outside' Is Prison: The World of American Hikikomori," *New York Magazine*, February 17, 2019.

57. W. Thomas Boyce, *The Orchid and the Dandelion: Why Sensitive Children Face Challenges and How All Can Thrive* (New York: Vintage, 2020).

58. Raj Chetty and others, "Race and Economic Opportunity in the United States: An Intergenerational Perspective," *Quarterly Journal of Economics* (May 2020), online appendix table V. In every race category, boys are less likely than girls to escape intergenerational poverty, measured in terms of household income.

59. Miles Corak, "'Inequality Is the Root of Social Evil,' or Maybe Not? Two Stories about Inequality and Public Policy," *Canadian Public Policy* (December 2016).

60. Raj Chetty and others, "Childhood Environment and Gender Gaps in Adulthood," *American Economic Review* (May 2016), p. 282.

61. Raj Chetty and Nathaniel Hendren, "The Impacts of Neighborhoods on Intergenerational Mobility II: County-Level Estimates," *Quarterly Journal of Economics* (February 2018), p. 1167.

62. David Autor and others, "Family Disadvantage and the Gender Gap in Behavioral and Educational Outcomes," *American Economic Journal: Applied Economics* (July 2019). See also David Autor and others, "School Quality and the Gender Gap in Educational Achievement," *American Economic Review* (May 2016); and David Autor and others, "Males at the Tails: How Socioeconomic Status Shapes the Gender Gap," Blueprint Labs, May 2020.

63. Richard V. Reeves and Sarah Nzau, "Poverty Hurts the Boys the Most: Inequality at the Intersection of Class and Gender," Brookings Institution, June 14, 2021.

64. Sue Hubble, Paul Bolton, and Joe Lewis, "Equality of Access and Outcomes in Higher Education in England," Briefing Paper 9195 (June 2021).

65. Colter Mitchell and others, "Family Structure Instability, Genetic Sensitivity, and Child Well-Being," *American Journal of Sociology* (January 2015).

66. William J. Doherty, Brian J. Willoughby and Jason L. Wilde, "Is the Gender Gap in College Enrollment Influenced by Nonmarital Birth Rates and Father Absence?," *Family Relations* (April 2016).

67. Marianne Bertrand and Jessica Pan, "The Trouble with Boys: Social Influences and the Gender Gap in Disruptive Behavior," Working Paper 17541 (Cambridge, MA: National Bureau of Economic Research, October 2011), p. 1.

68. Cameron Taylor, "Who Gets a Family? The Consequences of Family and Group Home Allocation for Child Outcomes," (unpublished paper, December 2021). Based on his analysis, Taylor suggests paying higher stipends to families who foster boys.

69. Autor and Wasserman, "Wayward Sons," p. 50.

70. Corak, "'Inequality Is the Root of Social Evil,'" p. 400.

6. NON-RESPONDERS

1. Michelle Miller-Adams, "About the Kalamazoo Promise," W.E. Upjohn Institute for Employment Research, 2015.

2. Timothy J. Bartik, Brad J. Hershbein, and Marta Lachowska, "The Merits of Universal Scholarships: Benefit–Cost Evidence from the Kalamazoo Promise," *Journal of Benefit–Cost Analysis* (November 2016).

3. Richard V. Reeves and Ember Smith, "Zig-Zag Men, Straight Line Women: Young Adult Trajectories in the U.S.," Brookings Institution, forthcoming. See also quotes in Derek Thompson, "Colleges Have a Guy Problem," *The Atlantic*, September 14, 2021.

4. William N. Evans and others, "Increasing Community College Completion Rates among Low-Income Students: Evidence from a Randomized Controlled Trial Evaluation of a Case-Management Intervention," *Journal of Policy Analysis and Management* (Fall 2020).

5. National Center for Education Statistics, Integrated Postsecondary Education Data System (IPEDS), "12-Month Enrollment Component 2019–20 provisional data," 2021. For a class breakdown, see Richard V. Reeves and Katherine Guyot, "And Justice for All: Community Colleges Serving the Middle Class," Brookings Institution, June 13, 2019.

6. National Center for Education Statistics, "Percentage Distribution of First-Time, Full-Time Degree/Certificate-Seeking Students at 2-Year Postsecondary Institutions 3 Years after Entry, by Completion and Enrollment Status at First Institution Attended, Sex, Race/Ethnicity, and Control of Institution: Cohort Entry Years 2010 and 2015," October 2019.

7. William N. Evans and others, "Increasing Community College Completion Rates," pp. 1 and 20.

8. Personal communication with author.

9. Robert W. Fairlie, Florian Hoffmann, and Philip Oreopoulos, "A Community College Instructor Like Me: Race and Ethnicity Interactions in the Classroom," *American Economic Review* (August 2014). See also Daniel Oliver and others, "Minority Student and Teaching Assistant Interactions in STEM," *Economics of Education Review* (August 2021).

10. Michael L. Anderson, "Multiple Inference and Gender Differences in the Effects of Early Intervention: A Reevaluation of the Abecedarian, Perry Preschool, and Early Training Projects," *Journal of the American Statistical Association* (2008), p. 1481.

11. Jonathan Guryan, James S. Kim, and David M. Quinn, "Does Reading during the Summer Build Reading Skills? Evidence from a Randomized Experiment in 463 Classrooms," Working Paper 20689 (Cambridge, MA: National Bureau of Economic Research, November 2014), p. 18.

12. David J. Deming and others, "School Choice, School Quality, and Postsecondary Attainment," *American Economic Review* (March 2014), p. 1008.

13. Scott Carrell and Bruce Sacerdote, "Why Do College-Going Interventions Work?," *American Economic Journal: Applied Economics* (July 2017), p. 136.

14. Vilsa E. Curto and Roland G. Fryer Jr., "The Potential of Urban Boarding Schools for the Poor: Evidence from SEED," *Journal of Labor Economics* (January 2014), p. 82.

15. Susan Dynarski, "Building the Stock of College-Educated Labor," *Journal of Human Resources* (Summer 2008), p. 598.

16. Joshua Angrist, Daniel Lang, and Philip Oreopoulos, "Incentives and Services for College Achievement: Evidence from a Randomized Trial," *American Economic Journal: Applied Economics* (January 2009), p. 136.

17. Angrist, Lang, and Oreopoulos, "Incentives and Services for College Achievement," p. 161.

18. Susan Scrivener and others, "Doubling Graduation Rates: Three-Year Effects of CUNY's Accelerated Study in Associate Programs (ASAP) for Developmental Education Students" (New York, NY: MDRC, February 2015). For one study showing positive outcomes for boys from preschool, see Guthrie Gray-Lobe, Parag A. Pathak and Christopher R. Walters, "The Long-Term Effects of Universal Preschool in Boston," Working Paper 28756 (Cambridge, MA: National Bureau of Economic Research, May 2021).

19. Mark Twain, "Letter from Mark Twain," *Daily Alta California*, June 16, 1867, p. 1.

20. Cynthia Miller and others, "Expanding the Earned Income Tax Credit for Workers without Dependent Children: Interim Findings from the Paycheck Plus Demonstration in New York City" (MDRC, September 2017), p. 46.

21. Emilie Courtin and others, "The Health Effects of Expanding the Earned Income Tax Credit: Results from New York City," *Health Affairs* (July 2020).

22. Miller and others, "Expanding the Earned Income Tax Credit," p. 49.

23. Another pilot in Atlanta seems not to have boosted employment for either men or women, at least based on an interim report. See Cynthia Miller and others, "A More Generous Earned Income Tax Credit for Singles: Interim Findings from the Paycheck Plus Demonstration in Atlanta" (MDRC, March 2020).

24. Joint Committee on Taxation, "Estimated Budget Effects of the Revenue Provisions of Title XIII—Committee on Ways and Means, of H.R. 5376, The 'Build Back Better Act'" (Congress of the United States, November 2021).

25. Gene B. Sperling, "A Tax Proposal That Could Lift Millions Out of Poverty," *The Atlantic*, October 17, 2017. See also Chuck Marr and Chye-Ching Huang, "Strengthening the EITC for Childless Workers Would Promote Work and Reduce Poverty," Center on Budget and Policy Priorities, February 20, 2015.

26. Sheena McConnell and others, *Providing Public Workforce Services to Job Seekers: 15-Month Impact Findings on the WIA Adult and Dislocated Worker Programs* (Washington, DC: Mathematica Policy Research, May 2016). See also Harry J. Holzer, "Higher Education and Workforce Policy: Creating More Skilled Workers (and Jobs for Them to Fill)," Brookings Institution, April 6, 2015.

27. Sheila Maguire and others, "Tuning In to Local Labor Markets: Findings from the Sectoral Employment Impact Study," Public/Private Ventures (2010).

28. Carolyn J. Heinrich, Peter R. Mueser, and Kenneth R. Troske, *Workforce Investment Act Non-experimental Net Impact Evaluation* (Columbia, MD: IMPAQ, December 2008).

29. Howard S. Bloom and others, "The Benefits and Costs of JTPA Title II-A Programs: Key Findings from the National Job Training Partnership Act Study," *Journal of Human Resources* (June 1997), p. 564.

30. Sheila Maguire and others, "Job Training That Works: Findings from the Sectoral Employment Impact Study," Public/Private Ventures, *P/PV In Brief* 7 (May 2009).

31. Sheila Maguire and others, "Tuning In to Local Labor Markets."

32. NAFSA: Association of International Educators, "Trends in U.S. Study Abroad 2019–2020." Nationally, the number of U.S. students studying abroad for credit during the 2019–2020 academic year declined 53% from 347,099 students to 162,633 students.

33. Ashley Stipek, Elaina Loveland, and Catherine Morris, *Study Abroad Matters: Linking Higher Education to the Contemporary Workplace through International Experience* (Stamford, CT: Institute of International Education and American Institute for Foreign Study, 2009). See also Peter Schmidt, "Men and Women Differ in How They Decide to Study Abroad, Study Finds," *Chronicle of Higher Education*, November 6, 2009.

34. National Center for Education Statistics, "Number of U.S. Students Studying Abroad and Percentage Distribution, by Sex, Race/Ethnicity, and Other Selected Characteristics: Selected Years, 2000–01 through 2018–19" (January 2021).

35. Lucas Böttcher and others, "Gender Gap in the ERASMUS Mobility Program," *PLoS One* (February 2016).

36. Mark H. Salisbury, Michael B. Paulsen, and Ernest T. Pascarella, "To See the World or Stay at Home: Applying an Integrated Student Choice Model to Explore the Gender Gap in the Intent to Study Abroad," *Research in Higher Education* (November 2010), p. 631.

37. "Fast Facts," Peace Corps, September 30, 2019. For Americorps, see Eric Friedman and others, *New Methods for Assessing AmeriCorps Alumni Outcomes: Final Survey Technical Report* (Cambridge, MA: Corporation for National and Community Service, August 2016), p. 22.

38. Over the five years from 2017–2018 to 2021–2022, 66% of recruited volunteers to VSO (Voluntary Service Overseas) were women. Personal communication from Sophie Scott, March 23, 2022.

7. MAKING MEN

1. Scott Barry Kaufman, "Taking Sex Differences in Personality Seriously," *Scientific American*, December 12, 2019.

2. Rong Su, James Rounds, and Patrick Ian Armstrong, "Men and Things, Women and People: A Meta-Analysis of Sex Differences in Interests," *Psychological Bulletin* (November 2009).

3. Stuart J. Ritchie and others, "Sex Differences in the Adult Human Brain: Evidence from 5216 UK Biobank Participants," *Cerebral Cortex* (August 2018), p. 2967.

4. Louann Brizendine, *The Female Brain* (New York: Harmony, 2007), p. 6.

5. Gina Rippon, *The Gendered Brain: The New Neuroscience That Shatters the Myth of the Female Brain* (New York: Random House, 2019), p. 353.

6. Melvin Konner, *Women After All: Sex, Evolution, and the End of Male Supremacy* (New York: W.W. Norton, 2015), p. 12.

7. Bryan Sykes, "Do We Need Men?," *The Guardian*, August 27, 2003.

8. Konner, *Women After All*, p. 24

9. Alice Dreger, *Galileo's Middle Finger: Heretics, Activists, and One Scholar's Search for Justice* (New York: Penguin Books, 2016), p. 21.

10. Selma Feldman Witchel, "Disorders of Sex Development," *Best Practice & Research Clinical Obstetrics & Gynaecology* (April 2018). See also Dreger, *Galileo's Middle Finger*, p. 29.

11. Konner, *Women After All*, p. 30.

12. Konner, *Women After All*, p. 213.

13. Raymond H. Baillargeon and others, "Gender Differences in Physical Aggression: A Prospective Population-Based Survey of Children Before and After 2 Years of Age," *Developmental Psychology* (February 2007).

14. Lise Eliot, "Brain Development and Physical Aggression: How a Small Gender Difference Grows into a Violence Problem," *Current Anthropology* (February 2021).

15. United Nations Office on Drugs and Crime, *Global Study on Homicide 2013* (United Nations, 2013).

16. As neurobiologist Robert Sapolsky puts it, testosterone "exaggerates the aggression that is already there." See Robert Sapolsky, *The Trouble with Testosterone* (New York: Simon and Schuster, 1997), p. 155.

17. Carole Hooven, *Testosterone: The Story of the Hormone that Dominates and Divides Us* (London: Octopus Publishing Group, 2022), chap. 7.

18. Desmond Morris, *The Naked Ape: A Zoologist's Study of the Human Animal* (New York: Random House, 1994).

19. Joyce Benenson, *Warriors and Worriers: The Survival of the Sexes* (Oxford University Press, 2014).

20. Severi Luoto and Marco Antonio Correa Varella, "Pandemic Leadership: Sex Differences and Their Evolutionary–Developmental Origins," *Frontiers in Psychology* (March 2021), p. 618.

21. Jason A. Wilder, Zahra Mobasher, and Michael F. Hammer, "Genetic Evidence for Unequal Effective Population Sizes of Human Females and Males," *Molecular Biology and Evolution* (November 2004).

22. John Tierney, "The Missing Men in Your Family Tree," *New York Times*, September 5, 2007.

23. Roy Baumeister, "Is There Anything Good About Men?," paper presented at the 115th Annual Convention of the American Psychological Association, January 1, 2007.

24. Joseph Henrich, *The WEIRDest People in the World* (New York: Farrar, Straus and Giroux, 2020), p. 164.

25. Lena Edlund and others, "Sex Ratios and Crime: Evidence from China," *Review of Economics and Statistics* (December 2013).

26. Carnegie Hero Fund Commission, www.carnegiehero.org.

27. Margaret Mead, *Male and Female: A Study of the Sexes in a Changing World* (New York: Morrow, 1949). The quote is from the introduction to the 1962 Pelican Edition, p. xxvii.

28. Konner, *Women After All*, p. 211.

29. Roy F. Baumeister, Kathleen R. Catanese, and Kathleen D. Vohs, "Is There a Gender Difference in Strength of Sex Drive? Theoretical Views, Conceptual Distinctions, and a Review of Relevant Evidence," *Personality and Social Psychology Review* (August 2001), p. 242.

30. Marianne Legato, *Why Men Die First: How to Lengthen Your Lifespan* (London: Palgrave Macmillan, 2009), p. 109.

31. Henrich, *WEIRDest People in the World*, p. 165.

32. For estimates of prostitution in the U.S., see *Prostitution: Prices and Statistics of the Global Sex Trade*, report (Havocscope Books, 2015), and *Sexual Exploitation: New Challenges, New Answers*, report (Scelles Foundation, May 2019). There are 260,000 clergy in the U.S. according the Bureau of Labor Statistics. See Bureau of Labor Statistics, "Employed Persons by Detailed Occupation, Sex, Race, and Hispanic or Latino Ethnicity," 2020 Labor Force Statistics from the Current Population Survey, January 22, 2021.

33. Riccardo Ciacci and María Micaela Sviatschi, "The Effect of Adult Entertainment Establishments on Sex Crime: Evidence from New York City," *Economic Journal* (January 2022).

34. Meredith Dank and others, "Estimating the Size and Structure of the Underground Commercial Sex Economy in Eight Major US Cities," The Urban Institute, June 2016.

35. Juno Mac and Molly Smith, *Revolting Prostitutes: The Fight for Sex Workers' Rights* (London: Verso Books, 2018).

36. "The Earliest Pornography?," *Science*, May 13, 2009.

37. Miranda A. H. Horvath and others, *Basically . . . Porn Is Everywhere: A Rapid Evidence Assessment on the Effects That Access and Exposure to Pornography Has on Children and Young People* (London: Office of the Children's Commissioner, 2013).

38. David Gordon and others, *Relationships in America Survey* (Austin Institute for the Study of Family and Culture, 2014).

39. Chyng Sun and others, "Pornography and the Male Sexual Script: An Analysis of Consumption and Sexual Relations," *Archives of Sexual Behavior* (May 2016). See also Michael Castleman, "How Much Time Does the World Spend Watching Porn?," *Psychology Today*, October 31, 2020.

40. Kevin Mitchell, "Sex on the Brain," *Aeon*, September 25, 2019.

41. Sean R. Womack and others, "Genetic Moderation of the Association between Early Family Instability and Trajectories of Aggressive Behaviors from Middle Childhood to Adolescence," *Behavior Genetics* (September 2021). See also Sara Palumbo and others, "Genes and Aggressive Behavior: Epigenetic Mechanisms

Underlying Individual Susceptibility to Aversive Environments," *Frontiers in Behavioral Neuroscience* 12 (June 2018), p. 117.

42. Zachary Kaminsky and others, "Epigenetics of Personality Traits: An Illustrative Study of Identical Twins Discordant for Risk-Taking Behavior," *Twin Research and Human Genetics* (February 2008).

43. Colter Mitchell and others, "Family Structure Instability, Genetic Sensitivity, and Child Well-Being," *American Journal of Sociology* (January 2015).

44. Henrich, *The WEIRDest People in the World*, p. 5.

45. Henrich, *The WEIRDest People in the World*, p. 268.

46. Lee T. Gettler and others, "Longitudinal Evidence That Fatherhood Decreases Testosterone in Human Males," *Proceedings of the National Academy of Sciences* (September 2011), p. 16198.

47. Henrich, *The WEIRDest People in the World*, pp. 278–81.

48. Sherry B. Ortner, "Is Female to Male as Nature Is to Culture?," in *Women, Culture, and Society*, ed. Michealle Zimbalist Rosaldo and Louise Lamphere (Stanford University Press, 1974), pp. 74–5.

49. Anthony W. Clare, *On Men: Masculinity in Crisis* (London: Arrow, 2001), p. 1

50. Leonard Kriegel, *On Men and Manhood* (New York: Dutton Adult, 1979), p. 14.

51. David D. Gilmore, *Manhood in the Making: Cultural Concepts of Masculinity* (Yale University Press, 1991), p. 230.

52. Gilmore, *Manhood in the Making*, p. 106

53. William Shakespeare, *The Tragedy of Coriolanus*, Act 5, Scene 3.

54. Roy F. Baumeister, *The Cultural Animal: Human Nature, Meaning, and Social Life* (Oxford University Press, 2005), p. 7.

55. Margaret Mead, *Male and Female: A Study of the Sexes in a Changing World* (New York: Morrow, 1949), p. 189.

56. Brian Kennedy, Richard Fry, and Cary Funk, "6 Facts about America's STEM Workforce and Those Training for It," Pew Research Center, April 14, 2021.

57. Rong Su, "Men and Things," p. 859. See also Steve Stewart-Williams and Lewis G. Halsey, "Men, Women, and STEM: Why the Differences and What Should Be Done?," *European Journal of Personality* (2021), pp. 3–39.

58. Gijsbert Stoet and David C. Geary, "The Gender-Equality Paradox in Science, Technology, Engineering, and Mathematics Education," *Psychological Science* (2018), pp. 581–93. In a related study, Geary and Stoet find a similar pattern for sex differences in expected occupations among adolescents in OECD countries. Gijsbert Stoet and David C. Geary, "Sex Differences in Adolescents' Occupational Aspirations: Variations across Time and Place," *PLoS One* (2022), doi.org/10.1371/journal.pone.0261438.

59. Armin Falk and Johannes Hermle, "Relationship of Gender Differences in Preferences to Economic Development and Gender Equality," *Science*, October 19, 2018, p. 5.

60. University of Gothenburg, News Release, October 2, 2018, www.gu.se/en/news
     /personality-differences-between-the-sexes-are-largest-in-the-most-gender
     -equal-countries. For the main study, see Erik Mac Giolla and Petri J. Kajonius,
     "Sex Differences in Personality Are Larger in Gender Equal Countries: Repli-
     cating and Extending a Surprising Finding," *International Journal of Psychology*
     (December 2019).

61. Olga Khazan, "The More Gender Equality, the Fewer Women in STEM," *The
     Atlantic*, February 18, 2018.

62. Rong Su, "Men and Things," p. 859.

63. Rong Su and James Rounds, "All STEM Fields Are Not Created Equal: People
     and Things Interests Explain Gender Disparities across STEM Fields," *Frontiers
     in Psychology* (February 2015).

64. American Psychological Association, "About APA," www.apa.org/about.

65. Stephanie Pappas, "APA Issues First-Ever Guidelines for Practice with Men and
     Boys," American Psychological Association, 2019, p. 2. See also American Psy-
     chological Association, Boys and Men Guidelines Group, *APA Guidelines for Psy-
     chological Practice with Boys and Men* (2018).

66. Pappas, "APA Issues First-Ever Guidelines, pp. 2–3.

67. Leonard Sax, "Psychology as Indoctrination: Girls Rule, Boys Drool?," Institute
     for Family Studies, January 15, 2019.

68. American Psychological Association, Twitter post, January 2019, 5:21 PM.

69. American Psychological Association, *Guidelines for Psychological Practice with Girls
     and Women* (2007).

70. *Juvenile Justice in a Developmental Framework: A 2015 Status Report* (New York:
     MacArthur Foundation, 2015).

71. John Fergusson Roxburgh, *Eleutheros; or, The Future of the Public Schools* (London:
     Kegan Paul, 1930).

72. "Titanic: Demographics of the Passengers," www.icyousee.org/titanic.html.

8. PROGRESSIVE BLINDNESS

1. "Most Educated Counties in the US Map," Databayou, https://databayou.com
    /education/edu.html.

2. Alice Park and others, "An Extremely Detailed Map of the 2020 Election," *New
    York Times*, updated March 30, 2021.

3. Valerie Bonk, "Montgomery Co. Schools Add Third Gender Option for Stu-
    dents," *WTOP News*, August 24, 2019.

4. Lindsey Ashcraft and Scott Stump, "Teen Girls at Maryland High School Fight
    Back after Finding List Ranking Their Looks," *Today*, March 28, 2019; Cathe-
    rine Thorbecke, "After Male Classmates Rated Their Appearances, These Teen

Girls Sparked a Movement to Change the 'Boys Will Be Boys' Culture," ABC News, March 28, 2019; Samantha Schmidt, "Teen Boys Rated Their Female Classmates Based on Looks. The Girls Fought Back," *Washington Post*, March 26, 2019.

5. Carly Stern, "Female Students on Hot or Not List Demand More Action from School," *Daily Mail*, November 8, 2021.

6. I am not going to name any of those involved here.

7. "First Amendment and Freedom," C-SPAN, December 17, 2019.

8. See, for example, Frank Pittman, *Man Enough: Fathers, Sons, and the Search for Masculinity* (New York: Putnam, 1993), and T. A. Kupers, "Toxic Masculinity as a Barrier to Mental Health Treatment in Prison," *Journal of Clinical Psychology* (June 2005). Kupers used the term to label "the constellation of socially regressive male traits that serve to foster domination, the devaluation of women, homophobia, and wanton violence," p. 714.

9. Carol Harrington, "What Is 'Toxic Masculinity' and Why Does It Matter?," *Men and Masculinities* (July 2020), p. 2.

10. Amanda Marcotte, "Overcompensation Nation: It's Time to Admit That Toxic Masculinity Drives Gun Violence," Salon, June 23, 2016.

11. Eldra Jackson III, "How Men at New Folsom Prison Reckon with Toxic Masculinity," *Los Angeles Times*, November 30, 2017.

12. Maggie Koerth, "Science Says Toxic Masculinity—More Than Alcohol—Leads to Sexual Assault," FiveThirtyEight, September 26, 2018.

13. Rachel Hosie, "Woke Daddy: The Feminist Dad Challenging Toxic Masculinity and Facing Right-Wing Abuse," *Independent,* June 20, 2017.

14. Danielle Paquette, "Toxic Masculinity Is Literally Bad for the Planet, According to Research," *Sydney Morning Herald*, September 1, 2016.

15. Dan Hirschman, "Did Bros Cause the Financial Crisis? Hegemonic Masculinity in the Big Short," *Scatterplot* (blog), August 27, 2016.

16. James Millar, "The Brexiteers Represent the Four Faces of Toxic Masculinity," *New Statesman*, July 5, 2018.

17. Jared Yates Sexton, "Donald Trump's Toxic Masculinity," *New York Times*, October 13, 2016.

18. Alisha Haridasani Gupta, "How an Aversion to Masks Stems from 'Toxic Masculinity,'" *New York Times*, October 22, 2020.

19. Peggy Orenstein, "The Miseducation of the American Boy," *The Atlantic*, January 2020.

20. Dan Cassino and Yasemin Besen-Cassino, "Of Masks and Men? Gender, Sex, and Protective Measures during COVID-19," *Politics & Gender* (August 2020). Note that there are some partisan differences in the strength of gender identity. Republican men and women are more likely to see themselves as "completely" masculine and feminine; Democrats and Independents are more likely to see themselves as "mostly" masculine or feminine.

21. Kim Parker, Juliana Menasce Horowitz, and Renee Stepler, "On Gender Differences, No Consensus on Nature vs. Nurture," Pew Research Center, December 2017.

22. Helen Lewis, "To Learn about the Far Right, Start with the 'Manosphere,'" *The Atlantic*, August 7, 2019.

23. PRRI Staff, "Dueling Realities: Amid Multiple Crises, Trump and Biden Supporters See Different Priorities and Futures for the Nation," PRRI, October 19, 2020.

24. PRRI Staff, "Dueling Realities." The precise figures are 60% and 63% agreeing to each question respectively among Republicans, compared to 24% and 23% among Democrats.

25. Catherine Morris, "Less Than a Third of American Women Identify as Feminists," Ipsos, November 25, 2019. There were large partisan differences, however: 48% of Democratic women adopted the feminist label, compared to just 13% of Republican women.

26. "Feminism: Fieldwork Dates: 3rd–6th August 2018," YouGov, August 2018.

27. ContraPoints, "Men," YouTube (video), August 23, 2019.

28. The Sex, Gender and COVID-19 Project, "The COVID-19 Sex-Disaggregated Data Tracker," Global Health 50/50, October 27, 2021.

29. Richard V. Reeves and Beyond Deng, "At Least 65,000 More Men Than Women Have Died from COVID-19 in the US," Brookings Institution, October 19, 2021. Figures updated from CDC.

30. José Manuel Aburto and others, "Quantifying Impacts of the COVID-19 Pandemic through Life-Expectancy Losses: A Population-Level Study of 29 Countries," *International Journal of Epidemiology* (September 2021).

31. UK Office for National Statistics, "Coronavirus (COVID-19) Related Deaths by Occupation, England and Wales: Deaths Registered between 9 March and 28 December 2020."

32. "The Vast Majority of Programmatic Activity to Prevent and Address the Health Impacts of COVID-19 Largely Ignores the Role of Gender," in *Gender Equality: Flying Blind in a Time of Crisis*, report (Global Health 50/50, 2021), p. 18.

33. George M. Bwire, "Coronavirus: Why Men Are More Vulnerable to COVID-19 Than Women," *SN Comprehensive Clinical Medicine* (June 2020).

34. Joanne Michelle D. Gomez and others, "Sex Differences in COVID-19 Hospitalization and Mortality," *Journal of Women's Health* (April 2021). See also Lina Ya'qoub, Islam Y. Elgendy, and Carl J. Pepine, "Sex and Gender Differences in COVID-19: More to Be Learned!," *American Heart Journal Plus: Cardiology Research and Practice* (2021); and Hannah Peckham and others, "Male Sex Identified by Global COVID-19 Meta-analysis as a Risk Factor for Death and ITU Admission," *Nature Communications* (December 9, 2020).

35. Marianne J. Legato, "The Weaker Sex," *New York Times*, June 17, 2006. See also her book, *Why Men Die First: How to Lengthen Your Lifespan* (London: Palgrave Macmillan, 2009).

36. Department of Health and Human Services, Fiscal Year 2022, www.hhs.gov /sites/default/files/fy2022-gdm-operating-plan.pdf.

37. Luke Turner, "Putting Men in the Frame: Images of a New Masculinity," *The Guardian*, February 16, 2020.

38. Kathryn Paige Harden, "Why Progressives Should Embrace the Genetics of Education," *New York Times*, July 24, 2018. The second quote is from her book *The Genetic Lottery: Why DNA Matters for Social Equality* (Princeton University Press, 2022), p. 179.

39. Raymond H. Baillargeon and others, "Gender Differences in Physical Aggression: A Prospective Population-Based Survey of Children Before and After 2 Years of Age," *Developmental Psychology* (January 2007).

40. Kate Manne, *Down Girl: The Logic of Misogyny* (New York: Oxford University Press, 2017), p. 79.

41. See, for example, Melvin Konner, *Women After All* (New York: W.W. Norton, 2015) and Daniel Amen, *Unleash the Power of the Female Brain: Supercharging Yours for Better Health, Energy, Mood, Focus, and Sex* (New York: Harmony, 2013).

42. Steve Stewart-Williams and others, "Reactions to Male-Favouring versus Female-Favouring Sex Differences: A Pre-registered Experiment and Southeast Asian Replication," *British Journal of Psychology* (July 2020).

43. Alice H. Eagly and Antonio Mladinic, "Are People Prejudiced against Women? Some Answers from Research on Attitudes, Gender Stereotypes, and Judgments of Competence," *European Review of Social Psychology* (1994), p. 13.

44. Konner, *Women After All*, p. 228.

45. Erin Spencer Sairam, "Biden, Harris Form a White House Gender Policy Council," *Forbes*, January 22, 2021.

46. National Strategy on Gender Equity and Equality, October 2021, https://www .whitehouse.gov/wp-content/uploads/2021/10/National-Strategy-on-Gender -Equity-and-Equality.pdf.

47. National Center for Education Statistics, "Table 233.28. Percentage of Students Receiving Selected Disciplinary Actions in Public Elementary and Secondary Schools, by Type of Disciplinary Action, Disability Status, Sex, and Race/ Ethnicity: 2013–14," U.S. Department of Education.

48. "Uninsured Rates for Nonelderly Adults by Sex 2019," Kaiser Family Foundation, State Health Facts.

49. "Fact Sheet: National Strategy on Gender Equity and Equality," The White House, October 22, 2021.

50. Helen Lewis, "The Coronavirus Is a Disaster for Feminism," *The Atlantic*, March 19, 2020.

51. Alicia Sasser Modestino, "Coronavirus Child-Care Crisis Will Set Women Back a Generation," *Washington Post*, July 29, 2020.

52. Email sent December 2, 2020, "Let's Fast Track for Gender Equity and Justice in the U.S. and Globally."

53. *Global Gender Gap Report 2021* (Geneva, Switzerland: World Economic Forum, 2021).

54. Richard Reeves and Fariha Haque, *Measuring Gender Equality: A Modified Approach* (Brookings Institution, forthcoming 2022).

55. Francisco Ferreira, "Are Men the New Weaker Sex? The Rise of the Reverse Gender Gap in Education," World Bank, June 26, 2018.

56. Hanna Rosin, "New Data on the Rise of Women," TED talk (video), December 2010.

9. SEEING RED

1. Josh Hawley, "Senator Hawley Delivers National Conservatism Keynote on the Left's Attack on Men in America," November 1, 2021, www.hawley.senate.gov/senator-hawley-delivers-national-conservatism-keynote-lefts-attack-men-america.

2. Daniel Villarreal, "Defense Bill Will Not Require Women to Sign Up for Draft After All," *Newsweek*, December 6, 2021.

3. Danielle Paquette, "The Unexpected Voters Behind the Widest Gender Gap in Recorded Election History," *Washington Post*, November 9, 2016.

4. Pew Research Center, "For Most Trump Voters, 'Very Warm' Feelings for Him Endure: An examination of the 2016 electorate, based on validated voters," August 9, 2018.

5. Paquette, "The Unexpected Voters," *Washington Post*, November 9, 2016.

6. Jane Green and Rosaline Shorrocks, "The Gender Backlash in the Vote for Brexit," *Political Behavior* (April 2021).

7. Jeremy Diamond, "Trump Says It's 'A Very Scary Time for Young Men in America,'" CNN, October 2, 2018.

8. PRRI, "Better or Worse Since the 1950s? Trump and Clinton Supporters at Odds over the Past and Future of the Country," October 25, 2016.

9. Evan Osnos, *Wildland: The Making of America's Fury* (New York: Farrar, Straus and Giroux, 2021), p. 256.

10. Pankaj Mishra, "The Crisis in Modern Masculinity," *The Guardian*, March 17, 2018.

11. "Men Adrift: Badly Educated Men in Rich Countries Have Not Adapted Well to Trade, Technology or Feminism," *The Economist*, May 28, 2015.

12. "The Anti-Immigrant Sweden Democrats Fail to Break Through," *The Economist*, September 13, 2018.

13. Katrin Bennhold, "One Legacy of Merkel? Angry East German Men Fueling the Far Right," *New York Times*, November 5, 2018.

14. S. Nathan Park, "Inside South Korea's Incel Election," UnHerd, February 16, 2022.

15. Raphael Rashid, "'Devastated': Gender Equality Hopes on Hold as 'Anti-feminist' Voted South Korea's President," *The Guardian*, March 11, 2022.

16. India Today, "Pakistan's Imran Khan Says Feminism Has Degraded the Role of a Mother," June 18, 2018. See also Siobhan O'Grady, "Erdogan Tells Feminist Summit That Women Aren't Equal to Men," *Foreign Policy*, November 24, 2014; Felipe Villamor, "Duterte Jokes About Rape, Again. Philippine Women Aren't Laughing," *New York Times*, August 31, 2018.

17. Ed West, "How Single Men and Women Are Making Politics More Extreme," *The Week*, August 4, 2017.

18. Christina Hoff Sommers, *The War Against Boys: How Misguided Feminism Is Harming Our Young Men* (New York: Simon & Schuster, 2001). See also Suzanne Venker, *The War on Men* (Chicago: WND Books, 2016).

19. Raphael Rashid, "South Korean Presidential Hopefuls Push Anti-feminist Agenda," *Nikkei Asia*, November 24, 2021.

20. Dan Cassino, "Why More American Men Feel Discriminated Against," *Harvard Business Review*, September 29, 2016.

21. Andrew Rafferty, "Cruz Attacks Trump for Transgender Bathroom Comments," NBC News, April 21, 2016.

22. Jeffrey M. Jones, "LGBT Identification Rises to 5.6% in Latest U.S. Estimate," Gallup, February 24, 2021.

23. Supreme Court of the United States, *Bostock v. Clayton County, Georgia*: Certiorari to the United States Court of Appeals for the Eleventh Circuit, No. 17–1618—Decided June 15, 2020, p. 1.

24. Lara Jakes, "M, F or X? American Passports Will Soon Have Another Option for Gender," *New York Times*, June 30, 2021.

25. Movement Advancement Project, "Equality Maps: Identity Document Laws and Policies," March 3, 2022, www.lgbtmap.org/equality-maps/identity_document _laws.

26. Laura Bates, *Men Who Hate Women* (London: Simon & Schuster, 2021), p. 10.

27. David Brooks, "The Jordan Peterson Moment," *New York Times*, January 25, 2018.

28. Jordan B. Peterson, *12 Rules for Life: An Antidote to Chaos* (New York: Penguin, 2018). See also Zack Beauchamp, "Jordan Peterson, the Obscure Canadian Psychologist Turned Right-Wing Celebrity, Explained," *Vox*, May 21, 2018.

29. "Jordan Peterson Explains His Theory of Lobster and Men," YouTube (video), January 31, 2018.

30. Robert Bly, *Iron John: A Book about Men*, 25th Anniversary Edition (Boston: Da Capo Press, 2004), pp. 2 and 6.

31. Geoff Dench, *Transforming Men: Changing Patterns of Dependency and Dominance in Gender Relations* (New Brunswick, NJ: Transaction, 1996).

32. "Jordan Peterson Debate on the Gender Pay Gap, Campus Protests and Postmodernism," *Channel 4 News*, January 16, 2018.

33. Henry Mance, "Jordan Peterson: 'One Thing I'm Not Is Naïve,'" *Financial Times*, June 1, 2018.

34. Charles Murray, *Human Diversity* (New York: Hachette, 2020), p. 302.

35. Juliana Menasce Horowitz and Ruth Igielnik, "A Century after Women Gained the Right to Vote, Majority of Americans See Work to Do on Gender Equality," Pew Research Center, July 7, 2020.

36. Dan Cassino, "Even the Thought of Earning Less Than Their Wives Changes How Men Behave," *Harvard Business Review*, April 19, 2016.

37. George Gilder, *Men and Marriage* (Gretna, LA: Pelican, 1992), p. 81.

38. Katie Hafner, "The Revolution Is Coming, Eventually," *New York Times*, October 19, 2003.

39. Gilder, *Men and Marriage*, pp. 13–15.

40. Dench, *Transforming Men*, p. 16.

41. Wendy Wang, Kim Parker, and Paul Taylor, "Breadwinner Moms," Pew Research Center, May 29, 2013. See also Pew Research Center, "The Harried Life of the Working Mother," October 1, 2009.

42. Arthur Schlesinger Jr., "The Crisis of American Masculinity," *Esquire Classic*, November 1, 1958.

43. Margaret Mead, *Some Personal Views* (New York: Walker, 1979), p. 48.

44. Ayaan Hirsi Ali, *Prey: Immigration, Islam, and the Erosion of Women's Rights* (New York: HarperCollins, 2021), pp. 242–43.

10. REDSHIRT THE BOYS

1. Margaret Mead, *Some Personal Views* (New York: Walker, 1979), p. 43. She wrote this in response to a reader question in *Redbook* magazine in October 1974.

2. Malcolm Gladwell, *Outliers: The Story of Success* (Boston: Little, Brown, 2008), p. 8.

3. EdChoice, "The Public, Parents, and K–12 Education," Morning Consult, September 2021.

4. EdChoice, "Teachers and K–12 Education: A National Polling Report," Morning Consult, October 2021 [conducted September 10–19, 2021], p. 19.

5. Diane Whitmore Schanzenbach and Stephanie Howard Larson, "Is Your Child Ready for Kindergarten?," *Education Next* (April 17, 2017).

6. Daphna Bassok and Sean F. Reardon, "'Academic Redshirting' in Kindergarten: Prevalence, Patterns & Implications," *Educational Evaluation and Policy Analysis* (February 2013). For data on teachers, I am drawing on the RAND poll of educators, which in fall 2021 included at my request some questions on redshirting. Teachers were three times as likely to have delayed school entry for their sons as for their daughters.

7. Schanzenbach and Larson, "Is Your Child Ready."

8. Bassok and Reardon, "'Academic Redshirting' in Kindergarten."

9. Thomas S. Dee and Hans Henrik Sieversten, "The Gift of Time? School Starting Age and Mental Health," Working Paper 21610 (Cambridge, MA: National Bureau of Economic Research, October 2015). See also Suzanne Stateler Jones, "Academic

Red-Shirting: Perceived Life Satisfaction of Adolescent Males," Texas A&M University, dissertation (May 2012). See also David Deming and Susan Dynarski, "The Lengthening of Childhood," *Journal of Economic Perspectives* (Summer 2008).

10. Elizabeth U. Cascio and Diane Whitmore Schanzenbach, "First in the Class? Age and the Education Production Function," *Education Finance and Policy* (Summer 2016), p. 244.

11. National Center for Education Statistics, "Table 17a. Percentage of Public School Students in Kindergarten through Grade 12 Who Had Ever Repeated a Grade, by Sex and Race/Ethnicity: 2007" (July 2010). See also Nancy Frey, "Retention, Social Promotion, and Academic Redshirting: What Do We Know and Need to Know?," *Special Education* (November 2005).

12. Philip J. Cook and Songman Kang, "The School-Entry-Age Rule Affects Redshirting Patterns and Resulting Disparities in Achievement," Working Paper 24492 (Cambridge, MA: National Bureau of Economic Research, April 2018).

13. Stateler Jones, "Academic Red-Shirting." See also Jennifer Gonzalez, "Kindergarten Redshirting: How Kids Feel about It Later in Life," *Cult of Pedagogy*, April 24, 2016.

14. William Ellery Samuels and others, "Predicting GPAs with Executive Functioning Assessed by Teachers and by Adolescents Themselves," *European Educational Researcher* (October 2019).

15. Deming and Dynarski, "The Lengthening of Childhood," p. 86.

16. Education Commission of the States, "Compulsory School Attendance Laws, Minimum and Maximum Age Limits for Required Free Education, by State: 2017," National Center for Education Statistics, nces.ed.gov/programs/state reform/tab1_2-2020.asp.

17. Deming and Dynarski, "The Lengthening of Childhood," p. 86.

18. Richard V. Reeves, Eliana Buckner, and Ember Smith, "The Unreported Gender Gap in High School Graduation Rates," Brookings Institution, January 12, 2021.

19. National Center for Education Statistics, "Graduation Rate from First Institution Attended within 150 Percent of Normal Time for First-Time, Full-Time Degree/Certificate-Seeking Students at 2-Year Postsecondary Institutions, by Race/Ethnicity, Sex, and Control of Institution: Selected Cohort Entry Years, 2000 through 2016" (August 2020).

20. Kristen Lewis, "A Decade Undone: 2021 Update," Measure of America of the Social Science Research Council (July 2021).

21. U.S. Equal Employment Opportunity Commission, "Title VII of the Civil Rights Act of 1964."

22. *United States v. Virginia et al.*, 518 U.S. 515 (1996), p. 517.

23. For the class of 2021, there were 60 female cadets and 420 male cadets. See "Enrollment Summary Fall 2017," Virginia Military Institute.

24. *United States v. Virginia et al.*, p. 515.

25. OECD, "The ABC of Gender Equality in Education: Aptitude, Behaviour, Confidence" (Paris: OECD Publishing, 2015).

26. National Center for Education Statistics, "Number of Students Receiving Selected Disciplinary Actions in Public Elementary and Secondary Schools, by Type of Disciplinary Action, Disability Status, Sex, and Race/Ethnicity: 2013–14."

27. National Center for Education Statistics, "Table 233.20, Percentage of Public School Students in Grades 6 through 12 Who Had Ever Been Suspended or Expelled, by Race/Ethnicity and Sex: Selected Years, 1993 through 2019." For the trend, see Richard M. Ingersoll and others, "Seven Trends: The Transformation of the Teaching Force—Updated October 2018," University of Pennsylvania, CPRE Research Reports, 2018.

28. Education and training statistics for the UK, "Full-Time Equivalent Number of Teachers for 'Teacher Numbers' for Primary, Secondary, Total Maintained, Female and Male in England, Northern Ireland, Scotland, United Kingdom and Wales between 2015/16 and 2019/20." See also Kim Hyun-bin, "Male Teachers Become Rare Breed," *Korea Times*, March 15, 2018.

29. Ingersoll and others, "Seven Trends," p. 14.

30. Quoted in Nathan Hegedus, "In Praise of the Dude Teaching at My Son's Preschool," Huffington Post, March 19, 2012.

31. Thomas S. Dee, "The Why Chromosome: How a Teacher's Gender Affects Boys and Girls," *Education Next* (Fall 2006). See also Sari Mullola and others, "Gender Differences in Teachers' Perceptions of Students' Temperament, Educational Competence, and Teachability," *British Journal of Educational Psychology* (2012).

32. Lauren Sartain and others, "When Girls Outperform Boys: The Gender Gap in High School Math Grades," University of North Carolina, 2022.

33. Ursina Schaede and Ville Mankki, "Quota vs Quality? Long-Term Gains from an Unusual Gender Quota," Working Paper presented to the Public Economics Program Meeting of the National Bureau of Economic Research, Spring 2022.

34. Siri Terjesen, Ruth V. Aguilera, and Ruth Lorenz, "Legislating a Woman's Seat on the Board: Institutional Factors Driving Gender Quotas for Boards of Directors," *Journal of Business Ethics* (February 2014).

35. Dee, "The Why Chromosome." See also Sari Mullola and others, "Gender Differences in Teachers' Perceptions of Students' Temperament, Educational Competence, and Teachability," *British Journal of Educational Psychology* (2012).

36. Seth Gershenson and others, "The Long-Run Impacts of Same-Race Teachers," Working Paper 25254 (Cambridge, MA: National Bureau of Economic Research, November, 2018, revised February 2021).

37. Lisette Partelow, "What to Make of Declining Enrollment in Teacher Preparation Programs," Center for American Progress, December 3, 2019.

38. National Center for Education Statistics, "Table 313.20, Full-Time Faculty in Degree-Granting Postsecondary Institutions, by Race/Ethnicity, Sex, and Academic Rank: Fall 2017, Fall 2018, and Fall 2019."

39. Jacqueline Bichsel and Jasper McChesney, "The Gender Pay Gap and the Representation of Women in Higher Education Administrative Positions: The Century So Far," College and University Professional Association for Human Resources, February 2017.

40. Melissa Trotta, "The Future of Higher Education Leadership," Association of Governing Boards of Universities and Colleges, September 14, 2021.

41. "Employed Persons by Detailed Occupation, Sex, Race, and Hispanic or Latino Ethnicity," U.S. Bureau of Labor Statistics.

42. Women account for 7% of pilots and 12% of navigators in the U.S. Air Force. See Air Force Personnel Center, "Air Force Active Duty Demographics," current as of September 30, 2021.

43. Kirsten Cole and others, "Building a Gender-Balanced Workforce," *Young Children* (September 2019).

44. Alia Wong, "The U.S. Teaching Population Is Getting Bigger, and More Female," *The Atlantic*, February 20, 2019.

45. See note 27.

46. Christina A. Samuels, "Building a Community for Black Male Teachers," *EdWeek*, February 17, 2021.

47. Esteban M. Aucejo and Jonathan James, "The Path to College Education: The Role of Math and Verbal Skills," *Journal of Political Economy* (January 2019).

48. See note 27.

49. Anthony P. Carnevale, Ban Cheah, and Emma Wenzinger, "The College Payoff: More Education Doesn't Always Mean More Earnings," Georgetown University Center on Education and the Workforce, 2021.

50. Bureau of Labor Statistics, "Employed Persons by Detailed Occupation, Sex, Race, and Hispanic or Latino Ethnicity," 2020 Labor Force Statistics from the Current Population Survey, January 22, 2021.

51. Fredrik deBoer, *The Cult of Smart: How Our Broken Education System Perpetuates Social Injustice* (New York: All Points Books, 2020).

52. Gijsbert Stoet and David C. Geary, "Gender Differences in the Pathways to Higher Education," *Proceedings of the National Academy of Sciences* (June 2020).

53. National Center for Education Statistics, "Table H175, Average Number of Credits and Percentage of Total Credits Public High School Graduates Earned in Each Curricular and Subject Area: 1992, 2004, and 2013."

54. Oren Cass, "How the Other Half Learns: Reorienting an Education System That Fails Most Students," Manhattan Institute, August 2018.

55. Joseph Fishkin, *Bottlenecks: A New Theory of Equal Opportunity* (Oxford University Press, 2014).

56. National Career Academy Coalition, "Career Academies Change Lives Every Day."

57. James J. Kemple with Cynthia J. Willner, "Career Academies: Long-Term Impacts on Labor Market Outcomes, Educational Attainment, and Transitions to Adulthood," MDRC, June 2008.

58. Eric Brunner, Shaun Dougherty, and Stephen L. Ross, "The Effects of Career and Technical Education: Evidence from the Connecticut Technical High School System," Working Paper 28790 (Cambridge, MA: National Bureau of Economic Research, May 2021).

59. Marianne Bertrand, Magne Mogstad, and Jack Mountjoy, "Improving Educational Pathways to Social Mobility: Evidence from Norway's 'Reform 94,'" Working Paper 25679 (Cambridge, MA: National Bureau of Economic Research, March 2019), p. 42.

60. Brian A. Jacob, "What We Know about Career and Technical Education in High School," Brookings Institution, October 7, 2017.

61. Perkins Collaborative Resource Network, www.cte.ed.gov/legislation/perkins-v.

62. DataLab, "Federal Investment in Higher Education," 2018.

63. National Center for Education Statistics, "Educational Institutions," Fast Facts, 2017–18.

64. Lucinda Gray, Laurie Lewis, and John Ralph, "Career and Technical Education Programs in Public School Districts: 2016–17," U.S. Department of Education, April 2018.

65. My $4 billion estimate is likely at the high end. The average high school has 847 students. I assume a federal government subsidy for the new technical schools of $5,000 per student (more than the $4,000 additional cost reported in Connecticut, a more expensive state than most). $1,000 \times 847 \times \$5,000 = \$4.2$ billion.

66. Education and Labor Committee, "Chairman Scott Praises Passage of the National Apprenticeship Act of 2021," press release, U.S. House of Representatives, February 5, 2021.

67. U.S. Department of Labor, "Data and Statistics: Registered Apprenticeship National Results Fiscal Year 2020," 2020. For international comparisons, see OECD/ILO, *Engaging Employers in Apprenticeship Opportunities* (2017), fig. 1.2.

68. Harry J. Holzer and Zeyu Xu, "Community College Pathways for Disadvantaged Students," *Community College Review* (April 15, 2021).

69. For a detailed proposal along these lines, see Austan Goolsbee and others, *A Policy Agenda to Develop Human Capital for the Modern Economy*, Aspen Economic Strategy Group, 2019.

70. Cass, "How the Other Half Learns," pp. 5–6.

71. Scottish Funding Council, "Gender Action Plan Annual Progress Report," January 30, 2019.

72. C. Kirabo Jackson, "The Effect of Single-Sex Education on Test Scores, School Completion, Arrests, and Teen Motherhood: Evidence from School Transitions," Working Paper 22222 (Cambridge, MA: National Bureau of Economic Research, May 2016).

73. Erin Pahlke, Janet Shibley Hyde, and Carlie M. Allison, "The Effects of Single-Sex Compared with Coeducational Schooling on Students' Performance and Attitudes: A Meta-Analysis," *Psychological Bulletin* (2014).

74. Michael Gurian and Patricia Henley with Terry Trueman, *Boys and Girls Learn Differently! A Guide for Teachers and Parents* (San Francisco: Jossey Bass, 2002).

11. MEN CAN HEAL

1. Margarita Torre, "Stopgappers? The Occupational Trajectories of Men in Female-Dominated Occupations," *Work and Occupations* (June 2018).
2. Gloria Steinem, *The Truth Will Set You Free, But First It Will Piss You Off!* (New York: Random House, 2019), p. 64.
3. Jerome Christenson, "Ramaley Coined STEM Term Now Used Nationwide," *Winona Daily News*, November 13, 2011.
4. According to the 2018 Standard Occupation Classification codes in the IPUMS American Community Survey data, the specific occupation "mathematicians" is grouped in with "Other mathematical science occupations" and "statisticians." Unless otherwise stated, all occupational analyses in this chapter are for prime age (25–54) full-time, year-round, civilian employees, with positive earnings, in 2019. Employment projections are from Bureau of Labor Statistics, "Occupational Projections, 2020–30, and Worker Characteristics, 2020," Table 1.7.
5. In defining HEAL occupations, I follow closely the approach taken by the Census Bureau in defining STEM as recommended by the Standard Occupational Classification (SOC) Policy Committee in 2012. See "Options for defining STEM occupations under the 2010 SOC system," Bureau of Labor Statistics, August 2012. For more details of my approach see Richard Reeves and Beyond Deng, "Women in STEM, Men in HEAL: Jobs for the Future," Brookings Institution, forthcoming 2022.
6. Note that women now make up the majority (64%) of social scientists, who are included in the STEM category.
7. The occupation category of social workers includes four subcategories: Child, Family, and School Social Workers; Healthcare Social Workers; Mental Health and Substance Abuse Social Workers; and All Other Social Workers. See also Jack Fischl, "Almost 82 Percent of Social Workers Are Female, and This Is Hurting Men," Mic, March 25, 2013.
8. David J. Deming, "The Growing Importance of Social Skills in the Labor Market," *Quarterly Journal of Economics* (November 2017), p. 1593.
9. Note that the BLS projections, on which these analyses are based, use a slightly different sample than the American Community Survey results I present elsewhere. See BLS, Table 1.7, "Occupational Projections, 2020–30, and Worker Characteristics," 2020. For more details, see Reeves and Deng, "Women in STEM, Men in HEAL."
10. All these earnings figures are at the median for prime age, full-time workers in these occupations in 2019.

11. U.S Department of Health and Human Services, Health Resources and Services Administration, *2018 National Sample Survey of Registered Nurses*.

12. Bureau of Labor Statistics, "Occupational Projections, 2020–30, and Worker Characteristics, 2020," table 1.7.

13. University of St. Augustine for Health Sciences, "Nurse Burnout: Risks, Causes, and Precautions," July 2020.

14. Louis Pilla, "This Might Hurt a Bit: The Chronic Nursing Shortage Is Now Acute," *Daily Nurse*, July 22, 2021.

15. Ernest Grant, letter to Honorable Xavier Becerra, Secretary, Department of Health and Human Services, American Nurses Association, September 1, 2021, p. 1.

16. Michael Topchik and others, *Crises Collide: The COVID-19 Pandemic and the Stability of the Rural Health Safety Net* (The Chartis Group, 2021). The specific figures I cite do not appear in the main report, but are in the full results of the survey, provided to me by Chartis and as reported by Dylan Scott, "Why the US Nursing Crisis Is Getting Worse," *Vox*, November 8, 2021.

17. Amandad Perkins, "Nursing Shortage: Consequences and Solutions," *Nursing Made Incredibly Easy* (September/October 2021).

18. Annie Buttner, "The Teacher Shortage, 2021 Edition," *Frontline Education*, April 19, 2021.

19. Rafael Heller and Teresa Preston, "Teaching: Respect but Dwindling Appeal," Kappan, September 2018.

20. Lisette Partelow, "What to Make of Declining Enrollment in Teacher Preparation Programs," Center for American Progress, December 3, 2019.

21. Morgan Lee and Cedar Attanasio, "New Mexico Asks Guard to Sub for Sick Teachers amid Omicron," AP News, January 19, 2022; David Schuman, "Twin Cities School Seeks Parents to Alleviate Substitute Teacher Shortage," CBS Minnesota, October 5, 2021; Justin Matthews, "60 International Educators Hired to Fill Teacher Shortages in Polk County," Fox 13 News Tampa Bay, October 11, 2021.

22. David Wimer and Ronald F. Levant, "The Relation of Masculinity and Help-Seeking Style with the Academic Help-Seeking Behavior of College Men," *Journal of Men's Studies* (October 2011).

23. Lea Winerman, "Helping Men to Help Themselves," American Psychological Association, June 2005.

24. Benedict Carey, "Need Therapy? A Good Man Is Hard to Find," *New York Times*, May 11, 2011.

25. For substance abuse, see SAMHSA Treatment Episode Data Set (TEDS), "Gender Differences in Primary Substance of Abuse across Age Groups" (2011). For special education, see "Students with Disabilities, Preprimary, Elementary, and Secondary Education," National Center for Education Statistics (May 2021).

26. Melinda French Gates, "Here's Why I'm Committing $1 Billion to Promote Gender Equality," *TIME*, October 5, 2019.

27. Building Blocks of STEM Act, Senate Report 116-78, Report of the Committee on Commerce, Science, and Transportation (August 2019), p. 7.

28. National Science Foundation, "Organizational Change for Gender Equity in STEM Academic Professions," NSF 20-057, March 10, 2020.

29. Financial data on the Society of Women Engineers are from Guidestar for Fiscal Year 2019. See www.guidestar.org/profile/13-1947735. Staff data from the SWE website. Both accessed March 28, 2022.

30. American Association for Men in Nursing, "Who We Are."

31. National Girls Collaborative Project, *Annual Report 2021*, p. 17.

32. See NSF awards 0631789 ($1.5 million) and 1103073 ($3 million).

33. Million Girls Moonshot, "Our Mission."

34. National Center for Education Statistics, "Table 318.30, Bachelor's, Master's, and Doctor's Degrees Conferred by Postsecondary Institutions, by Sex of Student and Discipline Division: 2017–18."

35. Specifically, 9th graders, according to data collected from 2009 to 2012. National Center for Education Statistics, "Data Point: Male and Female High School Students' Expectations for Working in a Health-Related Field," June 2020.

36. "Career and Technical Education: A Path to Economic Growth," in *Title IX at 45: Advancing Opportunity through Equity in Education* (Washington, DC: National Coalition for Women and Girls in Education, 2017), p. 6.

37. Mariah Bohanon, "Men in Nursing: A Crucial Profession Continues to Lack Gender Diversity," *INSIGHT Into Diversity*, January 8, 2019.

38. It is worth noting that there was no discernible impact on male students. Scott E. Carrell, Marianne E. Page, and James E. West, "Sex and Science: How Professor Gender Perpetuates the Gender Gap," *Quarterly Journal of Economics* (August 2010).

39. Wendy M. Williams and Stephen J. Ceci, "National Hiring Experiments Reveal 2: 1 Faculty Preference for Women on STEM Tenure Track," *Proceedings of the National Academy of Sciences* (April 2015), p. 5360.

40. Scholarships.org, "Scholarships for Women," accessed March 28, 2022.

41. Marie Curie Scholar Program (MCSP) at College of Saint Mary, see NSF Award 0630846.

42. National Center for Education Statistics, "Table 318.30."

43. Glenda M. Flores, and Pierrette Hondagneu-Sotelo, "The Social Dynamics Channeling Latina College Graduates into the Teaching Profession," *Gender, Work & Organization* (November 2014), p. 491.

44. These funds are mostly allocated under Title I of the WIOA law. See Daria Daniel, "Legislation Reintroduced to Address the Impacts of COVID-19 on the Nation's Workforce," National Association of Counties, February 10, 2021.

45. David H. Bradley, *The Workforce Innovation and Opportunity Act and the One-Stop Delivery System*, Congressional Research Service Report R44252 (2015, updated January 2021), p. 4.

46. Texas Workforce Commission, "Program Year 2018 Workforce Innovation and Opportunity Act Annual Report, Titles I and III" (2018), p. 12.

47. STEM RESTART Act, S.1297, 117th Congress (2021–2022).

48. The average salary of K–12 teachers in both 1999–2000 and 2020–2021 was $65,000 (in 2020/2021 dollars). National Center for Education Statistics, "Table 211.60, Estimated Average Annual Salary of Teachers in Public Elementary and Secondary Schools, by State: Selected Years, 1969–70 through 2020–21."

49. Madeline Will, "Joe Biden to Teachers: 'You Deserve a Raise, Not Just Praise,'" *Education Week*, July 2, 2021.

50. Meg Benner and others, "How to Give Teachers a $10,000 Raise," Center for American Progress, July 2018.

51. George A. Akerlof and Rachel E. Kranton, "Economics and Identity," *Quarterly Journal of Economics* (August 2000), p. 748.

52. For prime age (25–54) full-time workers. See also "Male Nurses Becoming More Commonplace, Census Bureau Reports," United States Census Bureau (February 2013).

53. Brittany Bisceglia, "Breaking the Stigma of the Male Nurse," *Nursing License Map* (blog), December 3, 2020.

54. Wally Bartfay and Emma Bartfay, "Canadian View of Men in Nursing Explored," *Men in Nursing* (April 2007).

55. Quoted in Andrew Clifton, Sarah Crooks, and Jo Higman, "Exploring the Recruitment of Men into the Nursing Profession in the United Kingdom," *Journal of Advanced Nursing* (March 2020), p. 1879.

56. Aaron Loewenberg, "There's a Stigma around Men Teaching Young Kids. Here's How We Change It," *Slate*, October 18, 2017.

57. Jill E. Yavorsky, "Uneven Patterns of Inequality: An Audit Analysis of Hiring-Related Practices by Gendered and Classed Contexts," *Social Forces* (December 2019). Note that these were not HEAL jobs specifically.

58. Martin Eisend, "A Meta-analysis of Gender Roles in Advertising," *Journal of the Academy of Marketing Science* (November 2009).

59. Claudia Goldin, "A Pollution Theory of Discrimination: Male and Female Differences in Occupations and Earnings," in *Human Capital in History: The American Record*, ed. Leah Platt Boustan, Carola Frydman, and Robert A. Margo (University of Chicago Press, 2014), p. 324.

60. Edward Schiappa, Peter B. Gregg, and Dean E. Hewes, "Can One TV Show Make a Difference? *Will & Grace* and the Parasocial Contact Hypothesis," *Journal of Homosexuality* (November 2006).

61. Melissa S. Kearney and Phillip B. Levine, "Media Influences on Social Outcomes: The Impact of MTV's 16 and Pregnant on Teen Childbearing," *American Economic Review* (December 2015).

62. On evaluation of these marketing campaigns, see Doug McKenzie-Mohr, *Fostering Sustainable Behavior: An Introduction to Community-Based Social Marketing* (Gabriola Island, BC: New Society, 2013).

63. Cass R. Sunstein, *How Change Happens* (MIT Press, 2020); Robert H. Frank, *Under the Influence: Putting Peer Pressure to Work* (Princeton University Press, 2020).

64. In 2008–2009, 13% of enrolled nursing students in Oregon were male, compared to 11% of registered nurses, a rise that was at best in line with national trends. See Tamara Bertell and others, *Who Gets In? Pilot Year Data from the Nursing Student Admissions Database* (Portland: Oregon Center for Nursing, 2009), table 5, p. 11.

65. Kimberley A. Clow, Rosemary Ricciardelli, and Wally J. Bartfay, "Are You Man Enough to Be a Nurse? The Impact of Ambivalent Sexism and Role Congruity on Perceptions of Men and Women in Nursing Advertisements," *Sex Roles* (April 2015).

66. Marci D. Cottingham, "Recruiting Men, Constructing Manhood: How Health Care Organizations Mobilize Masculinities as Nursing Recruitment Strategy," *Gender & Society* (February 2014).

67. Tara Boyle and others, "'Man Up': How a Fear of Appearing Feminine Restricts Men, and Affects Us All," NPR, October 1, 2018.

68. Ben Lupton, "Maintaining Masculinity: Men Who Do 'Women's Work,'" *British Journal of Management* (September 2000), pp. 33–48.

12. NEW DADS

1. Hanna Rosin, *The End of Men: And the Rise of Women* (New York: Riverhead Books, 2012), p. 9.

2. Matt Gertz, "Tucker Carlson's Snide Dismissal of Paternity Leave Is in Stark Contrast to His Colleagues' Fervent Support," Media Matters for America, October 15, 2021.

3. "Piers Morgan Mocks Daniel Craig for Carrying Baby," BBC, October 16, 2018.

4. Serena Mayeri, *Reasoning from Race: Feminism, Law, and the Civil Rights Revolution* (Harvard University Press, 2014), p. 123. Reflecting on the case decades later, Ginsburg said: "This is my dream for society. . . . Fathers loving and caring for and helping to raise their kids." See Erika Bachiochi, "What I Will Teach My Children about Ruth Bader Ginsburg," *America Magazine*, September 24, 2020.

5. Eric Michael Johnson, "Raising Darwin's Consciousness: An Interview with Sarah Blaffer Hrdy on Mother Nature," *Scientific American*, March 16, 2012.

6. Anna Machin, *The Life of Dad: The Making of the Modern Father* (New York: Simon & Schuster, 2018), pp. 17–18.

7. William H. Jeynes, "Meta-Analysis on the Roles of Fathers in Parenting: Are They Unique?," *Marriage & Family Review* (April 2016); Sara McLanahan and

Christopher Jencks, "Was Moynihan Right?," *Education Next* (Spring 2015); Kevin Shafer, *So Close, Yet So Far: Fathering in Canada & the United States* (University of Toronto Press, 2022), especially chap. 2.

8. Kathleen Mullan Harris, Frank F. Furstenberg, and Jeremy K. Marmer. "Paternal Involvement with Adolescents in Intact Families: The Influence of Fathers over the Life Course," *Demography* (June 1998).

9. Rebecca M. Ryan, Anne Martin, and Jeanne Brooks-Gunn, "Is One Good Parent Good Enough? Patterns of Mother and Father Parenting and Child Cognitive Outcomes at 24 and 36 Months," *Parenting: Science and Practice* (May 2006).

10. James A. Gaudino Jr., Bill Jenkins, and Roger W. Rochat, "No Fathers' Names: A Risk Factor for Infant Mortality in the State of Georgia, USA," *Social Science & Medicine* (January 1999).

11. Marc Grau-Grau and Hannah Riley Bowles, "Launching a Cross-disciplinary and Cross-national Conversation on Engaged Fatherhood," in *Engaged Fatherhood for Men, Families and Gender Equality: Healthcare, Social Policy, and Work Perspectives*, ed. Marc Grau-Grau, Mireia las Heras Maestro, and Hannah Riley Bowles (New York: Springer, 2022), p. 2.

12. William H. Jeynes, "Meta-Analysis on the Roles of Fathers," p. 17. See also Harris, Furstenberg, and Marmer, "Paternal Involvement with Adolescents in Intact Families."

13. Kim Parker, Juliana Menasce Horowitz, and Renee Stepler, "Americans Are Divided on Whether Differences between Men and Women Are Rooted in Biology or Societal Expectations," Pew Research Center, December 5, 2017.

14. Pauline Hunt, *Gender and Class Consciousness* (London: MacMillan, 1980), p. 24.

15. National Academies of Sciences, Engineering, and Medicine, *The Promise of Adolescence: Realizing Opportunity for All Youth* (Washington, DC: The National Academies Press, 2019), p. 37.

16. Rob Palkovitz, "Gendered Parenting's Implications for Children's Well-Being," in *Gender and Parenthood: Biological and Social Scientific Perspectives*, ed. W. Bradford Wilcox and Kathleen Kovner Kline (Columbia University Press, 2013), p. 11.

17. Deborah A. Cobb-Clark and Erdal Tekin, "Fathers and Youths' Delinquent Behavior," *Review of Economics of the Household* (June 2014).

18. Eirini Flouri and Ann Buchanan, "The Role of Father Involvement in Children's Later Mental Health," *Journal of Adolescence* (February 2003).

19. Stephen D. Whitney and others, "Fathers' Importance in Adolescents' Academic Achievement," *International Journal of Child, Youth and Family Studies* (2017).

20. Machin, *The Life of Dad*, p. 111.

21. Shafer, *So Close, Yet So Far*, p. 68.

22. David J. Eggebeen, "Do Fathers Uniquely Matter for Adolescent Well-Being?," in *Gender and Parenthood: Biological and Social Scientific Perspectives*, ed. W. Bradford Wilcox and Kathleen Kovner Kline (Columbia University Press, 2013), p. 267.

23. Paul R. Amato and Joan G. Gilbreth, "Nonresident Fathers and Children's Well-Being: A Meta-analysis," *Journal of Marriage and Family* (August 1999).

24. William Marsiglio and Joseph H. Pleck, "Fatherhood and Masculinities," in *Handbook of Studies on Men and Masculinities*, ed. Michael S. Kimmel, Jeff Hearn, and Robert W. Connell (Thousand Oaks, CA: Sage, 2004), p. 253.

25. Alan Booth, Mindy E. Scott, and Valarie King, "Father Residence and Adolescent Problem Behavior: Are Youth Always Better Off in Two-Parent Families?," *Journal of Family Issues* (May 2010).

26. Kathryn Edin and Timothy J. Nelson, *Doing the Best I Can: Fatherhood in the Inner City* (University of California Press, 2013), p. 216.

27. Gretchen Livingston and Kim Parker, "A Tale of Two Fathers: More Are Active, but More Are Absent," Pew Research Center, June 15, 2011.

28. Jo Jones and William D. Mosher, "Fathers' Involvement with Their Children: United States, 2006–2010," National Health Statistics Reports, no. 71 (Hyattsville, MD: National Center for Health Statistics, 2013). See also Edin and Nelson, *Doing the Best I Can*, p. 215.

29. Calvina Z. Ellerbe, Jerrett B. Jones, and Marcia J. Carlson, "Race/Ethnic Differences in Nonresident Fathers' Involvement after a Nonmarital Birth," *Social Science Quarterly* (September 2018), p. 1158.

30. Janet Gornick and Marcia Meyers, "Institutions That Support Gender Equality in Parenthood and Employment," in *Gender Equality: Transforming Family Divisions of Labor* (New York: Verso, 2009), pp. 4–5.

31. Heather Boushey, "Home Economics," *Democracy Journal* (Spring 2016).

32. Tanya Byker and Elena Patel, "A Proposal for a Federal Paid Parental and Medical Leave Program," Brookings Institution, May 2021.

33. House Bill 2005 was signed into law on July 1, 2019, in the 80th Oregon Legislative Assembly. Note that the implementation of the policy in 2023 has been delayed.

34. OECD, Parental Leave Systems, "Paid Leave Reserved for Fathers," OECD Family Database, October 2021.

35. Ankita Patnaik, 'Daddy's Home!' Increasing Men's Use of Paternity Leave," Council on Contemporary Families, April 2, 2015.

36. Quoted in Gornick and Meyers, *Institutions That Support Gender Equality*, p. 437.

37. "The effect of fertility on [maternal] labor supply is . . . large and negative at higher levels of development." Daniel Aaronson and others, "The Effect of Fertility on Mothers' Labor Supply over the Last Two Centuries," *Economic Journal* (January 2021).

38. Claudia Goldin, *Career and Family: Women's Century-Long Journey toward Equity* (Princeton University Press, 2021), p. 234.

39. U.S. Bureau of Labor Statistics, "Employment Status of Mothers with Own Children under 3 Years Old by Single Year of Age of Youngest Child and Marital Status, 2019–2020 Annual Averages," in *Employment Characteristics of Families 2020*, April 2021.

40. Juliana Menasce Horowitz, "Despite Challenges at Home and Work, Most Working Moms and Dads Say Being Employed Is What's Best for Them," Pew Research Center, September 12, 2019.

41. Daly is quoted in Marsiglio and Pleck, "Fatherhood and Masculinities," p. 257.

42. Edin and Nelson, *Doing the Best I Can*, p. 216.

43. Maria Cancian and others, "Who Gets Custody Now? Dramatic Changes in Children's Living Arrangements after Divorce," *Demography* (May 2014), p. 1387.

44. This is an approximate figure, based on interviews with lawyers in each U.S. state. See "How Much Custody Time Does Dad Get in Your State?," Custody Xchange, 2018.

45. Heather Hahn, Kathryn Edin, and Lauren Abrahams, *Transforming Child Support into a Family-Building System* (US Partnership on Mobility from Poverty, March 2018).

46. Office of Child Support Enforcement, "Preliminary Report for FY 2020," tables P-29 and P-85, U.S. Department of Health and Human Services, June 2021.

47. For more details on this reform, see Hahn and others, *Transforming Child Support*, pp. 13–16.

48. Timothy Nelson, unpublished analysis drawing on data from interviews with 429 fathers across the country, quoted in Hahn and others, *Transforming Child Support*, p. 5.

49. Oregon Secretary of State, Department of Justice, "Chapter 137: Parenting Time Credit," *Oregon State Archives*. I made a similar proposal in "Non-resident Fathers: An Untapped Childcare Army?," Brookings Institution, December 9, 2015.

50. Edin and Nelson, *Doing the Best I Can*, p. 227.

51. Michael Young and Peter Willmott, *The Symmetrical Family* (New York: Pantheon, 1973), p. 278.

52. Alexander Bick, Bettina Brüggemann, and Nicola Fuchs-Schündeln, "Hours Worked in Europe and the United States: New Data, New Answers," *Scandinavian Journal of Economics* (October 2019), pp. 1381–1416.

53. Julie Sullivan, "Comparing Characteristics and Selected Expenditures of Dual- and Single-Income Households with Children," *Monthly Labor Review*, U.S. Bureau of Labor Statistics, September 2020, https://doi.org/10.21916/mlr .2020.19.

54. Richard V. Reeves and Isabel V. Sawhill, *A New Contract with the Middle Class* (Brookings Institution, 2020), pp. 46–56.

55. Goldin, *Career and Family*, p. 17.

56. Kim Parker and Wendy Wang, *Modern Parenthood: Roles of Moms and Dads Converge as They Balance Work and Family*, report prepared for the Pew Research Center, March 2013.

57. Richard Weissbourd and others, "How the Pandemic Is Strengthening Fathers' Relationships with Their Children," Harvard Graduate School of Education, Making Caring Common Project, June 2020.

58. Grant R. McDermott and Benjamin Hansen, "Labor Reallocation and Remote Work during COVID-19: Real-Time Evidence from GitHub," Working Paper 29598 (Cambridge, MA: National Bureau of Economic Research, December 2021).

59. Goldin, *Career and Family*, p. 9.

60. Goldin, *Career and Family*, figure 9.1, p. 178.

61. Goldin, *Career and Family*, p. 191.

62. Claudia Goldin and Lawrence F. Katz, "A Most Egalitarian Profession: Pharmacy and the Evolution of a Family-Friendly Occupation," *Journal of Labor Economics* (July 2016).

63. Stephanie Vozza, "How These Companies Have Made Four-Day Workweeks Feasible," *Fast Company*, June 17, 2015.

64. Karen Turner, "Amazon Is Piloting Teams with a 30-Hour Workweek," *Washington Post*, August 26, 2016.

65. *The 2016 Deloitte Millennial Survey: Winning over the Next Generation of Leaders* (London: Deloitte, 2016).

66. Claire Cain Miller, "Paternity Leave: The Rewards and the Remaining Stigma," *New York Times*, November 7, 2014. 62% of fathers or father-to-be agree there is an "unspoken rule that men at their job should not take full paternity leave" according to a Harris Poll survey, conducted May 26–June 3, 2021. The poll was conducted for Volvo cars.

67. Shane Barro, "Gender Equality Won't Just Change Women's Lives—It'll Change Everyone's," Huffington Post, September 30, 2015.

EPILOGUE

1. Richard V. Reeves and Ember Smith, "Americans Are More Worried about Their Sons Than Their Daughters," Brookings Institution, October 7, 2020.

INDEX

Figures are indicated by "f" following the page numbers.

Abecedarian program, 76
Abraham, Katharine, 62
Accelerated Study in Associate Programs
  (ASAP), 77
Administration. *See* HEAL fields
Adolescents. *See* Children and adolescents
Affirmative action, 14–15, 144, 160
Affordable Care Act of 2010, 110
African Americans. *See* Black men and boys;
  Black women and girls
Agency, 81, 87, 96–98
Aggression, 85–86, 88–90, 94, 101, 111, 124
Akerlof, George, 162–63
Akyurek, Gokcen, 9
Alcohol-related deaths. *See* Deaths of despair
Alger, Horatio, 70
Amazon, 181
American Association for the Advancement of
  Men in Nursing, 158, 161
American Council on Education, 3, 142–43
American Enterprise Institute, 26, 49, 68
American Family Survey, 183
American Institute for Boys and Men, ix, x
American Institute for Foreign Study, 80
American Nursing Association, 154–55
American Psychological Association (APA)
  guidelines, 100–01
Americorps, 81
Angrist, Josh, 77
Anomie, 37, 127
Apprenticeships, 147–48
Arbery, Ahmaud, 54
ASAP (Accelerated Study in Associate
  Programs), 77
Aucejo, Esteban, 15
Auras of gender, 164
Automation, 21–22
Autor, David, 16, 19, 65, 72

Bannon, Stephen, 120, 127
Bartik, Timothy, 73
Bates, Laura, 122
Baumeister, Roy, 91, 97
Beaty, Daniel, 55

Beauvoir, Simone de, xv
Benenson, Joyce, 90
Bertrand, Marianne, 27, 37, 71, 147
Biases. *See* Discrimination; Stereotypes
Biden, Joe: supporter demographics, 105; on
  teacher pay raise, 162; White House
  Gender Policy Council created by, 112
Big Think, x
Binder, Ariel, 38
Bisexuals. *See* LGBTQ community
Black men and boys, 45–59; college degrees
  held by, 50, 51*f*; Commission on the Social
  Status of, 58; criminalization of, 54, 55;
  discrimination against, xiii, 46; economic
  mobility of, 3, 49; education initiatives for,
  76, 146; employment rates for, 50, 55; as
  engaged fathers, 56, 173; gendered racism
  experienced by, xiii, 47, 54, 59; in HEAL
  fields, 158, 161; incarceration of, 48, 50,
  53–55; intersectionality and, 47, 53–54;
  masculinity of, 45, 47, 54; neighborhood
  influences on, 71; provider role for, 56–57;
  structural barriers facing, 40; in teacher
  workforce, 142–44; threat stereotype of,
  53–56; Trump supported by, 119; wage
  distribution for, 50–51, 52*f*
Black women and girls: births outside of
  marriage, 56; college degrees held by, 50,
  51*f*; economic mobility of, 49; economic
  role within families, 56; education
  initiatives for, 76; employment rates for, 50;
  gendered racism experienced by, 47, 52;
  high school graduation rates for, 50;
  intersectionality and, 47; marriage trends
  among, 49, 56–57; provider role for, 56–57;
  wage distribution for, 51, 52*f*; "welfare
  queen" archetype of, 47
Blankenhorn, David, 37–38
Bly, Robert, 124
Bolotnyy, Valentin, 28
Bosson, Jennifer, 165
Bound, John, 38
Boushey, Heather, 64, 174
Bowles, Hannah Riley, 170

Boys. *See* Men and boys
Brain development, 8–11, 16, 85, 101
Breadwinners. *See* Provider role
Brizendine, Louann, 87
Brown, Michael, 57–58
Budig, Michelle, 27
Building Blocks of STEM Act of 2019, 157
Bureau of Labor Statistics, U.S., 22, 23
Burgos, Christian Alexander, 92
Burton, Deborah, 164
Busette, Camille, xiii, 53
Buttigieg, Pete, 168

Call Me MISTER program, 161
Cancian, Maria, 177
Career and technical education (CTE),
    146–47, 159
Carlson, Tucker, 168
Carnegie Hero Fund, 92
Carnevale, Anthony, 145
Cascio, Elizabeth, 136, 137
Case, Anne, 60, 62
Cashin, Sheryll, 48
Cass, Oren, 148
Cassino, Dan, 126
Castile, Philando, 54
Ceci, Stephen, 160
Centrifugal gender politics, 128–29
Cherlin, Andrew, 36, 38, 65
Chetty, Raj, 49, 50, 52, 70, 71
Childcare: in COVID-19 pandemic, 20, 113;
    equal allocation of, xii, 174, 176; gender
    pay gap and, 27–29; redshirting and, 138;
    testosterone levels and, 95
Children and adolescents: adversity faced by,
    70–72; births outside of marriage, 35–36,
    56, 65; co-residency with fathers, xii, 38,
    41, 94–95, 172; custody arrangements for,
    125, 177; fathers, importance to, 169–72; of
    incarcerated parents, 55, 94; meaning and
    fulfillment from, 39; one-child policy in
    China, 91; orchid/dandelion dichotomy
    and, 70–71; in single-parent households,
    55, 71. *See also* Childcare; Education;
    Families
Child support, 176–78
China, one-child policy in, 91
Chingos, Matthew, 15–16
Civil Rights Act of 1964, Title VII, 121, 139
Clare, Anthony, 96
Clark, Roy Peter, 23–24
Class status: economic mobility and, 49, 72;
    educational performance and, 3, 7, 50, 71;
    employment trends and, 18; family life
    and, 62, 64–66; income differences and, 61;
    marriage rates and, 65; nonmarital births

and, 36; redshirting and, 135–38. *See also*
    Poverty; Working-class men and boys
Clinton, Hillary, 126
Coates, Ta-Nehisi, 53, 54
Code-switching, 40
Cole, Kirsten, 143
College education: admissions process, 7, 14;
    degree attainment, xii, 3, 11–13, 12–13*f*, 50,
    51*f*, 71; dropouts and stop outs, 15–16, 75;
    enrollment statistics, 3, 12, 15, 50, 76, 114,
    148; free programs, xiv, 17, 73–75; in
    HEAL fields, 159; mentoring and support
    programs, 75, 77; Moving the Needle
    initiative, 142–43; scholarship programs,
    76, 144, 158, 160–61; in STEM fields,
    13, 160; WEF gender parity score for,
    114
Commission on Civil Rights, 14, 58
Commission on the Social Status of Black
    Men and Boys, 58
Conservatives. *See* Political Right
Conversion therapy, 100
Cook, Philip, 137
Corak, Miles, 70, 72
Cottingham, Marci, 165
Council of Economic Advisers, 29, 64
COVID-19 pandemic: childcare concerns in,
    20, 113; economic impact of, 19–21;
    educational trends during, 3, 20, 114;
    employment rates during, 20–21; gender
    gap in mortality rates, ix, 109–10, 114;
    healthcare system burdened by, 154;
    remote work during, 179; toxic masculinity
    during, 107
Cowen, Tyler, 123
Cox, Daniel, 68
Craig, Daniel, 168
Creation stories, 85, 88
Crenshaw, Kimberlé, 46, 47
Criminal justice system, xiii, 46, 58
CTE (career and technical education),
    146–47, 159
Cultural diversity. *See* Racial and ethnic
    differences
Culture wars, xiv, 121, 126, 129, 168
Curnock Cook, Mary, 16, 17
Curry, Tommy, 47
Custody arrangements, 125, 177

Daly, Mary, 176
Dandelion/orchid dichotomy, 70–71
Davis, Baron, 144
Deaths of despair, xii, 60–63, 63*f*
Deaton, Angus, 60, 62
Dee, Thomas, 141–42
Delahunty, Jennifer, 14, 15

Deming, David, 138, 154
Democrats. *See* Political Left
Dench, Geoff, 33, 34, 37, 124, 127
Direct model of fatherhood, 172–82
Discrimination: in employment, xiii, 50, 55, 121, 139; intersectionality and, 46; statistical, 87. *See also* Racism; Sexism; Stereotypes
Diversity. *See* Racial and ethnic differences
Division of labor, 33, 125, 170, 180
Divorce, 35, 39, 177
Dunn, Irina, 35
Duterte, Rodrigo, 120
Dynarski, Susan, 138

Eagly, Alice, 112
Early Training Project, 76
Earned Income Tax Credit (EITC), 78
Earnings: class gap in, 61; education level and, xiii; gender gap in, xii, 4, 18, 23–29, 25*f*, 60–61, 180; in HEAL fields, 154, 162; in paid leave policies, 173–74; race gap in, 50–51, 52*f*; subsidy programs, 77–78.
Economic inequality, 61, 66, 72
Economic mobility, 3, 49, 72
Edin, Kathryn, 64, 67, 172–73, 176, 178
Edlund, Lena, 91
Education, 3–17; affirmative action in, 14–15, 144, 160; brain development and, 8–11, 16, 85; class status and, 3, 7, 50, 71; COVID-19 pandemic and, 3, 20, 114; employment in relation to, 3, 19; gender gap in, xii, 3–8, 11–17, 50, 71, 80, 85; high school graduation rates, 7–8, 50, 138; income in relation to, xiii; marriage trends and, 37, 65–66; nonmarital births and, 36, 65; OECD survey of, 4–5; policy interventions, xiv, 17, 73–77; race gaps in, 7, 48, 50; redshirting of boys (starting school a year later), 134–40; in single-sex schools, 148; structural challenges in, xiii, 4, 11; study abroad programs, 80; Title IX legislation and, 3, 11, 14; vocational training, 145–48, 159. *See also* College education; Education initiatives; Grade point average; HEAL fields; Teachers; *specific subject areas*
Education Amendments of 1972, Title IX of, 3, 11, 14
Education initiatives, 133–49; apprenticeships, 147–48; free college programs, xiv, 17, 73–75; mentoring programs, xiv, 75–77; overview, 133–34; redshirting, 134–40; sex differences and, 149; teacher diversity, 140–45; vocational training, 145–48, 159
Eggebeen, David, 171–72

EITC (Earned Income Tax Credit), 78
Elan, Maika, 69
Emanuel, Natalia, 28
Emotional intelligence (EQ), 21
Employment, 18–30; auras of gender in, 164; automation and, 21–22; class status and, 18; in COVID-19 pandemic, 20–21; discrimination in, xiii, 50, 55, 121, 139; education level and, 3, 19; father-friendly, 178–82; free trade and, 21–23; gender gap in, 19–21, 20*f*, 51; male provider role as incentive for, 38; meaning and fulfillment from, 39; opioid use and, 62; paid leave, xii, 173–76, 179; policy interventions, 77–79, 157–66; race gap in, 51; redshirting effects on, 138–39; in remote settings, 179; sex differences in choice of, 86, 97–100, 99*f*, 124–25; in STEM fields, 22, 97–100, 99*f*, 124–25, 152, 153*f*; structural challenges in, xiii, 4; training programs for, 78–79; trends for women in, 29–30; work/life balance and, 181. *See also* HEAL fields; Income
Engaged fatherhood, 56, 169–73
Engineering. *See* STEM fields
EQ (emotional intelligence), 21
Equality. *See* Gender equality; Inequality
Erdoğan, Recep Tayyip, 119
Ethnicity. *See* Racial and ethnic differences

Falk, Armin, 98
Faludi, Susan, xiii, 19
Families: American Family Survey, 183; childcare responsibilities within, 27, 64; class differences and, 62, 64–66; division of labor within, 33, 125, 170, 180; provider role within, xiii, 32–38, 41, 56–57, 64–65, 127; racial differences and, 56–57; traditional model of, 33–34, 37, 128. *See also* Children and adolescents; Fathers; Mothers
Fathers, 31–42, 167–82; child support from, 176–78; conservative views of, 168; co-residency with children, xii, 38, 41, 94–95, 172; direct model of fatherhood, 172–82; dislocation of, xiii, 36; engaged, 56, 169–73; family-friendly work for, 178–82; gender pay gap for, 28; importance of, 169–72; in joint custody arrangements, 177; mature masculinity of, 41–42; paid leave for, xii, 173–76, 179; progressive views of, 168; provider role for, xiii, 32–38, 41, 56–57; stay-at-home, 66, 167; structural barriers facing, 40. *See also* Families
Femininity: robustness of, 95–96; stereotypes related to, 141; traditional ideas of, 119;

usefulness of traits associated with, 87; women's identification with, 107–08

Feminism: criticisms of, 108, 119, 121, 127–28, 184; on economic success of women, 30; on gender pay gap, 26; on gender-specific medicine, 110; in identity economics, 163; on marriage, 31, 34; pathologizing of, 129; on working mothers, 36. *See also* Women's movement

Ferreira, Francisco, 115

Fine, Cordelia, xii

Finland, student performance in, 4–5, 142

Fishkin, Joseph, 146

Flores, Glenda, 161

Ford, Tiffany N., 47

Frances, Carol, 3

Frank, Robert, 164

Free trade, 21–23

Friendships, 68–70

Gaming habits, 19–20

Gap instinct, 24–25, 86

Gates, Melinda French, 157

Geary, David, 98

Gender bias. *See* Sexism

Gender differences. *See* Sex differences

Gender economics, 72

Gendered racism, xiii, xv, 47, 52, 54, 59

Gender equality: advocacy for, xii, 115–16; compatibility with masculinity, xiv; in education, 3, 11, 114; in HEAL fields, 165; narratives of, 72; in paid leave policies, 173–76; paradox of, 98; progress toward, 38; in STEM fields, 152; wage distribution and, 25–26

Gender gaps: in 2016 election results, 118; childhood adversity and, 70; conservative views of, 26, 124–26; in COVID-19 mortality rates, ix, 109–10, 114; in deaths of despair, xii, 60–63, 63f; in education, xii, 3–8, 11–17, 50, 71, 80, 85; in employment, 19–21, 20f, 51; Global Gender Gap Report, 114–15; in income, xii, 4, 18, 23–29, 25f, 60–61, 180; in policy intervention outcomes, xiii–xiv, 17, 73–79; progressive views of, xiv, 26, 106, 112–16; in teacher workforce, xi, 8, 140–45, 141f; in volunteer organizations, 81

Gender politics, 128–29, 176

Gender roles: in advertisements, 164; conformity to, 98; incongruity of, 165; socialization and, 27; traditional, xiv, 98, 122, 126–28. *See also* Sex differences

General Social Survey, 36

Genghis Khan, 90–91

Gestsdottir, Steinunn, 12

Gilder, George, 41–42, 127

Gilmore, David, 32–34, 96

Ginsburg, Ruth Bader, 139, 168

Girls. *See* Women and girls

Gladwell, Malcolm, 134

Global Gender Gap Report, 114–15

Goldin, Claudia, 26, 28, 164, 179, 180

Goode, William, 36

Gornick, Janet, 173–76

Gorsuch, Neil, 121

Grade point average (GPA): brain development and, 10; education initiatives and, 76; gender gap in, 6–7, 6f, 15, 142; redshirting and, 137

Grand gender convergences, 26

Grau-Grau, Marc, 170

Grievance politics, 118–22

Grossbard, Shoshana, 66

Gudmundsson, Eyjolfur, 12

Gurian, Michael, 148–49

Haldane, Andy, 21

Haphazard self, 67–68

Haque, Fariha, 114–15

Harden, Kathryn Paige, 111

Harrington, Carol, 107, 109

Harris, Kamala, 58–59

Hawley, Josh, xi, 117–18, 120, 122, 125

HEAL (health, education, administration, and literacy) fields, 150–66; college degrees in, 159; description of, 152; funding for men in, 157–58, 161–62, 165–66; gender matching of providers and users, 155–57; income levels within, 154, 162; job growth within, 13, 154–55; male representation in, 153, 153f, 156–58, 156f; overview, 150–51; pipeline of men for, 158–60; service-learning opportunities in, 158; stereotypes of men in, 163–65; teacher gender in, 159–60; vocational training in, 159; women's dominance of, 22, 151, 153, 159. *See also* Nursing; Teachers

Health care. *See* HEAL fields

Hemingway, Ernest, 69

Henrich, Joseph, 91, 95

Heriot, Gail, 14

Hermle, Johannes, 98

Hershbein, Brad, 73, 74

Higher education. *See* College education

High-investment parenting (HIP) marriages, 66

High school graduation rates, 7–8, 50, 138

Hikikomori (shut-ins), 69–70

Hillman, Nick, 61

Hispanic men and boys: education initiatives for, 76, 146; fatherhood approach of, 173; in HEAL fields, 158, 161; Trump supported by, 119
Hispanic women and girls: births outside of marriage, 56; in HEAL fields, 161
Hochschild, Arlie, 64
Hoff Sommers, Christina, 26
Homegrown STL initiative, 57–58
Homosexuality. *See* LGBTQ community
Hooven, Carole, 89–90
Hrdy, Sarah Blaffer, 169
Hunt, Pauline, 170
Hyde, Janet, 40

Iceland, gender equality in, 12, 114
Identity economics, 162–63
Incarceration, 48, 50, 53–55, 94
Income. *See* earnings
Individualism, xiii, 106, 108–10
Inequality: economic, 61, 66, 72; intergenerational patterns of, 49; intersectionality and, 46; racial differences in family life and, 56. *See also* Gender gaps
Ingersoll, Richard, 141
Institute for Women's Policy Research, 52
Institute of International education, 80
Intersectionality, 46–47, 53–54
Intersex persons, 89
Interventions. *See* Education initiatives; Policy interventions

Jackson, Jerlando F. L., 50
Jail. *See* Incarceration
James, Charles, 26
James, Jonathan, 15
Japan, *hikikomori* (shut-ins) in, 69
Jean-Pierre, Charles, 144
Jensen, Frances, 10
Jeynes, William, 170
Jobs. *See* Employment
Job Training Partnership Act of 1982, 78
Joe, Sean, 57–58
Joint custody arrangements, 177
Jones, Suzanne Stateler, 137

Kajonius, Petri, 98
Kalamazoo Promise program, 73–76, 79
Kang, Songman, 137
Kearney, Melissa, 18, 62
Kefalas, Maria, 64
Kendi, Ibram X., 54
Khan, Imran, 119
Khazan, Olga, 98
Killewald, Alexandra, 37
Kimbrough, Gray, 20

Kimmel, Michael, 68
Klein, Ezra, ix
"Knock, Knock" (Beaty), 55
Konner, Melvin, 88, 89, 92, 111–12
Köpping, Petra, 119
Kranton, Rachel, 162–63
Kriegel, Leonard, 96
Kristof, Nicholas, 62
Krueger, Alan, 62
Kunjufu, Jawanza, 55

Labor, division of, 33, 125, 170, 180
Labor market. *See* Employment
Lachowska, Marta, 73
Lamont, Michèle, 38
Larson, Stephanie Howard, 135
Latinos/Latinas. *See* Hispanic men and boys; Hispanic women and girls
Left. *See* Political Left
Legato, Marianne J., 93, 110
Leira, Arnlaug, 175
Lesbians: as parents, 27. *See also* LGBTQ community
Lewis, Helen, 108, 113
LGBTQ community: conversion therapy and, 100; employment discrimination and, 121; marriage equality for, 65, 164; trans rights issues, 120–21, 123
Liberals. *See* Political Left
Life/work balance, 181
Literacy: engaged fatherhood and, 169; gender gap in, 5, 15, 141–42, 144; initiatives for improvement of, 76; OECD survey of, 4–5; psychological impact of, 95; redshirting and, 135, 137. *See also* HEAL fields
Lundberg, Shelly, 66

MacArthur Foundation, 101
Machin, Anna, 169, 171
Males. *See* Men and boys
Manne, Kate, 111
Manosphere, 106, 121–22
Marriage: births outside of, 35–36, 56, 65; breadwinning potential of possible mate, 56–57; class differences in, 65; conservative views of, 34, 37–38; declining rates of, 34, 37, 65; education level and, 37, 65–66; feminist views of, 31, 34; liberalization of social norms for, 41; male benefits of, 39; polygynous, 91; racial differences in, 49, 56–57; same-sex, 65, 164; shotgun marriages, 35–36; symbolic power of, 65; testosterone levels following, 95; in traditional family model, 34, 37
Marsiglio, William, 172

Masculinity: APA guidelines on, 100; Black, 45, 47, 54; compatibility with gender equality, xiv; cultural lag in conceptualizations of, 36; fragility of, 95–97; haphazard self and, 67–68; mature, 38, 41–42, 67; men's identification with, 107–08; pathologizing of, xv, 106, 108, 117, 129; in postfeminist world, 184; prosocial, 182; provider role as element of, 33, 36, 38; role incongruity and, 165; Schlesinger on recovery of, 128; as social construction, 96, 100, 111; stereotypes related to, 141; testosterone and aggression as part of, 89; toxic, xiv, 54, 105–09, 117, 122; traditional ideas of, 100, 117, 119; usefulness of traits associated with, 87. *See also* Men and boys

Mathematics. *See* STEM fields

Math problem of surplus men, 91

MBK Alliance, 52

McConnaughy, Corrine, 53

McGhee, Heather, 57

McMichael, Gregory and Travis, 54

McMillan, Kendra, 154

Mead, Margaret, 31, 92, 97, 128–29, 134

Men and boys: APA guidelines on working with, 100–01; brain development in, 8–11, 16, 85, 101; college degrees held by, xii, 3, 11–13, 12–13f, 50, 51f, 71; economic relations between women and, 31–32, 36, 118; friendship deficit among, 68–70; gaming habits of, 19–20; GPA rank among, 6–7, 6f; in HEAL fields, 153, 153f, 156–66, 156f; high school graduation rates for, 7–8; marriage benefits for, 39, 95; math problem of surplus men, 91; on meaning of life, 39–40; physical strength of, 22; "prime" working age for, 19; provider role for, xiii, 32–38, 41, 56–57, 127; wage distribution for, 24–26, 25f, 50–51, 52f. *See also* Black men and boys; Fathers; Gender *entries*; Hispanic men and boys; Masculinity; Patriarchy; Sex differences; Working-class men and boys

Men Going Their Own Way (MGTOW), 121, 122

Mentoring programs, xiv, 75–77, 162, 165

#MeToo movement, 107

Meyers, Marcia, 173–76

Mill, Harriet Taylor, 47

Mill, John Stuart, 34, 47, 183

Miller, Arthur, 34

Million Girls Moonshot, 158–59

Minorities. *See* Racial and ethnic differences

Mishra, Pankaj, 119

Misogyny, 17, 106, 119–20, 122

Mitchell, Kevin, 94

Mladinic, Antonio, 112

Moberg, Ylva, 27

Modestino, Alicia Sasser, 113

Modi, Narendra, 119

Mogstad, Magne, 147

Moore, James L., 50

Morgan, David, 33, 67

Morgan, Piers, 168

Morris, Desmond, 90

Mothers: births outside of marriage, 35–36, 56, 65; in COVID-19 pandemic, 20; custody of children awarded to, 125, 177; gender pay gap for, 27–29; paid leave for, xii, 173, 179; provider role for, 32, 35, 56–57, 64–65; second shift of domestic labor for, 64; stay-at-home, 36; welfare system support for, 35; working, 29–30, 35, 36, 64, 167. *See also* Families

Mountjoy, Jack, 147

Moving the Needle initiative, 142–43

Moynihan, Daniel Patrick, 49, 53, 57

Murakami, Haruki, 69

Muro, Mark, 21

Murray, Charles, 125

My Brother's Keeper initiative, 52

National Academies of Sciences, Engineering, and Medicine, 10, 170

National Coalition for Women and Girls in Education, 159

National Girls Collaborative Project, 158

National Organization for Women, 26, 127

National Science Foundation, 151–52, 157, 158, 160, 165

Naturalistic fallacy, 88

Nature-nurture debate, 86–87, 94–97

Negativity instinct, 24

Nelson, Timothy, 172–73, 176, 178

New York Times, ix

Nightingale, Florence, 163

No fault divorces, 35

Nursing: college degrees for, 159; gender gap in, 124–25, 163; recruitment of men into, 158, 161, 164–65; shortages within, 154–55; stereotypes of men in, 163

Nussbaum, Martha, 47

Obama, Barack, 40, 52, 55

Objectification of women, 105–06

Occupations. *See* Employment

One-child policy (China), 91

Opioids, 62, 68

Opportunity pluralism, 146

Oppression: intersectionality and, 46, 47; patriarchy and, 34, 110, 121; sex differences as justification for, 87; of women by men, 128

Orchid/dandelion dichotomy, 70–71
Orenstein, Peggy, 107
Organization for Economic Cooperation and Development/OECD countries, 3–5, 13, 13f, 140, 174
Ortner, Sherry, 95–96
Overdoses. See Deaths of despair

Pager, Devah, 55
Paid leave, xii, 173–76, 179
Palkovitz, Rob, 171
Pan, Jessica, 71
Pandemic. See COVID-19 pandemic
Parenting time credits, 178
Parents. See Fathers; Mothers
Partelow, Lisette, 142
Patriarchy: Black masculinity and, 47; feminist upending of, 128; gender pay gap and, 26; oppression and, 34, 110, 121
Pay. See Earnings
Paycheck Plus pilot program, 77–78
Peace Corps, 81
Perry program, 76
Peterson, Jordan, 123–25
Pew Research Center, 39, 107, 127, 170
Pharmacy profession, egalitarian nature of, 180
Pieri, Jules, 176
PISA (Programme for International Student Assessment), 4–5
Pleck, Joseph H., 172
Policy interventions: for direct model of fatherhood, 173–82; employment initiatives, 77–79, 157–66; gender gap in outcomes of, xiii–xiv, 17, 73–79; by White House Gender Policy Council, 112–13, 115. See also Education initiatives
Political Left, 105–16; centrifugal gender politics and, 129; on conformity to gender roles, 98; on fatherhood, 168; on gender gaps, xiv, 26, 106, 112–16; on individualism, 106, 108–10; partisan politics and, 108, 184; pathologizing of masculinity by, xv, 106, 108, 117, 129; on sex differences, 106, 110–12; on toxic masculinity, xiv, 106–09, 117, 122; victim-blaming by, 108–10
Political Right, 117–29; APA guidelines criticized by, 100; centrifugal gender politics and, 129; on fatherhood, 168; on gender gaps, 26, 124–26; on gender roles, xiv, 98, 118, 122, 126–28; grievance politics and, 118–22; on individualism, 110; on marriage, 34, 37–38; partisan politics and, 108, 120, 184; pathologizing of feminism by, 129; on sex differences,

118, 123–26; on toxic masculinity, 108, 117
Polygyny, 91
Populism, xv, 23, 118–19, 122
Pornography, 93–94, 117
Poverty, 49, 50, 70, 172
Prejudice. See Discrimination; Sexism; Stereotypes
Prison. See Incarceration
Programme for International Student Assessment (PISA), 4–5
Progressives. See Political Left
Project READS, 76
Project STAR, 76
Prosocial masculinity, 182
Prostitution, 93
Provider role, xiii, 32–38, 41, 56–57, 64–65, 127
Public Religion Research Institute, 108

Queer persons. See LGBTQ community

Racial and ethnic differences: in births outside of marriage, 56; in educational performance, 7, 48, 50; in employment trends, 51; in family life, 56–57; in grade retention, 136; in marriage trends, 49, 56–57; in redshirting, 135–37; in study abroad participants, 80; in teacher workforce, 142–44; in wage distribution, 50–51, 52f. See also specific racial and ethnic groups
Racism: as barrier to equality, 46, 48; binary models of, 58; gendered, xiii, 47, 52, 54, 59
Raley, Kelly, 56
Ramaley, Judith A., 151–52
Ray, Rashawn, 53
Reading skills. See Literacy
Reardon, Sean, 6
Redshirting (starting school a year later), 134–40
Remote work, 179
Republicans. See Political Right
Right. See Political Right
Rippon, Gina, 87
Risk-taking, 85–86, 90–92, 94, 101, 171
Ritchie, Stuart, 86
Robinson, Nicholas, 61
Rodgers, Shawn, 163
Romney, Mitt, 62
Roosevelt, Eleanor, 31
Rosin, Hanna, 3, 12, 15, 17, 30, 116, 167
Rosling, Hans, 24
Rounds, James, 99–100, 125
Roxburgh, J. F., 101
Ruggles, Steve, 37
Russell, Bertrand, 74

Salaries. *See* Income
Same-sex marriage, 65, 164
Sapolsky, Robert, 9
Sawhill, Isabel, 65
Schanzenbach, Diane Whitmore, 135–37
Schlesinger, Arthur, Jr., 128
Scholarship programs, 76, 144, 158, 160–61
Schooling. *See* College education; Education
Schwammenthal, Daniel, 129
Science. *See* STEM fields
Self-complexity, 40
Sen, Amartya, 47
Sex differences, 85–102; agency as driver of,
    87, 96–98; in aggression, 85–86, 88–90, 94,
    101, 111, 124; APA guidelines on, 100–01;
    in brain development, 8–11, 16, 85, 101;
    conservative views of, 118, 123–26;
    COVID-19 mortality rates and, ix, 109–10;
    creation story depictions of, 85, 88;
    education initiatives and, 149; in
    employment choice, 86, 97–100, 99*f*,
    124–25; fragility of masculinity vs.
    femininity, 95–97; in maturation process,
    101–02; nature–nurture debate on, 86–87,
    94–97; progressive views of, 106, 110–12;
    in risk-taking, 85–86, 90–92, 94, 101; in
    sex drive, 85, 92–94, 111, 112, 124. *See also*
    Gender roles
Sexism: binary models of, 58; in education
    system, 11, 14–15; institutionalization of,
    27, 87; justifications for, 99, 111, 125; men
    as victims of, 120, 163; misogyny, 17, 106,
    119–20, 122; Title VII legislation on, 121,
    139
Sexual orientation. *See* LGBTQ community
Shafer, Kevin, 171
Shakespeare, William, 96
Shand, Fiona, 63
Shared custody arrangements, 177
Shotgun marriages, 35–36
Shut-ins (*hikikomori*), 69–70
Silva, Jennifer, 67–68
Silverio Mendoza, Lucas Y., 92
Single-sex schools, 148
Slaughter, Anne Marie, 182
Small, Delrawn, 54
Social class. *See* Class status
Society of Women Engineers, 157–58
South Korea: discrimination against men in,
    120; right-wing political parties in, 119;
    teacher gender statistics in, 140
Sperling, Gene, 78
Statistical discrimination, 87
Stay-at-home mothers/fathers, 36, 66, 167
Stay the Course program, 75–76

Steinbeck, John, 69
Steinberg, Laurence, 8–9
Steinem, Gloria, 31–35, 37, 65, 141, 151
STEM (science, technology, engineering, and
    math) fields: college degrees in, 13, 160;
    employment within, 22, 97–100, 99*f*,
    124–25, 152, 153*f*; funding for women in,
    157–62; gender-equality paradox and, 98;
    gender gap in, 5–6, 13; OECD survey of,
    4–5; pipeline of women for, 158–59;
    teacher gender in, 145, 159–60; vocational
    training in, 148
STEM RESTART Act (proposed), 162
Stereotypes: of Black men and boys, 53–56; of
    marriageability, 56; of masculine and
    feminine, 141; of men in HEAL fields,
    163–65; sex differences and, 87. *See also*
    Discrimination; Gender roles; *specific racial
    and ethnic groups*
Sterling, Alton, 54
Stevenson, Adlai, 31, 32
Stevenson, Betsey, 21
Stoet, Gijsbert, 98
Storr, Krystnell, 10
Straight line instinct, 24
Study abroad programs, 80
Su, Rong, 99–100, 125
Suicide. *See* Deaths of despair
Sullivan, James, 75
Sunstein, Cass, 164
Swanson, Barrett, 63
Sweden: gender pay gap in, 27–28; right-wing
    political parties in, 119; student perfor-
    mance in, 5
Sweeney, Megan, 56
Sykes, Brian, 88

Tach, Laura, 33
Tax Cuts and Jobs Act of 2017, 23
Taylor, Cameron, 71
Teachers: college degrees for, 159; gender of,
    xi, 8, 140–45, 141*f*; in HEAL fields,
    159–60; identity matching with learners,
    75; pay raises for, 162; race and ethnicity
    of, 142–44; recruitment efforts, 142–45,
    161; redshirting of children by, 135;
    shortages of, 155; in STEM fields, 145,
    159–60; stereotypes of men as, 163. *See also*
    Education
Technology. *See* STEM fields
Temporary Assistance for Needy Families,
    178
Teo, Alan, 69–70
Testosterone, 88–90, 95, 100, 111
Titanic sinking (1912), 101

Title VII (Civil Rights Act of 1964), 121, 139
Title IX (Education Amendments of 1972), 3, 11, 14
Toobin, Jeffrey, 93
Toxic masculinity, xiv, 54, 105–09, 117, 122
Trade, employment impacted by, 21–23
Transgender persons. *See* LGBTQ community
Trump, Donald: Council on Women and Girls abolished by, 112; inaugural address of, 61–62; supporter demographics, 67, 118, 119, 126; toxic masculinity and, 107; on trans rights, 120
Turner, Luke, 110
Twain, Mark, 77

Unilateral divorces, 35
United Kingdom (UK): Brexit and, 107, 118; COVID-19 mortality rate for men in, 109; doctor gender statistics in, 150; educational gender gap in, 12, 50, 71, 148; free trade and employment in, 22; Office of the Children's Commissioner, 93; teacher gender statistics in, 140; Voluntary Service Overseas program, 81
Universities. *See* College education
Urban boarding schools, 76
Urban Institute, 15–16, 93

Vaghul, Kavya, 64
Van Pelt, Toni, 26
Verbal skills, 5, 15, 144
Victim-blaming, 108–10
Video games, 19–20
Vincent-Lancrin, Stephan, 3
Violence: Black men stigmatized as dangerous, 53; cultural valorization of, 86; gender gap in committing acts of, 89; misogyny and, 122; social decrease in, 90; testosterone suppression system of marriage on, 95; toxic masculinity and, 107; traditional masculinity and, 100
Vocational training, 145–48, 159
Voluntary Service Overseas program (UK), 81

Wages. *See* Earnings
Wasserman, Melanie, 19, 65, 72
WEF (World Economic Forum), 12, 114–15
Weinberger v. Wiesenfeld (1975), 168
Welfare system, 35, 47, 98, 174, 178
"What Is A Bachelor Like?" (poem), 38–39
White, Ismail, 53
White House Gender Policy Council, 112–13, 115

Willetts, David, 35
Williams, Wendy, 160
Willmott, Peter, 178–79
Wilson, William Julius, 56
Winship, Scott, 49
WIOA (Workforce Innovation and Opportunity Act of 2014), 161–62
Women and girls: APA guidelines on working with, 101; brain development in, 9–11, 16, 85, 101; college degrees held by, xii, 3, 11–13, 12–13f, 50, 51f, 71; economic relations between men and, 31–32, 36, 118; friendship networks among, 69; GPA rank among, 6–7, 6f; in HEAL fields, 22, 151, 153, 159; high school graduation rates for, 7–8, 50; Hispanic, 56, 161; on meaning of life, 39–40; objectification of, 105–06; physical strength of, 22; in prostitution, 93; in senior positions, 21, 27, 29–30; in STEM fields, 13, 22, 97–100, 99f, 124–25, 152, 153f, 157–62; wage distribution for, 24–26, 25f, 51, 52f; in workforce, 29–30, 35, 36, 64. *See also* Black women and girls; Femininity; Feminism; Gender *entries*; Mothers; Sex differences
Women-are-wonderful (WoW) effect, 112
Women's movement: conservative views of, 127; on economic independence, 31–32; educational system and, 11; on power held by men, 19; rallying cries of, 35; success of, 37, 129. *See also* Feminism
Wondra, Danielle, 56
Work. *See* Employment
Workforce Innovation and Opportunity Act of 2014 (WIOA), 161–62
Workforce Investment Act of 1998, 78
Working-class men and boys, 60–72; childhood adversity of, 70–72; deaths of despair among, 60–63; dislocation of, 63, 78; economic struggles of, 61, 62; employment trends and, 18; family life for, 61, 64–66; friendship deficit among, 68–70; haphazard self of, 67–68; marriage trends for, 37, 65; provider role for, 38
Working mothers, 29–30, 35, 36, 64, 167
Work/life balance, 181
World Economic Forum (WEF), 12, 114–15
World Trade Organization, 22
WoW (women-are-wonderful) effect, 112
WuDunn, Sheryl, 62
Wynn, Natalie, 109

Yavorsky, Jill, 163
Yoon Suk-yeol, 119
Young Michael, 178–79